Praise for *Note to Self*

. . . .

"What a dazzling rainbow of wisdom Laurie Buchanan has assembled into one volume! Drawing on a wide range of spiritual teachers and scientific discoveries, Buchanan guides the reader on an exciting journey of self-discovery. She is a modern oracle at Delphi, and this book a modern temple with 'Know Thyself' written on every page. Highly recommended for daily spiritual practice (a list of 365 questions at the end will guide journal writing). Leaders of retreats, and spiritual seekers will be sharing well-thumbed, dog-eared copies soon."

—SHIRLEY HERSHEY SHOWALTER, former president of Goshen College and author of *Blush: A Mennonite Girl Meets a Glittering World*

"Laurie Buchanan has a knack for helping others find positive, creative, and clear solutions to life's challenges. Reading this book was like watching the sun rise for me; every page had bright rays of wisdom that made me smile. Delightful indeed!"

—CHRISTINE DESMET, author, screenwriter, and writing teacher at University of Wisconsin-Madison Continuing Studies

"*Note to Self: A Seven-Step Path to Gratitude and Growth* is a book where we jot down big ideas in the margins as we turn the pages, repeatedly, until the corners become soft and familiar under our fingertips. Laurie Buchanan has given us a pinch-and-dollop recipe for thriving that is refined with science and verified through practice. Each precisely selected word of each well-organized chapter is underscored by Buchanan's conviction and compassion and her respect for a job that none of us can delegate—the self. Her knowledgeable, concise, and sometimes humorous approach is alchemy for what she accurately describes as 'the business of being.' *Note to Self* is a scholarly work that I shall keep within arm's reach and recommend often."

—TERRILL WELCH, artist, photographer, leadership coach, and author of *Leading Raspberry Jam Visions Women's Way: An Inside Track for Women Leaders*

"If you're ready to take charge of your life, Laurie will guide you all the way."
—JULIE MURPHY CASSERLY, President of JMC Wealth Management, motivational speaker, financial healer, and author of *The Emotion Behind Money: Building Wealth from the Inside Out*

"Relevant to our times, this important read can easily be considered a manual for intentional living; allowing us to embrace a well-crafted plan for revival, beyond the hypnotic hold of the human condition. *Note to Self* offers an inspired jumpstart into conscious living for both the beginner, as well as an enthusiastic reminder for the seasoned traveler on the path."
—ALISON ELLIOT, international speaker, energy enrichment coach, and author of *Hot Flashes Cool Wisdom: A Rumble Through the Jungle of Midlife*

"Laurie has me hooked with 'Whatever you are not changing, you are choosing.' Here's a book packed full to the brim with wisdom and compassion. Keep *Note to Self* beside you and you'll reach what's best in your life."
—HEATHER SHUMAKER, author of *It's OK Not to Share* and *It's OK to Go Up the Slide*

"For the self-help addict, Laurie Buchanan's *Note to Self: A Seven-Step Path to Gratitude and Growth* is the motherlode. What would normally take seven books to achieve, Laurie has done in one. She offers affirmations, guided meditations, aromatherapy, even suggestions on which physical ailments to have your own health care provider check out. It's an encyclopedia of holistic health care, useful as a reference for when a particular ailment or issue appears. It's also a book to devour from cover to cover, just not in one sitting."
—JANET GIVENS, author of *At Home on the Kazakh Steppe*, 2015 winner of the Moritz Thomsen Peace Corps Experience award

"Laurie Buchanan leads us on a beautiful journey to the seven aspects of 'self,' namely, OURSELVES. Guide yourself to this book. You'll thank your 'self' for years."
—PAMELA S. WIGHT, author of *The Right Wrong Man* and *Twin Desires*, and creative writing instructor

"Laurie Buchanan offers us gentle companionship, insightful guidance, and wise humor that will warm the less-than-intrepid adventurer embarking on a life change. Laurie is the person you want next to you as you decide what stays and what needs to be released on every level of our beings—physical, relational, and spiritual. Throughout *Note to Self,* Laurie offers clear sustainable practices that assure us of a lighter brighter future."
—SUZI BANKS BAUM, writer, artist, teacher and editor of *An Anthology of Babes: 36 Women Give Motherhood a Voice*

"Laurie Buchanan has a remarkable gift for addressing complex and deeply personal issues, with wit and wisdom. Anyone who is on the path of self-discovery and spiritual growth will find *Note to Self* an invaluable resource and companion."
—DOROTHY SANDER, philosopher, theologian, poet, author, and founder of Aging Abundantly

"Laurie's motto is "whatever you are not changing, you are choosing" and it is my suggestion that this book becomes part of your daily practice in life so you too will know what you need to change—and choose—to live at your highest vibration. You will learn about each of your seven selves through real-life examples and exercises that take you down the path of mind-body connection, color therapy, diet, aromatherapy, affirmations, breathwork, and more. This book is a cornucopia of wellness affluence. Your authentic life is waiting, read this book now and let your beautiful new you flow through a joy-filled, abundant life."
—LAURIE SCHEER, media goddess, director of the annual UW-Madison Writers' Institute, and author of *The Writer's Advantage: A Toolkit for Mastering Your Genre*

"I had a difficult time closing the book; I eagerly turned each page, anticipating Laurie's wisdom and wit."
—SHEILA GLAZOV, personality expert, professional speaker, educator, and award-winning author of *What Color Is Your Brain? A Fun and Fascinating Approach to Understanding Yourself and Others*

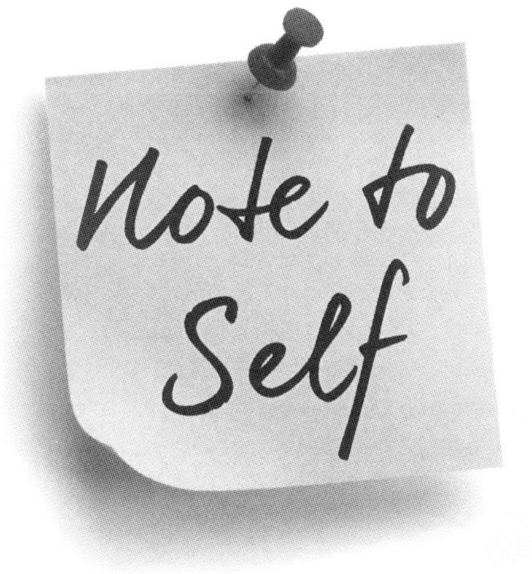
Note to
Self

Published 2016
Printed in the United States of America
ISBN: 978-1-63152-113-3
Library of Congress Control Number: 2016941778

Cover design by © Julie Metz, Ltd./metzdesign.com
Interior design by Tabitha Lahr

For information, address:
She Writes Press
1563 Solano Ave #546
Berkeley, CA 94707

She Writes Press is a division of SparkPoint Studio, LLC.

A Seven-Step Path
to Gratitude and Growth

Note to Self

Laurie Buchanan, PhD

SHE WRITES PRESS

Contents

Foreword xv

Preface xvii

Introduction xix

CHAPTER 1: Abundance: The Crème de la Crème 1

CHAPTER 2: How to Use This Book to
Unlock Your Highest Potential 5

CHAPTER 3: Self #1: Self-Preservation 11

CHAPTER 4: Keys to Self-Preservation: Enhance Your
Sense of Groundedness 31

CHAPTER 5: Self #2: Self-Gratification 41

CHAPTER 6: Keys to Self-Gratification: Increase Your
Sense of Delight 61

CHAPTER 7: Self #3: Self-Definition 69

CHAPTER 8: Keys to Self-Definition: Cultivate Your
Inner Landscape 91

CHAPTER 9: Self #4: Self-Acceptance 101

CHAPTER 10: Keys to Self-Acceptance: Develop Your

Emotional Empowerment. 123

CHAPTER 11: Self #5: Self-Expression 133

CHAPTER 12: Keys to Self-Expression: Unleash Your

Creative Flair 153

CHAPTER 13: Self #6: Self-Reflection 163

CHAPTER 14: Keys to Self-Reflection: Boost Your Insight 185

CHAPTER 15: Self #7: Self-Knowledge 195

CHAPTER 16: Keys to Self-Knowledge: Strengthen the

Connection with Your Higher Self 219

CHAPTER 17: Integrating the Seven Selves: A Rainbow of Color 229

CHAPTER 18: It's an Inside Job: Internal Inventory Questions 249

Acknowledgments. 263

About the Author. 265

Bibliography. 267

For Len,

my true north

Note to readers: In my private practice, I'm not always familiar with a person's faith background. With this in mind, I use the terms "divine love" or "source energy" when referring to divinity. I've chosen to do the same throughout this book.

Please mentally substitute what's more comfortable for you: God, Goddess, Yahweh, Jehovah, Jesus, Moses, Allah, Krishna, Light, Mohammed, Supreme Being, Buddha, All That Is, Source Energy, Shiva, Universe, Higher Self, Creator, Brahman, Spirit, Mother Earth, or Father Sky.

It's my experience that the name we use isn't as important as our relationship and interaction.

—LAURIE BUCHANAN, author of *Note to Self: A Seven-Step Path to Gratitude and Growth*

Foreword

The whole essence of Laurie Buchanan's book is timely and timeless. I had a difficult time closing the book; I eagerly turned each page, anticipating Laurie's wisdom and wit. This book helps readers understand how they can easily unpack the emotional baggage they persistently pack and cautiously carry on their journey through life.

Note to Self engages the reader with personal self-awareness inventories, affirmations, action steps, practical tips, tools, and exercises. The well-organized chapters and structure of the book make it easy and comfortable to read and to reflect upon the topics that it offers to the reader. Chakra rainbow colors enhance the research data and genuine stories within each chapter.

Laurie's effective use of bibliotherapy teaches life lessons and how to deal with problems through examples to which the reader can realistically relate. The drawing of personal energy circles helps readers envision and record the healthy and/or healing attributes, abilities, purpose, mission, paths, and/or passions in their lives on the inside of the circle, and the harmful or unhealthy behaviors, attitudes, or people on the outside of the circle. Readers also learn effective life skills to reduce negative feelings and reinforce positive, creative problem-solving skills.

Readers feel as if their problems are less threatening and learn how to handle difficulties when they realize that others have encountered similar problems and successfully overcome their tribulations. The self-expression, mindfulness, and positive statements on which Laurie focuses are encouraging and essential elements, treasures just waiting for readers to discover them. The fascinating quotes and facts on the pages and in the sidebars are effective prompts that sparked me to write dozens of "don't forget" notes that made this book mine.

The book concludes with 365 introspective and thought-provoking "Internal Inventory Questions." There are no must-do directions or right or wrong answers—just a lovely and simple invitation to explore gratitude, growth, and delight every day.

Note to Self is an invaluable resource to help individuals transform life's obstacles into opportunities, develop a healthier level of self-esteem, and cultivate a splendid sense of joy, *now!*

—SHEILA GLAZOV, personality expert, professional speaker, educator, and award-winning author of *What Color Is Your Brain? A Fun and Fascinating Approach to Understanding Yourself and Others* (Slack Inc., 2007)

Preface

"The most effective way to do it, is to do it."

—TONI CADE BAMBARA, American author,
documentary filmmaker, social activist, and college professor

Running full speed along the people mover at the Dallas/Forth Worth International Airport, with my brief bag slung over my shoulder and bouncing against my back, my carry-on biting my heels, I realized that no matter how light I pack, baggage is not only frustrating but inconvenient and was slowing me down.

Hooking a left, I galloped up the escalators, narrowly avoiding people like me who had luggage draped over their bodies and following disobediently behind.

I didn't encounter any smiling faces.

I'm going to miss my connecting flight! was the thought that hammered my splitting head with every pounding step. The faint smell of jet exhaust and fast food, and the heady mixture of perfumes and colognes that hung like an invisible cloud over the throng of bustling people, didn't help.

Breathless, I arrived at the gate, boarding pass clenched firmly between my teeth, only to be informed by the smiling airline agent that there was a delay. Apparently to avoid the checked-bag fees, passengers had overstuffed their carry-ons and couldn't deplane quickly.

Tension and frustration in the gate area were thick. Tempers were getting hot. Those with short fuses were getting loud and argumentative.

Baggage! We all carry it with us through life.

It comes in a wide variety of styles, shapes, and colors—more than enough to accommodate the stuff that we accumulate through life. And no matter how we dress it up, it's still frustrating and inconvenient and slows us down.

In fact, it's downright disruptive. Some airlines are implementing a "bags fly free" strategy. That's great for traveling. This book is about becoming baggage free. That's great for life, especially when we realize that we don't just pack for one; we pack for seven.

"Each of us has the right and the responsibility to assess the roads which lie ahead and those over which we have traveled, and if the future road looms ominous or unpromising, and the roads back uninviting, then we need to gather our resolve and, carrying only the necessary baggage, step off that road into another direction. If the new choice is also unpalatable, without embarrassment, we must be ready to change that one as well."

—MAYA ANGELOU, American author and poet

Introduction

The baggage we carry on life's journey is tied to a specific self, its core characteristic, an associated wellness, and a shadow side. These include:

1. Self-preservation, survival, physical wellness, and self-destruction
2. Self-gratification, pleasure, occupational wellness, and self-denial
3. Self-definition, personal power, social wellness, and self-importance
4. Self-acceptance, love, emotional wellness, and self-rejection
5. Self-expression, creativity, environmental wellness, and self-repression
6. Self-reflection, intuition, intellectual wellness, and self-absorption
7. Self-knowledge, divine connection, spiritual wellness, and self-unawareness

As a holistic health practitioner and transformational life coach, I work with a wide range of clients—from young children to seniors and every age in between. My specific areas of focus are energy medicine, inner alchemy (personal transformation), and spiritual awareness.

I've done a tremendous amount of research on human energy. This includes the energetic shell around us, known as the aura; the energy pathways in our body, referred to as meridians; and the seven energy stations that run parallel to our spine, called chakras.

Hundreds of books have been written about human energy, but none of them talks about the "self" associated with each of the chakras.

This book will introduce you to each of your seven selves and will help you to offload baggage, regardless of the contents—negative people, places, things, behaviors, events, and emotions that keep you topsy-turvy—so that, unencumbered, you can wrap your arms around a joy-filled, abundant life.

In thinking about the term "baggage," I realized that while it might sound cliché, it's an expression that everyone recognizes. It has an abiding truth, one we relate to because, big or small, it's something we all carry.

Think of the things that you lug around. Do they include fear, current or past abuse, rejection, or mistrust? Or maybe it's possessiveness, anger, a painful childhood, or inconsolable grief due to loss.

Are you weighed down by an overpacked schedule, a relationship that's bankrupting your heart, spending more than you earn, extensive family obligations, embracing beliefs that aren't true (e.g., *I'm not attractive* or *I'm not good enough*), a demanding job you don't enjoy, or chasing after unrealistic goals?

These things are like clothes that no longer fit: they're tight and uncomfortable and never looked good in the first place, because they didn't suit you.

Tooth by tooth, the zipper that tucks away emotional baggage slides open, exposing what we hoped to pack away. When anger, non-forgiveness, and fear slip out, the stomach clenches in dread.

It doesn't have to be that way.

Eileen, age fifty-eight, is in the upper-management echelon of a large pharmaceutical company. She shared, "I know I'm supposed to 'live in the present,' but I'm so obsessed with the previous actions of others that I just can't. I can see it's affecting the employees in my region, and I'm scared that it's going to impact my job. But I can't let them express their ideas; I can't trust anyone because of what happened before. I have to maintain tight control of the situation. But it's causing low morale, and there's no teamwork, no new ideas. What am I going to do?"

It's clear that Eileen and the employees in her region can't move forward while she's still looking back.

If you're reading this book, you've probably come to the realization that you're tired of carrying around so much baggage and you're looking for a healthy way to offload it. In my private practice, I work with clients to help them examine the contents they've stowed in their bags so they can empty them.

....

"Carrying your negative emotional baggage requires energy that could be put to much better use—say good-bye to it, let it go, and get on with your life."

—LUCY MACDONALD, Canadian certified counselor and author

....

This happens through deep exploration of oneself.

This book is based on the Life Harmony wellness program I designed to help people turn intention into action—the discipline of getting on track and staying there—a program that takes people from where they are to where they want to be.

Like the program, this book facilitates empowerment by identifying the baggage we carry and illuminating the path to whole, unencumbered health—body, mind, and spirit. Using real-life examples, it provides practical tips, techniques, and exercises to help you offload your bags.

LIFE LUGGAGE

Barbara, age fifty-three, shared this story: "I think I was born old. Somehow I managed to get myself born to parents whom I didn't trust at all. I remember, when I was four years old, riding my tricycle while my mother was walking. We lived in Fort Bliss, Texas. We had to cross railroad tracks. I almost refused to cross them. I kept asking my mother, 'Are you *sure* there's no train coming?'

"It was the desert. You could see for miles and miles. But I didn't trust her word. She had already lied to me on many occasions by then, and I knew from early on that I was pretty much on my own. My father was absent most of the time, and my siblings were in the same predicament I was. I don't feel sorry for myself. This was my path, for whatever reason, and I have learned very well how to take good care of me."

We are spiritual beings on a human journey who learn lessons as we go along. We arrive empty-handed and unencumbered. Yet somehow, as we travel life's path we start to acquire baggage—be it family, academia, business, or pleasure—to accommodate the journey. This runs the gamut of backpack, fanny pack, brief bag, garment bag, accessory bag, duffel bag, tote bag, book bag, gym bag, camera bag, and handbag.

Sandi shared, "I believe I'm here to finish with many issues, including the emotional issues that block me from living as my authentic self. This human existence is far too short to waste time reliving the past, and carrying emotional baggage just weighs me down. When I leave this body, I want to leave as light as possible."

I'm sure you can remember a situation where you overheard part of a whispered conversation that went something like this: "I should tell you, he's got baggage."

Red flags went up immediately. You got the distinct impression that the guy's trouble. What you probably didn't know was whether it was with relationships, addictions, diseases, or debt. And that's only the beginning. The potential list of "baggage" is lengthy, and none of us is immune.

Many of the bags we carry are small and easy to manage. They're the type easily stowed in the overhead compartment or under the seat in front of us for easy access when we travel by plane. They carry our essentials, the things we want to keep close at hand, such as medication, toiletries, a change of clothes, a book, a laptop, a cell phone, an iPod—the items we don't want to be without.

> "Everyone's got emotional baggage; the question is, what are you doing to unpack that trunk and put it away, so your lovers, friends, and relatives don't have to keep tripping over it?"
>
> —SHARI SCHREIBER, life strategist

The baggage that's bulky or much too heavy to lug around is checked in upon arrival at the airport, where we receive a claim check for identification and pickup at our destination. These pieces typically contain items that we could do without if we had to. We want them, but they're nonessential. They're loaded into the cargo hold for the flight and then offloaded onto a conveyor belt in the baggage claim area, where they await retrieval.

As we travel through life, the overhead compartment–size baggage that we tend to keep within arm's reach is a word picture for smaller, daily concerns that affect us. The emotional equivalent of these might include frustration, stubbornness, anger, boredom, and jealousy.

The contents are dependent on the "self" the luggage is associated with. Because of the mind-body connection, even these seemingly small items, left unresolved, can negatively impact our body.

The larger, cumbersome pieces that are placed in the freight area are a symbol for deep, burdensome issues that have a profound, underlying impact. The emotional equivalent of these might include non-forgiveness, depression, revenge, and guilt.

Because of the mind-body connection, these items, left unresolved, can have tremendous negative physical ramifications on our body. Physical illness that stems from emotional wounds requires emotional healing to occur along with physical healing.

AN INVITATION

I invite you to take a journey—a journey to evaluate the seven aspects of self that comprise your personality; a journey to examine the contents of your baggage through the filter of your soul.

In doing so, you'll discover the who, what, when, where, why, and how that truly benefit you. You'll learn the four elements that determine whether a person, place, or thing is for your highest and best good.

In turn, you'll discover the value that you provide as well. You'll be able to gauge where changes need to be made—people, places, and things you need to add, alter, or remove from your life—so that you can move forward unencumbered and unleash your potential.

People oftentimes ask me what my role is in this process. My answer is always the same:

I won't walk in front of you.
I won't walk behind you.
I won't carry you.
I will, however, walk beside you.

As you read these pages, I'll help you to explore the contents of the luggage you've acquired to date, find out why you're still carrying it, and determine the life lesson it's taught you, then provide you with techniques to release it and move forward—lighter and freer—so that you can create a joyful and abundant life—*now!*

CHAPTER 1

Abundance: The Crème de la Crème

The following thought-provoking questions are not meant for quick yes or no answers, so enjoy a cup of coffee or tea while you contemplate and write your responses.

1. Are you willing to invest in yourself?
2. Are you willing to become stronger than your history?
3. Are you willing to forgive yourself?
4. Are you willing to forgive others?
5. Are you willing to stop being held hostage by the opinion of others?
6. Are you willing to be motivated by trust instead of fear?
7. Are you willing to let go of anger?
8. Are you willing to let go of your need to control?
9. Are you willing to know the truth?
10. Are you willing to be transformed?
11. Are you willing to function from a place of authenticity?
12. Are you willing to live an inspired life?

If you answered yes to these questions, you're ready to live an abundant life.

Abundance isn't to be confused with prosperity. There's absolutely nothing wrong with prosperity. This book, however, is about offloading emotional baggage so that you can live a joyful life of abundance.

Let's take a look at the difference:

Abundance is *inner wealth*; it's something that brings a return value to the heart. It benefits your inner self with intangible dividends. Examples include love, peace of mind, health, wellness, wisdom, integrity, respect, quality relationships, joy, gratitude, humor, a positive attitude, and contentment—being satisfied.

When I asked my friend Christine how her father's brain surgery went, she responded, "My dad's surgery went awry, and they almost lost him. His heart stopped for four minutes after the apparatus on his head turned his neck in such a way that his breathing was cut off. He's got a strong heart, for being seventy-six, and the doctors are so confident, and so is he, that they're going to do the surgery again in three weeks. They feel that they at least found the area that will work in this last operation before all heck broke loose in the operating room.

"My dad's a positive sort, so he was kidding very soon about 'seeing the light and coming back.' My mother was less enthusiastic, of course. She got quite a scare, as we all did.

"But he's at home, resting up now for the next version of the surgery in three weeks. He's a dogged kind of guy—he never gives up—and he also always laughs about these things in life. Truly a man to admire."

Christine's father is a perfect example of someone with a storehouse of abundance—inner wealth.

Prosperity is *material wealth*; it's something that brings a return value to the wallet and/or bank account. It's on the outside of self and has tangible dividends. You can touch it, hold it, drive it, live in it, wear it, swim in it, take it to the bank, or invest it. Examples include money, jewelry, real estate, cars, boats, recreational vehicles, collections, and investments.

One of my clients, Hank, has an eight-thousand-square-foot house and a second home, of over ten thousand square feet. Both residences contain boxes of purchased items that are yet to be opened because he already has so much "stuff."

"The National Association of Professional Organizers says we have so much 'stuff' that each person spends approximately one year of their life looking for lost items.

"As a society we've acquired so much 'stuff' over the last three decades that the self-storage industry is the fastest-growing new industry in the United States. It's grown so fast that in the last twelve years, the use of self-storage space has grown from one in every seventeen households to one in every ten. That's an increase of 65 percent.

He owns multiple luxury vehicles and drives a different one to each of his weekly appointments, depending on his mood; sometimes it's the Bentley, other times it's the Hummer, and sometimes it's the vintage Cadillac he had restored for Sally, his wife. When he's feeling casual, it's the souped-up pickup with a five-hundred-cubic-inch engine, and when the weather's really nice, he rides his favorite motorcycle, a custom Indian Chief.

A person can have abundance and not prosperity, or a person can be prosperous and not have abundance. A person can be both or neither.

Dr. Wayne Dyer said, "Abundance is not something we acquire. It is something we tune into." In other words, *abundance is a state of being*. All we need to do is learn how to connect with it, but it's all too easy to let life's clutter—internal and external—define our days, to become the critical factor in the choices we make.

In his book *The Geography of Bliss: One Grump's Search for the Happiest Places in the World*, Eric Weiner tells us that the size of a person's bank account doesn't really have that much of an impact on a person's happiness quotient. For instance, a person who's sitting in first class isn't necessarily happier than those of us in coach.

What's true for everyone, regardless of income, is that "stuff"—material trappings—brings fleeting joy at best, while joy and peace of mind begin and reside in the heart. Like a seedling, they have to be nurtured and cultivated in order to grow.

When our inner landscape is well tended, we are able to face our stories and face our fears. We can allow ourselves to dream, to explore our understanding of who we are, and to determine our purpose in life.

Each of us carries a system of energy within us, a system that guides us toward a greater understanding of who we are, what we need, and how we can choose the best course of action. When we make time for stillness, ask questions, and listen to our soul's voice—our internal compass—we receive clear direction.

CHAPTER 2

How to Use This Book to Unlock Your Highest Potential

The seven selves are constantly moving in and out of balance. This is normal, but when an imbalance lasts too long, we can experience illness—of body, mind, and spirit. To remedy this, we need simply to set an intention to reconnect with the self in question, and then use effective healing strategies to restore balance.

Keys serve two purposes: to lock and to unlock something. The "key" chapters that follow the descriptions of each of the seven selves are designed to assist you in unlocking your highest potential. They provide realistic, easy-to-use techniques, tips, exercises, and thought-provoking questions designed to help you offload baggage associated with each self.

....

"The will to win, the desire to succeed, the urge to reach your full potential . . .
These are the keys that will unlock the door to personal excellence."
—CONFUCIUS, Chinese teacher, philosopher, and political theorist

....

Start with the suggestion you think is the easiest, and then, as you gain momentum, try another one, and then another. You'll be amazed at how quickly you get rid of baggage you've been lugging around.

Each "key" chapter includes ten sections:

1. Mind-Body Connection
2. Color Therapy
3. Diet

4. Aromatherapy
5. Affirmations
6. The Business of Being
7. Breathwork
8. Wellness Inventory and Vitality Check
9. Action Steps
10. Personal Energy Signature

MIND-BODY CONNECTION

Many people consider physical illness to stem from a mind-body connection. This link isn't static; it varies based on the disease. For more than thirty years, Harvard psychologist and author Ellen Langer has studied this connection, revealing that changing one's mind—becoming mindful of subtle changes and being aware of the power of possibility—could lead one's body to optimize health and turn back the clock psychologically and physically.

....

"There is no question that the things we think have a tremendous effect upon our bodies. If we can change our thinking, the body frequently heals itself."
—C. EVERETT KOOP, MD, and thirteenth surgeon general of the United States

....

This section points to the physical body systems associated with each self. If you're experiencing issues with any of the areas listed, it's time to make an appointment with your health care provider.

COLOR THERAPY

Each of the seven selves is associated with—and influenced by—a specific color. Every color has a different wavelength and individual properties, both positive and negative.

Color is simply energy, *energy made visible*. Different colors stimulate or inhibit the functioning of different parts of our body. Treatment with the appropriate color can restore balance and normal functioning.

This section provides information about the color to use for each self. It offers easy-to-implement suggestions for how to weave that color into the tapestry of your life.

DIET

In this book, the word "diet" refers to what we eat, as opposed to being a term used for weight loss. What we consume is the way we provide fuel to our body. Most healthy diets are rich in fruits, nuts, and vegetables—foods that offer an incredible array of vitamins, minerals, and phytonutrients, whether eaten raw, sautéed, steamed, or grilled.

This section provides a list of food items and a vitamin or mineral supplement to help support each self.

AROMATHERAPY

Essential oils are the fragrant, highly concentrated natural constituents that are found in plants. They're what give the plant its characteristic odor and contain the healing power of the plant they're extracted from. Used correctly, essential oils bring a wide range of health benefits without causing side effects.

This section provides a brief list of essential oils for encouraging each self.

AFFIRMATIONS

Belleruth Naparstek—psychotherapist, author, and guided-imagery pioneer—tells us, "Affirmations are positive statements, spoken in the first person, designed to combat negative thinking and set the stage for first attitude, and then behavioral, change. Repetition, over time, can result in profound personal changes."

This section provides examples of affirmations for each self.

THE BUSINESS OF BEING

This book isn't about being in business; it's about the business of being. But when you really stop to think about it, each of us is similar to a small business.

Any successful business owner will tell you that it's in their best interest to implement strategies that improve their prospects for success. Similarly, as human beings, we are well served by implementing guiding principles that inspire us to live our purpose and reach our goals.

This section points to a business concept that, when put into practice on a personal basis, is useful for strengthening each self and encourages living on purpose—by intent.

BREATHWORK

This section provides easy-to-follow breathing exercises designed to help you relax and release stress. By looking at the individual needs of each self, you'll learn how to weave simple breathwork techniques into your daily life—offloading baggage and increasing joy.

WELLNESS INVENTORY AND VITALITY CHECK

This section asks thought-provoking questions designed to trigger an internal inventory, check your vitality level, and motivate action for the wellness associated with each self.

ACTION STEPS

Here you'll find a list of suggestions and healthful exercises for each self. Some are so simple you'll be able to do them right away (I call those "quick hits"), while others will take a little bit of planning.

PERSONAL ENERGY SIGNATURE

At the end of each "key" chapter, you'll find a circle that represents your personal energy signature. Taking into consideration what you learned in the previous chapter, you'll list inside the circle the key people, places, things, and actions that are for the highest and best good of each self—positive, uplifting, constructive, and healing.

On the outside of the circle, you'll list the people, places, things, and actions you need to avoid to keep that self healthy and balanced.

Now that you know how to use this book, the easiest place to begin is the physical package we reside in—our body. Let's get started.

> "To will is to select a goal, determine a course of action that will bring one to that goal, and then hold to that action till the goal is reached. The key is action."
>
> —MICHAEL HANSON, author

CHAPTER 3

Self #1: Self-Preservation

Self-preservation is responsible for survival and physical wellness; its purpose is to enhance our sense of groundedness. When healthy, this self functions from a place of courage. Corresponding to the base chakra, it resonates with the color red. An inspiring affirmation for this self is: *I am safe.* Its shadow side is self-destruction.

❖ ❖ ❖

Maggie shared that she interviewed for a job at a different company—one that pays more—not because she's unhappy with her current position, but because she's been spending more than she makes for quite some time, and if she doesn't earn more money quickly, she'll have to file for bankruptcy.

"I desperately need this new job," she said. "My out-of-control spending has finally caught up with me. It was never a matter of 'if'; it was a matter of 'when.'"

Do you trust most people?

Do you feel insecure in body, mind, or spirit?

Do you feel lacking in money, time, health, love, food, or friends?

Do you rely on substances to get you through the day—alcohol, nicotine, marijuana, prescription or recreational drugs?

This self, self-preservation, is the force that grounds and empowers our being—our foundation. The developmental stage begins somewhere between the second trimester in utero and one year of age.

Self-preservation is concerned with security, survival, and trust. As we mature, this often translates to money, home, and job.

When our senses of survival and self-preservation are in balance, we enjoy qualities from the constructive side of this self. These include passion, courage, spontaneity, love, and hope.

THE SHADOW SIDE: SELF-DESTRUCTION

When our senses of survival and self-preservation are out of balance, we can experience feelings of self-destruction.

Many things are cued to self-destruct under a specific set of predefined circumstances. Humans are no different.

The conditions we need to avoid include insufficient sleep; lack of exercise; an unhealthy diet; and addictive substances, such as nicotine, drugs, and excess alcohol. Some people use these as coping mechanisms for stress or a sense of hopelessness, while others even turn to self-injury, such as cutting or burning oneself, or to thoughts or attempts of suicide. None of these methods addresses the source—the underlying issue.

Self-destruction can manifest itself in a number of harmful ways that become items we tuck into our life's baggage. Depending on their size and impact, we may slip them into a tote that we keep within arm's reach, for handy retrieval, or stuff them into a large suitcase that comes around on the baggage carousel only occasionally. These can include:

> *Physical:* immune-related disorders, lower-back pain, rectal tumors, sciatica, and varicose veins.

> *Mental:* arrogance, dominance, superstition, depression, and a frantic sense of survival or impending doom.

> *Emotional:* frustration, anger, instinct, loyalty, a lack of trust or family security, and a sense of abandonment.

> *Spiritual:* material-world lessons, lack (a sense of scarcity), and excess.

Logan's mother, Peggy, was heartbroken as she told me about her son. "He started out like a shiny new penny, full of promise. He was doing so well until he got into high school. To fit in with his new 'friends,' he started smoking and drinking and he quit putting in any effort. At the end of four years, we weren't even sure he'd graduate, but he did—barely.

"In college, he started doing drugs. He dropped out of school soon after he began. We don't know if it was from indifference or not being able to keep up. Since then, he's gone from one fast-food job to another, and through multiple relationships. At twenty-seven, he's still living at home. We don't see him very often, because he's usually 'out.' When we do see him, he's in the garage, smoking pot. When his father and I confronted him about this, he said, 'You've got your choice: it's pot or suicide. Which one do you want? It really doesn't matter to me.'"

"Being defeated is often a temporary condition. Giving up is permanent."

—MARILYN VOS SAVANT, American magazine columnist, author,
lecturer, and playwright

In a group session, Penny's son, Gary, admitted that he was self-medicating to numb his lack of hope for and belief in a positive outcome for himself. His father, Kevin, countered by saying, "Hope by itself leads nowhere unless it's accompanied by action. Hope that doesn't include action is illusory and condemns a person to an endless continuation of the status quo."

Christine shared, "My mojo is gone. I just want to sit in a corner and wither away. I'm existing, not living. I simply go through the motions. I can't seem to get myself out of it. My addiction is depression—sitting down and doing absolutely nothing."

Bailey was in a car accident with her husband and two young children. She was the only one who survived. For years, she's been ashamed of being alive. She shared, "That shame, which is bigger than the pain—than anything else—will last forever."

Survival and self-preservation work hand in hand with physical wellness—our ability to preserve a healthy quality of life that enables us to weather our daily activities without unnecessary fatigue or physical stress. They also include an ability to recognize that our behaviors have a direct impact on our physical wellness, and that by embracing healthful habits, we can protect our body. These include getting plenty of rest, relaxation, and sound sleep; routine checkups; eating a balanced diet; and exercise.

Physical wellness means that we bring the unhealthy aspects of our body to light—take them out of our baggage—for examination so that we can find the mind-body correlation and work through them in a healthy and productive way, offloading baggage and increasing joy.

Physical wellness encompasses all of the ways in which we care for the package we reside in—our body. This includes breathing, what we ingest (water, food, and supplements), weight management, and exercise.

TAKE A DEEP BREATH AND RELAX

Our breath is a major source of energy. Eastern cultures have explored the power inherent in the breath and speak of that energy as "chi" or "prana."

In Latin, the word for "breath" and "spirit" is the same: *spirare*. The term "spirit" or "life force" in the Hebrew language can be translated into the word "breath." About sixteen to seventeen times per minute, we say yes to continuing our life here on Earth by taking another breath. Our breath is quite literally our life force. We breathe about ten thousand quarts of air per day, oxygenating some twenty-seven trillion cells.

Breathing is paramount to survival and self-preservation. Our body can go without food and water for a few days—at best—but it can't go without oxygen for more than a few minutes. Oxygen is the source of our sustenance. Within the breath, we encounter the rhythm of energy that all life emits.

....

"If I had to limit my advice on healthier living to just one tip, it would be simply to learn how to breathe correctly. From my own experience and from working with patients, I have come to believe that proper breathing is the master key to good health."

—DR. ANDREW WEIL, physician, founder and program director of the Arizona Center for Integrative Medicine, and best-selling author

....

We breathe in and out some twenty-two thousand times per day—inhalation followed by exhalation. The actual job of breathing is done mainly by the diaphragm, the sheet of muscles between the chest and the abdomen. These muscles contract when we breathe in, expanding the lungs and drawing in air. We breathe out simply by relaxing the diaphragm; the lungs deflate like balloons.

Deep, circular breathing—belly breathing—happens when we inhale through our nose and exhale through our mouth. However, the ideal breath isn't quite as simple as that. A true, cleansing breath is one that directs the breath energy all the way down into the lower belly, about two inches below the navel. This area is known as the lower *tan tien,* meaning "stove," "furnace," or "cauldron." Follow this inhalation by expelling waste products up and out through the mouth with a long, slow exhalation.

The key to healthy breathing is to have longer exhalations than inhalations. In fact, they should be twice as long. This not only purges toxins but promotes vital energy, relaxation, and healing. The average adult utilizes only about one quart of their six-to-seven-quart lung capacity.

Inhaling slowly, deeply, and evenly through both nostrils and exhaling through the mouth—mindful breathing—helps to synchronize both hemispheres of the brain. It promotes whole-body integration of our physical, mental, emotional, and spiritual states of being. When we don't use our breath effectively, our other systems have to work overtime to compensate. This overwork can set the stage for serious illness.

Healthy breathing increases vitality, lowers blood pressure, enhances mental concentration and the ability to retain information, unleashes creativity, improves circulation, diminishes anxiety, and promotes relaxation.

Mindful breathing can be used anytime, anywhere. If you sit in front of a computer all day or have a long commute, lower your shoulders periodically and breathe mindfully. The difference in your energy and stress level at the end of the day will be noticeable.

With regular practice, mindful breathing becomes our natural way of breathing: relaxed, rhythmic, flowing, and open.

So sit back, relax, and inhale deeply through your nostrils, drawing the breath fully into the pit of your stomach. In doing so, you just sent a powerful dose of oxygen to your brain and every single cell in your body and rid yourself of some excess baggage.

WATER: THE ELIXIR OF LIFE

Water is the main component of all living beings and the major constituent of human cells. It's vital to survival and self-preservation.

How can we know how much water is the *right* amount of water to drink? It's easy: simply divide your body weight by two. The resulting number is the number of ounces of water you should drink every twenty-four hours.

Next to the air we breathe, water is the most important thing we'll ever put into our body. Here are some of the benefits of drinking the *right* amount of water every day:

- Reduces back pain
- Slashes cancer risk
- Provides a whole-body cleanse
- Diminishes digestive problems
- Boosts energy
- Enhances the effectiveness of exercise
- Diminishes the frequency of headaches
- Enhances heart health
- Improves memory
- Enhances skin health
- Promotes weight loss

Dr. Masaru Emoto, author of *The Hidden Messages in Water*, found that water from clear springs and water that has been exposed to loving words shows brilliant, complex, and colorful snowflake patterns.

In contrast, polluted water, or water exposed to negative thoughts, forms incomplete, asymmetrical patterns with dull colors. The implications of this research create a new awareness of how we can positively impact the earth and our personal health.

DIET: A FOUR-LETTER WORD

You've heard the saying "you are what you eat." That sentiment isn't far from the truth. A more accurate statement is "you are what you assimilate." A body that's not healthy can't assimilate all the nutrients it needs from the foods and supplements it ingests.

Research shows that people who eat a variety of brightly colored fruit, leafy vegetables, certain fish, and nuts packed with omega-3 fatty acids can improve focus and decrease their risk of getting Alzheimer's disease.

Eating well is also one of the keys to a positive outlook, emotional balance, and a joyful life. The benefits of healthy eating include increased mental acuteness, resistance to illness and disease, higher energy levels, a more robust immune system, faster recuperation times, and better management of chronic health problems.

Good nutrition keeps muscles, bones, organs, and other body parts strong for the long haul. Eating foods that are rich in vitamins and minerals boosts immunity and fights illness-causing toxins. A healthy diet reduces the risk of heart disease, stroke, high blood pressure, type 2 diabetes, bone loss, cancer, and anemia.

The American Institute for Cancer Research recommends, "People concerned with reducing cancer risk and managing their weight cover two-thirds (or more) of their plate with vegetables, fruit, whole grains, and beans, and one-third (or less) with animal protein. One of the best possible choices for that 'one-third or less' is fish."

Top Ten Anticancer Foods:
- Cruciferous vegetables—broccoli, cabbage, and Brussels sprouts
- Tomatoes
- Berries—blueberries, açaí berries, raspberries, cranberries, and strawberries
- Onions and leeks
- Red beets
- Spinach and watercress
- Garlic
- Whole grains
- Oranges
- Beans—all types of beans, including soybeans and lentils

Other fruits and vegetables that help to protect against cancer include pumpkin, pineapple, rhubarb, apples, carrots, sweet potatoes, squash, red onions, radishes, apricots, grapefruit, red grapes, lemons, mangoes, papayas, peaches, and persimmons.

In the United States, we tend to live in the fast lane—hurry, hurry, hurry—and often eat on the run. How and what we eat affects the pleasure we take, or miss, in the eating experience. Many of our global neighbors have already discovered this and have offloaded "food baggage" by treating food with healthy respect and joy. They share meals with others, lingering over each course and savoring the taste, thus fostering a deep appreciation for the pleasure of eating wholesome and delicious foods.

Our food choices, our attitude, and the environment we're eating in all affect healthy digestion and our assimilation of nutrition. Bringing more attention and thought to our meals helps us to make healthier food choices and enhances our eating pleasure.

CHOOSING NUTRITIONAL SUPPLEMENTS: MORE THAN "EENY, MEENY, MINY, MOE"

No matter how well we eat, there are usually some nutritional gaps in our diet. Multivitamins and minerals are an easy and convenient way to help fill those gaps and ensure that our bodies get all of the nutritional support they need every day.

There are thirteen vitamins classified as either water soluble (C and B-complex) or fat soluble (A, D, E, and K), and each plays a key role for our body:

Water-soluble vitamins are stored in the body for a brief period of time and then excreted by the kidneys. The one exception is vitamin B_{12} which is stored in the liver. Water-soluble vitamins need to be taken daily.

Fat-soluble vitamins are absorbed—along with fat from the intestine—into the circulation. Any disease or disorder that affects the absorption of fat, such as celiac disease, can lead to a deficiency of these vitamins. Once absorbed into the circulation, these vitamins are carried to the liver, where they're stored.

In addition to vitamins, our bodies need several minerals to achieve proper makeup of bone and blood and for maintenance of normal cell function. These are divided into two groups:

> **Major minerals,** which include phosphorous, calcium, sodium, potassium, chlorine, sulfur, and magnesium.

> **Trace minerals,** which include iron, iodine, cobalt (from vitamin B_{12}), chromium, selenium, copper, fluorine, manganese, zinc, and molybdenum.

A variety of multivitamin and mineral formulas can address the specific nutritional needs of each gender and stage of life. Nutritional requirements change with age, especially for women, as they experience various changes in their life cycle (e.g., menstruation, pregnancy/lactation, and menopause).

The idea of taking a single pill every day to cover all of our multivitamin and mineral needs is nice, but I recommend finding a formula that's designed for your life stage and has a suggested dose of one or two tablets, three times per day—preferably one that delivers more than the Food and Drug Administration's Recommended Daily Allowance (RDA) minimums.

And remember, multivitamin and mineral formulas are designed to supplement a healthy eating plan; they were never designed to be used as a substitute for a healthy diet.

THE WEIGHT IS OVER

The largest contributor to our weight—or lack thereof—is the amount of food we eat. Whether we're overweight, underweight, or just right:

- To **gain** weight, we have to consume more fuel (calories) than we burn.

- To *maintain* weight, we have to consume and burn the same amount of fuel.

- To *lose* weight, we have to consume less fuel than we burn.

A multitude of healthy eating styles exist. Some examples are:

Food combining is the process of separating particular foods and eating specific ones at certain meals, for better digestive health and weight loss.

Blood-type eating agrees that "you are what you eat" but, further, that we should "eat what we are." Eating by blood type means we eat a diet compatible with our blood type for optimal health and digestion.

Dosha-type eating has our specific mind-body constitution in mind.

There are three ayurvedic doshas:

- *Vata*—controls movement
- *Pitta*—controls metabolism
- *Kapha*—controls structure

Personally, I try to avoid food that comes from a package—bag, box, bottle, can, or jar—and enjoy eating a wide variety of foods that are fresh and unprocessed, as close to the source as possible.

....

"The American society has become 'obesogenic,' characterized by environments that promote increased food intake, nonhealthful foods, and physical inactivity.

"Obesity plays a significant role in causing poor health in women, negatively affecting quality of life, and shortening quantity of life. More than half of adult US women are overweight, and more than one-third are obese.

"The life expectancy of women in the United States is approaching eighty years of age, and more women than ever are expected to turn sixty-five in the second decade of the new millennium. Prevention and early treatment of obesity are crucial to ensuring a healthy population of women of all ages."

—THE AMERICAN OBESITY ASSOCIATION

....

Two of the healthiest and easiest techniques to implement with *any* eating style are to start your day with a large glass of water and to make lunch the largest meal of your day.

What works for one person may not work for another. There's a *right* number of calories for you. That number depends on your age, your physical activity level, and whether you're trying to lose, gain, or maintain weight. According to the National Institute on Aging, a woman over fifty who is:

- Not physically active needs about 1,600 calories a day.
- Somewhat physically active needs about 1,800 calories a day.
- Very active needs about 2,000 calories a day.

Eating healthfully gives us more energy, keeps our weight in check, and helps us look better, which boosts self-esteem. It's all connected—when our body feels good, we feel happier inside and out.

EXERCISE—FOR THE HEALTH OF IT

The human body burns fuel just like a car. We can't continuously fill it with fuel; we have to burn fuel between fill-ups. The best way to burn fuel is with exercise.

First and foremost, exercise should improve our health, not risk it. We need to exercise intelligently and cautiously. When choosing an exercise, we need to keep in mind factors like our strengths, our schedule, the complexity of the exercise, our current stress level, and our available time. By selecting an exercise that fits well with these variables, we increase our likelihood of stick-to-itiveness.

....

"After four hours of sitting, the body starts to send harmful signals because the genes that regulate the amount of glucose and fat in the body start to shut down.

"Australian researchers tracked the lifestyle habits of 8,800 adults and found that each hour spent sitting in front of the television daily was associated with:

- An 11 percent increased risk of death from all causes
- A 9 percent increased risk of cancer death
- An 18 percent increased risk of cardiovascular disease (CVD)-related death

"Compared with people who watched less than two hours of television daily, those who watched more than four hours a day had a 46 percent higher risk of death from all causes and an 80 percent increased risk for CVD-related death.

"This association held regardless of other independent and common cardiovascular disease risk factors, including smoking, high blood pressure, high blood cholesterol, unhealthy diet, excessive waist circumference, and leisure-time exercises."

—SCIENCEDAILY.COM

Karla shared, "I've been nursing an injury for about a year and during that time have done nothing but sit, sit, sit. I'm better now and ready to move. Unfortunately, it caught up with me, big-time. My lab tests came back, revealing that I'm now prediabetic and fifty pounds overweight. This could have been avoided if I'd exercised every day—just a little bit each day."

Countless people exercise to control their weight, to get into better physical condition, to become healthier, or to look physically attractive. But exercise also offers a distraction from stressful situations, an outlet for frustration, and an endorphin lift.

Many of us in today's world dance a wicked two-step with a very ungracious partner named stress. Stress flings us through our days and muddles up our mind with lists of things to do; worries about bills, potential layoffs, or the responsibilities of being a parent or grandparent; concerns about providing eldercare for aging parents . . . and the list goes on.

Excess stress negatively affects the body, mind, and spirit. In fact, it's been estimated that more than 90 percent of health problems that bring people into a doctor's office are stress related. And while virtually all of us could benefit from adding healthy habits to our lifestyle, it's harder to begin a new habit than it seems, especially if we're overscheduled and overstressed.

"Fat located in the abdominal area functions differently than fat located elsewhere in the body. It has a greater blood supply, as well as more receptors for cortisol, a stress hormone.

"Cortisol levels rise and fall throughout the day, but when we're under constant stress—the kind created by a marriage that's unraveling, a job you hate, or financial worries—the amount of the hormone we produce remains elevated. With high stress and, consequently, high cortisol levels, more fat is deposited in the abdominal area, since there are more cortisol receptors there.

"Chronically high cortisol levels also kill neurons in the brain and interfere with feel-good neurotransmitters—such as dopamine and serotonin—that can lead to depression and feeling more stressed.

"The fat at our waist—what researchers call central obesity—is associated with higher rates of cardiovascular disease, type 2 diabetes, and several types of cancer. And while it's true that heredity plays a role in overall body type, genetics accounts for only 25–55 percent of the tendency to develop the most serious diseases associated with abdominal fat—the remainder is lifestyle."

—BRENDA DAVY, PhD, RD, assistant professor, Virginia Tech

The American Counsel on Exercise tells us that:

1. Exercise can make us feel less anxious.
2. Exercise is relaxing.
3. Exercise increases alertness.
4. Exercise makes us feel better about ourselves.
5. Exercise reduces depression.
6. Exercise helps us to sleep more restfully.
7. Exercise increases energy, which in turn helps us to better deal with stressful events.
8. Exercise rids the body of stress-causing adrenaline.
9. Exercise encourages us to follow a healthier diet.
10. Exercise helps us take time for ourselves—often difficult when we're stressed out.

Deepak Chopra said, "If you don't take care of your health today, you will be forced to take care of your illness tomorrow."

In taking an active role in our physical wellness, we come to understand and value the direct relationship between exercise, quality nutrition, and the way our body performs. We appreciate that the physical benefits of regular hygiene routines, looking good and feeling terrific, lead to the psychological benefits of enhanced self-esteem, determination, and a sense of direction.

SO, HOW'S YOUR NEST EGG?

In addition to physical wellness, this self—self-preservation—is responsible for how we handle our finances.

Financial stress is widespread and growing. Concerns and anxiety over bills, debt, high mortgages, interest rates, late fees, and other financial hardships are the leading cause of stress in Americans.

....

"The average US household credit card debt stands at $16,140, counting only those households carrying debt. Based on an analysis of Federal Reserve statistics and other government data, the average household owes $7,529 on their cards; looking only at indebted households, the average outstanding balance rises to $16,140. Current as of October 2015, here is the US household consumer debt profile:

- Average credit card debt: $16,140
- Average mortgage debt: $155,361
- Average student loan debt: $31,946"

—NERDWALLET.COM

....

Finances cover a broad spectrum, from shaky and unstable to secure and steady. Regardless, our financial position has a large, corresponding impact on our sense of survival and self-preservation. Let's take a look:

Spendthrift

We'll refer to the person who operates from a weak financial position as Spendthrift. This person puts very little thought into their spending habits. Consequently, they're overextended financially.

Spendthrift hasn't planned for the future. They haven't saved any money for their retirement years. If Spendthrift were to lose their job unexpectedly, they wouldn't have enough savings set aside to tide them over for very long—one to two months, perhaps.

Spendthrift is the type of person who bases their expenditures on what they *want*, as opposed to what they *need*. Sometimes they buy things just for the sake of having them. Maybe it's to "keep up with the Joneses;" maybe it's to keep up with oneself.

Oftentimes, Spendthrift charges items they can't otherwise afford. They put their purchases on a credit card and end up paying interest because they don't have the ability to pay off their card at the end of the month.

By struggling to live within their means, Spendthrift adds weight to their life's baggage and minimizes their joy.

Jack is the epitome of Spendthrift. His philosophy is "money is round and meant to roll!" He shared, "Help! I've got too much stuff, and I'm running out of storage space. Not only is my garage packed to the rafters, but my bedroom closets are a disaster, and I'm also having problems in my kitchen pantry, linen closet, and laundry room. I'm drowning in clutter at my house."

Pennywise

We'll refer to the person who operates from a strong financial position as Pennywise. They're thoughtful in their spending habits. More accurately, they're thoughtful in their saving habits. Consequently, they aren't overextended financially.

Pennywise has planned for the future. They've saved money for their retirement years. If Pennywise were to lose their job unexpectedly, they'd have enough savings set aside to tide them over for a long time—long enough for them to find another job.

....

It appears that more and more of us are moving to a Pennywise mentality. "The majority of Americans continue to enjoy saving money more than spending it, by 62 percent to 34 percent. The 2014 saving-spending gap is the one of the widest since Gallup began tracking Americans' preferences in 2001."

—BRENDAN MOORE, gallup.com

....

Pennywise is the type of person who bases their expenditures on what they need first. They don't buy things just for the sake of having them. When they do find something they want, they may use their charge card so they can earn air miles or other types of incentives, but they always pay their card off at the end of every month.

If Pennywise can't afford it, Pennywise doesn't buy it. They don't carry a balance on their charge card, so they never incur interest fees.

Pennywise lives within their means, making more money than they spend.

Nadine is the epitome of Pennywise. Her philosophy is "the less we have, the more room we have to live right-sized lives." The "less is more" attitude adds exponentially to her joy factor.

How would you answer the following questions?

Are your financial habits more like Spendthrift's, more like Pennywise's, or somewhere in between?

Are you satisfied with what you have, or are you more concerned with what you don't have yet?

Do you have a written budget where you've listed your income and all of your expenses and calculated the difference?

Do you live within your means, or do you spend more money than you earn?

One of the best books I've ever read about establishing a budget and financial planning is Julie Murphy Casserly's *The Emotion Behind Money: Building Wealth from the Inside Out*. If you feel overwhelmed at the idea of creating a personal budgeting plan, this easy-to-read and enjoyable book offers a foolproof way to create, organize, and maintain a personal budget. It's a step-by-step guide to getting yourself on track financially and staying there for the rest of your life.

Creating a financial budget is establishing a boundary. But in order to be effective, the boundary must be maintained. Establishing and maintaining boundaries are two very different things:

> ***Establishing a boundary*** is defining it and setting it in place.

> ***Maintaining a boundary*** is implementing it, weaving it into your lifestyle, and checking it often to ensure that it holds.

As a pilot would say, "Plan your flight and fly your plan."

Establish a solid, realistic financial plan and follow it. Doing so goes a long way toward ensuring that you won't run out of money before you run out of years. A boundary is effective only if it's maintained.

DRAWING A LINE IN THE SAND

All boundaries, not just financial, are governed by this self—self-preservation.

In their book *Healing the Scars of Emotional Abuse*, Gregory L. Jantz, PhD, and Ann McMurray share results from a playground study that was conducted at several elementary schools from different demographics across the United States. The purpose of the study was to determine the effects of having a fence—or not—around the perimeter of a playground.

The questions were:

> Is having a fence around the playground a healthy boundary, one that enables a child to flourish?
>
> Does having a fence around the playground promote feelings that diminish, constrict, and limit?

Observations of children in first through fifth grades were made before and after, with and without the fence.

Before the Fence Was Removed

Before the fence was removed, the children were boisterous, laughing, giggling, and running around. They jumped rope, played on the monkey bars and teeter-totter, and were actively engaged in handball and tetherball. They used the entire playground, right up to the fence line. When the bell rang, it was a chore for the playground supervisors to get them lined up and ready to go back to our classrooms.

After the Fence Was Removed

Over a school break, and without notification, the fence around the playground perimeter was removed. When the children returned to school, in almost all instances, it was observed that they were more soft-spoken, their laughter was diminished, and they used very few pieces of playground equipment. They didn't venture near the area where the fence had been. Rather, they tended to congregate in the center. When the bell rang, they lined up with limited supervision and were ready to return to their classrooms.

Conclusion

The conclusion of the nationwide study was that with healthy boundaries in place, the children felt safe, and within that sense of safety, they felt free. Subsequently, they displayed behaviors of children who are comfortable and confident.

....

"Boundaries are a measure of self-esteem. Standing your ground increases your credibility. It makes you more desirable because it allows you to remain open and receptive to the other person, as well as retain a sense of separate identity. Good boundaries say you are very selective because you value yourself—and value the people you let into your life."

—YANGKI CHRISTINE AKITENG, relationship coach and author

....

THERE ARE MANY TYPES OF BOUNDARIES

The word "boundary" is defined as "an indicated border or limit." Boundaries can be physical or emotional and can be applied to many different areas in life, including relationships (platonic and intimate), environments, finances, social life, exercise, children, workplace, home, food, and recovery (such as in twelve-step programs).

Petra shared, "Fundamental self-care demands that if I want to be concerned about the welfare of others, I need to also consider my own. For much of my life, I've found it difficult to set and protect my boundaries. Poorly defined and frequently violated during childhood, they didn't develop until I was in my fifties. People could easily walk over me—and still can, just less often."

Somewhat like the beds in the story of *Goldilocks and the Three Bears*, boundaries can be too hard, too soft, or just right. Using relationships as the illustration, here's how those boundaries look:

Too Hard

People with relationship boundaries that are too strict tend to shut everyone out of their lives. They appear unapproachable and cold and don't discuss their feelings or display their emotions. They exhibit excessive self-sufficiency and don't ask for help. They don't allow others to get emotionally or physically close to them. They have, in fact, barricaded themselves behind an invisible barrier that has no point of entry.

Rigid boundaries are exclusive, rather than inclusive. Partners in this type of relationship are self-contained and make very little emotional impact and connection. If they experience intimacy, it tends to be cold and detached. The characteristics of unyielding boundaries include:

- Saying no if the request involves close interaction
- Avoiding intimacy
- Fear of rejection or of being consumed
- Not sharing personal information
- Struggling to identify wants, needs, and feelings
- Meager social life at best
- Rarely asking for help

Too Soft

People with relationship boundaries that are too lax are inclined to get very close to others too fast. They have a tendency to take on others' feelings as their own. As a result, they can quickly become overwhelmed, give too much, take too much, and need constant reassurance.

Typically, people with boundaries that are too loose lead chaotic, drama-filled lives. They don't have any type of barrier around themselves; every place is an entry point.

Collapsed boundaries are so inclusive that it's difficult to distinguish one person from the other. Oftentimes, partners in this type of relationship seek to lose themselves in the other person or expect the other person to become lost in them. They project their pain onto others and often take on others' pain in return. The characteristics of weak boundaries include:

- Not saying no, for fear of rejection

....

"'No' is a complete sentence."

—ANNE LAMOTT, political activist, public speaker, writing teacher, and author

....

- Being held hostage by the opinions of others
- Being overly responsible and controlling, or passive and dependent
- Sharing personal information before establishing mutual trust
- Taking on the feelings of others
- Tolerating abuse and disrespect
- Compromising values to please others

Just Right

People with relationship boundaries that are just right tend to be firm yet flexible. They give and receive support. They respect their feelings, needs, opinions, and rights—and those of others—but they're clear about their separateness.

They're responsible for their own happiness. Likewise, they give other people the gift of being responsible for their personal happiness as well.

They're comfortable with themselves and thus are able to negotiate and compromise. By invitation only, their barrier has windows and doors that allow access to those who respect their boundaries.

Healthy boundaries are flexible; they grow and change. They can be lowered to enhance intimacy or raised to promote safety.

The line between partners in this relationship is easily identifiable. They're independent people, yet they're close enough to be connected and to have a positive impact on each other's lives. The characteristics of healthy boundaries include:

- Self-respect
- Not tolerating abuse or disrespect—of any kind
- Communicating personal wants, needs, and feelings
- Responsibility for exploring and nurturing their full potential
- Not allowing others to define their limits
- Expectations of reciprocity in relationships; sharing responsibility and power
- Asking for help when it's needed

As with the children in the playground-safety study, healthy boundaries create a safe space that allows us to freely enjoy life.

Just as we expect others to value our boundaries, it's equally important for us to respect the boundaries of others. Barbara shared, "Because I believe in karma—the law of return—I have to ask myself periodically, in what way have I knowingly violated another person's boundaries with the intent to get something for myself, even if it caused another distress?"

HOME IS WHERE WE ARE

This self—self-preservation—also governs "home." When we're young, we can't wait to leave it. When we're finally out on our own, many of us yearn for it. There are numerous definitions for home. For some, it's a geographic location—the place they were born or grew up, or maybe where they currently reside. For others, it's a feeling; as the saying goes, "home is where the heart is."

Patricia shared with a sigh, "I'd always planned to follow the conventional wisdom and not move for at least a year after my life mate died, but here I am, two months into my grief, and I'm moving—not by choice, but by circumstance. Right now I'm rattling around in an empty house, filling it with tears. Though I'm mostly moved and packed and the house is cleaned, I'm not ready to go—it's way too soon.

"But even if I could stay, it wouldn't change anything. My mate would still be dead, and I'd still be homeless—he was my home, not this house."

I believe that no matter where we go, when our internal compass—our inner guidance system—is divine love, we're at home within ourselves. Home is anywhere we are.

When we're confident in our survival and self-preservation, we're empowered. When this self is healthy and in balance, there's an abundant return value to the heart. In this case, the dividends include tangibles such as financial freedom, physical fitness, strength, vitality, flexibility, and stamina.

The added bonus is not just longevity but *quality* longevity. There's a tremendous difference between existing and thriving. Regardless of our age, we need the life force of joy—*joie de vivre*. And security allows joy to flower more fully.

In the following chapter, you'll find several keys—practical tips, tools, and exercises—to enhance your sense of groundedness and offload baggage associated with self-preservation.

....

"Self-preservation is the first law of nature."

—SAMUEL BUTLER, English novelist, essayist, and critic

....

CHAPTER 4

Keys to Self-Preservation: Enhance Your Sense of Groundedness

"The body is a sacred garment."

—MARTHA GRAHAM, American dancer and choreographer, whose influence on dance has been compared to the influence Picasso had on modern visual arts, Stravinsky had on music, or Frank Lloyd Wright had on architecture

1. MIND-BODY CONNECTION

Self-preservation is associated with the immune system, lymphatic system, spinal column, rectum, feet, and legs. If you're experiencing issues in any of these areas, it's time to make an appointment with your health care provider.

2. COLOR THERAPY

Red is associated with self-preservation, survival, and physical wellness.

It enhances vitality, energy, and courage. It's the color of blood. Think of mouthwatering strawberries, the inside of a ripe watermelon, flaming maple trees, iron-rich soils, a juicy beefsteak tomato, fire-engine red, or the brilliant shade of a cardinal against a snowy backdrop. Remember the sweet, rich taste of red licorice at the movies?

The *positive* properties of red are expressed as energetic, assertive, powerful, exciting, passionate, strong-willed, courageous, and self-motivated.

The *negative* properties of red are described as aggressive, domineering, impatient, insensitive, and self-centered.

The healing properties of red are stimulating and vitalizing and address physical symptoms such as tiredness, poor circulation, colds/chills, and negative states of mind like apathy, fear, and lack of initiative. Red boosts brain activity and increases heart rate, respiration, and blood pressure.

When you need a boost in the areas of survival and self-preservation, indulge yourself with this color. Its frequency refreshes crucial earth energy by stirring the base chakra and stimulating all of the body's energy centers. Like the deep root system of a healthy tree, red stabilizes our foundation and can help to bring our energetic body "down to earth." It gives us legs to stand on. When our energy wavers or we feel used up or indifferent, red helps us ground and center our energy so that we can realize our goals.

The vibration of red is warming, energizing, and stimulating—what shade are you drawn to?

True primary red is a statement color, dramatic, vibrant, and stimulating. Or maybe you enjoy more muted tones—cozy and intimate, with just a hint of passion and romance.

What we do with our physical environment—our personal space—speaks to our heart and helps us to flourish:

- Accessorize with a piece of red clothing or jewelry.
- Add a splash of red to your decor. Fill a clear vase with bright red marbles and set it on an end or coffee table.
- Do something bold—paint your headboard red.
- Take advantage of the healing frequency of red crystals, such as garnet, red jasper, and ruby.

3. DIET

A quick and easy way to make sure you're eating the right amount of food is to use the *plate method*. Look at your plate; it should have:

- one-half fruits and veggies
- one-quarter lean meat or protein
- one-quarter grains or starches (like rice or pasta)

Plates have actually gotten bigger over the last forty years. Most plates are twelve inches wide, but the plate method uses a nine-inch plate. This means you'll need to leave space around the outside of your plate to make sure you're not eating too much. Although it's used primarily for diabetics' meal planning, the plate method is great for anyone who's interested in weight management and good nutrition.

Foods that enhance our senses of survival and groundedness include:

- **Root vegetables**—carrots, potatoes, parsnips, radishes, beets, onions, and garlic
- **Protein-rich foods**—eggs, meats, beans, tofu, soy products, and peanut butter
- **Spices**—horseradish, hot paprika, chives, cayenne, and peppers
- **Supplements**—a good multivitamin and mineral supplement that improves general body function and boosts physical and mental health and well-being

Tip: limit unhealthy fats by using olive oil.

4. AROMATHERAPY

The use of myrrh, patchouli, vetiver, rosewood, ylang-ylang, cinnamon, thyme, or balsam de Peru helps to eliminate fears associated with survival and self-preservation. These essential oils encourage fortitude, courage, peace, calm, sympathy, acceptance, and mastery.

5. AFFIRMATIONS

When we encounter threats to our sense of safety, effective affirmations to speak out loud are:

I am grounded and safe, life is safe, and I'm not afraid.
I am capable of providing for my life's necessities.
Well-being is my number-one priority.
I am healthy, full of energy and vitality.
I stand up for myself.
My body is a safe and pleasurable place for me to be.
My body is my temple; I love and respect it.
I trust my body's wisdom.
I honor my uniqueness.
I function from a place of courage.

6. THE BUSINESS OF BEING

Survival and self-preservation in the business world are strengthened with a business plan. For a moment, think of your life as a business and write the answers to the following questions:

> What's your personal business plan?
> How do you want to conduct your life?
> What are your parameters?
> What are your ethics and practices?
> What will you become involved in?
> What will you refrain from becoming involved in?

7. BREATHWORK: CIRCULAR BREATHING

Whenever you recognize that you're hosting an unwanted, draining emotion related to issues of survival, self-preservation, or physical wellness, stop what you're doing and focus on your breath. Breathe deeply, slowly, and steadily. Place a hand on your lower belly to ensure that you're breathing past your chest.

An effective breathing exercise to do is circular breathing. Here's how it's done:

- Lie with your back on the floor.
- Place a large, flat stone or brick horizontally just below your ribs, as a focus point. Few people realize that the lungs extend beyond the rib cage. In fact, two-thirds of the lungs sit below the lowest rib. Filling the larger portion of the lungs will enhance your energy.
- Inhale slowly and deeply through your nose, filling your lower abdomen with breath, causing the stone or brick to rise.
- Exhale deeply and slowly through your mouth; the stone or brick will lower as your abdomen naturally contracts.
- Once you've established a rhythm, identify a replacement attitude. Imagine that with each inhalation, you're breathing in the color red and the feeling of that new attitude—increasing joy.
- When you exhale, imagine that you're releasing the toxins associated with the unwanted emotion—offloading baggage.

- Repeat for several minutes, drawing the red breath and replacement feeling down into your lower belly to anchor the new feeling.

8. PHYSICAL WELLNESS INVENTORY AND VITALITY CHECK

- Do you drink the *right* amount of water every day? It's easy. Simply divide your body weight by two. The resulting number is the number of ounces of water you should drink every twenty-four hours.
- Do you get a sufficient amount of sleep each evening?
- Do you burn more calories than you ingest? This is easy to calculate if you wear a fitness tracker. There are many excellent choices on the market.
- You are what you assimilate—have you changed your eating style for health? For life?
- Have you started and maintained a realistic exercise program?
- Have you had a physical examination in the last eighteen months?
- Do you know your numbers: cholesterol, blood pressure, and blood sugar levels?

If you answered no to any of these questions, it may indicate an area of opportunity for you to improve the quality of your physical wellness.

On a scale of one to nine, where do you rate yourself on the current level of your physical vitality, if one represents low energy (frail, fatigued, drained) and nine represents high energy (strong, energetic, vibrant)?

Is there a difference between where you currently are and where you want to be? If so, write down how you'll close the gap. Be specific.

9. ACTION STEPS

To enhance your senses of survival and groundedness, reconnect with your body by doing physical activities:

- **Quick hits:** Do some squats or stomp your feet on the ground to connect to the earth. Go outside, get some fresh air, and connect with nature to relieve stress and gain new creative ideas.

- **With a little planning:** Start aerobics, working with weights, or running. Plant a garden; go hiking, camping, climbing, kayaking, or horseback riding. Get restful sleep.

Water

This bears repeating: *drink the right amount of water every day*. To calculate the amount that's right for you, simply divide your body weight by two. The resulting number is the number of ounces that you need to drink every twenty-four hours. Remember that caffeine and alcohol are dehydrators.

Body Weight

Do you need to lose, maintain, or gain weight? Ideal weight is determined by many factors, including age, gender, and height.

Body mass index (BMI) is a mathematical calculation often used to determine if a person is overweight. A BMI between 25 and 29.9 is considered overweight; a BMI of 30 or more is considered obese. BMI is calculated by dividing a person's body weight by their height in inches (squared), and then multiplying that number by 703.

Note: this number can be misleading for very muscular people, pregnant women, or breastfeeding mothers.

Here's how the calculation would look for a woman who's five feet, seven inches tall and weighs 135 pounds: 135 (weight)/4,489 (height in inches $(67)^2$) x 703 = 21.14.

Exercise

Start and maintain an exercise regimen, one that's fun so you'll stick with it. Be realistic about what you can do. You don't need to be an athlete; almost anyone can exercise.

Consider your current state of physical fitness. If you haven't exercised in years, start with something modest, like stretching. Stretching each morning is a great way to wake up your body and get your muscles ready for the day. Start with a small block of time, maybe twenty minutes. As you get into your routine, you won't mind increasing to twenty-five and then thirty minutes. In order to be most effective, you need to be consistent. Consistency and breathing are key to any type of exercise.

Relax, and avoid holding your breath. Warm up your muscles by holding gentle stretches for about thirty seconds; direct attention to your breath, and focus. This helps settle a busy mind into a state of relative quiet. If you feel pain, you've gone too far. Ease up until you're free of pain, and then hold the stretch for thirty seconds.

Begin at the top of your body and work your way down through the muscle groups until you reach your feet—neck, shoulders, elbows, wrists, back, waist, thighs, knees, and ankles—working both sides of your body evenly. Avoid bouncing, as that can cause micro-tears in the muscle.

Pretzel Poses—NOT!

We'd all do well to take lessons from our dog and cat companion animals. Have you ever noticed the first thing they do when they wake up? They bow forward and backward in a deep stretch, similar to the "downward-facing dog" yoga pose. It's not as easy as it looks, but it's worth learning because it tones and strengthens your entire body and can also help to alleviate back pain. Here's how it's done:

- Start on your hands and knees. Your knees should be directly below your hips, and your hands should be slightly in front of your shoulders, with your fingers spread out. Curl your toes under.
- Exhale and lift your knees off the floor. At first, your leg muscles may be tight. Don't force the pose. If your heels don't naturally drop toward the floor, or if the pose feels tight, slowly "walk" your legs: keep your feet still, but alternately bend and straighten each leg, like you're walking in place. After a few stretches, you'll feel looser. If your heels still don't touch the floor, put a rolled towel under them. By the way, there's no shame in learning the pose with bent knees and straightening them when you're ready.
- Push your thighs back and straighten your knees without locking them. Again, a rolled towel can help with this until you get the hang of it.
- Keep your head between your upper arms; don't let it hang. It's tempting to let your shoulders hunch up toward your ears, but the position is much more comfortable if you pull them down. Concentrate on maintaining a long neck. If you're new at this, you can stack yoga blocks under your head for support. Also, rotat-

ing your upper arms out can help to release the tension in your
shoulders.

- One problem that many people experience is slippery or shaky
hands. Generally, this is caused by not shifting your weight far
enough back. Lift your pelvis a little higher, causing a slight arch
in your lower back. This will move your center of gravity back and
will help to keep your hands still.
- To come out of the downward dog pose, bend your knees toward
the floor and return to a kneeling position.

They make it look so easy! The next time you see your dog or cat do this healthy pose, you'll look at them with a whole new respect.

Detox

For the next twenty-one days, refrain from caffeine, soda, and alcohol. For a whole detox, drink your water with fresh-squeezed lemon in it. (I prefer mine at the temperature of hot tea.) Lemon is antiseptic and antiscorbutic. These qualities work toward correcting the system and cleansing impurities, including the efficient elimination of waste. Side benefits are lemon's potassium content, which nourishes the brain and nerve cells, and calcium, which builds strong bones.

Money

Is your income greater than your expenses, or do you spend more money than you make? Establish and work toward maintaining a written financial budget.

Boundaries

Creating healthy boundaries is a process that takes time and practice. Determination and persistence are essential. Here are a few tips to help you get on track and stay there:

- When you recognize the need to set a boundary, put it in place.
- Clearly communicate the boundary in a dignified and respectful
manner.

- Don't justify or apologize for any boundaries that you set.
- When a boundary is tested—and it will be—stand firm; sometimes this means ending a relationship.
- Detoxify your personal energy signature; this means removing people, places, and things that manipulate, abuse, and/or try to control you.

10. PERSONAL ENERGY SIGNATURE

On a sheet of paper, draw a circle that represents your personal energy circle. Considering what you've learned about self-preservation, survival, and physical wellness, on the inside of the circle list the people, places, and things that are for this self's highest and best good—positive, uplifting, constructive, and healing.

On the outside of the circle, list the people, places, things, and actions you need to avoid to keep this self healthy and balanced. The examples on the following page will help you get started.

SELF-PRESERVATION, SURVIVAL, AND PHYSICAL WELLNESS
PERSONAL ENERGY SIGNATURE

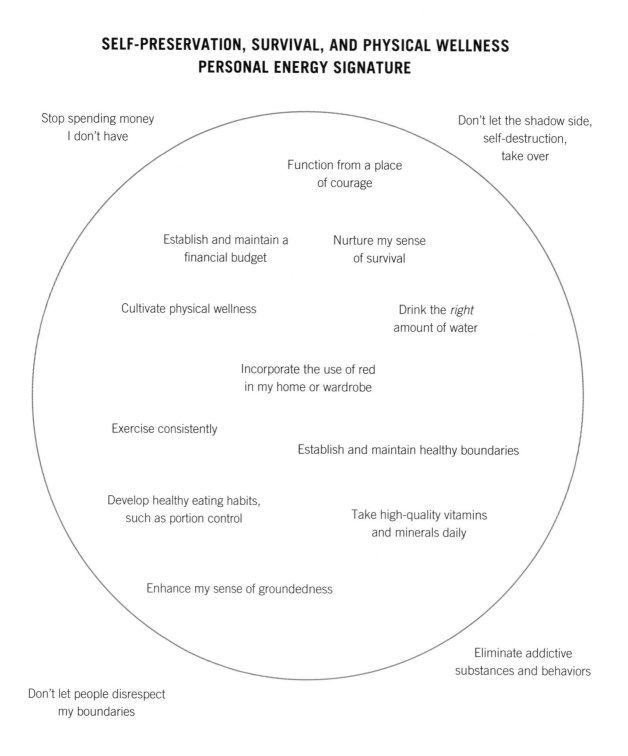

Stop spending money
I don't have

Don't let the shadow side,
self-destruction,
take over

Function from a place
of courage

Establish and maintain a
financial budget

Nurture my sense
of survival

Cultivate physical wellness

Drink the *right*
amount of water

Incorporate the use of red
in my home or wardrobe

Exercise consistently

Establish and maintain healthy boundaries

Develop healthy eating habits,
such as portion control

Take high-quality vitamins
and minerals daily

Enhance my sense of groundedness

Eliminate addictive
substances and behaviors

Don't let people disrespect
my boundaries

CHAPTER 5

Self #2: Self-Gratification

Self-gratification is responsible for pleasure and occupational wellness; its purpose is to increase our sense of delight. When healthy, this self functions from a place of personal respect. Corresponding to the sacral chakra, it resonates with the color orange. An inspiring affirmation for this self is: *I am radiant*. The shadow side is self-denial.

❖ ❖ ❖

Rhonda shared, "Will I ever outgrow my fear of intimacy? I'm forty-seven, and I'm scared. Don't get me wrong, I'm not scared of sex, but I'm startled by holding hands. If a guy wants to get to know me more, compliments me, or crosses the line from being sweet to me to being sweet on me, I get flustered—I stutter or look at my feet; I run away.

"It seems to go only one way. I'm okay with administering affection, just not receiving it. I'm all about actually being a friend, whether it's a guy sharing his problems with me postcoitally or going out for the occasional drink or friendly outing. I'm the gal who can actually do 'friends with benefits' and not want anything more—really."

- Are you comfortable with intimacy?
- Do you struggle to see yourself as "sexy" and wonder how anyone could desire you?
- Do you see sex in a positive light—healthy and pleasurable?
- Does guilt overshadow your life?

This self—self-gratification—enables us to make changes in our life through personal choices to effect pleasure, passion, and purpose. The developmental stage begins somewhere between six and twenty-four months of age.

Self-gratification presents us with the opportunity to lessen our need to control and to enjoy balance in our lives. As we continue to grow, this often translates to food and intimacy (specifically sex).

When our senses of pleasure and self-gratification are in balance, we enjoy qualities from the constructive side of this self. These include happiness, enthusiasm, sociability, and self-assuredness.

THE SHADOW SIDE: SELF-DENIAL

When our senses of pleasure and self-gratification are out of balance, we can experience negative things, such as self-denial.

Vastly different from self-discipline—controlling one's impulses—or forgoing something for the benefit of someone else, self-denial is triggered by negative thought patterns such as:

- I'm not good enough; therefore, I can't have, be, or do this.
- If I can't have, be, or do this, then I don't deserve to have, be, or do that.
- I'm going to deny myself this to prove to you that . . .

Sometimes the martyr attitude is manipulative, in that it garners sympathy or, even better, vengeance for the "willing victim."

Self-denial can manifest itself in a number of harmful ways that become items we tuck into our life's baggage. Depending on their size and impact, we may slip them into a tote that we keep within arm's reach, for handy retrieval, or stuff them into a large suitcase that comes around on the baggage carousel only occasionally. These can include:

Physical: urinary problems, pelvic pain, libido, and issues with reproductive organs, including concerns with fertility.

Mental: ethics, blame, power, control, poor choices, and irresponsibility.

Emotional: fear, guilt, selfishness, emotional disconnect, and destructive behaviors.

Spiritual: manifesting, not honoring relationships, not learning to "let go."

Through angry tears, Emily shared, "I'm forty-two, and I have no friggin' clue what I'm supposed to be doing with my life!"

With a sigh of affectionate regret, Leslie, age sixty, shared, "I wish I could begin over again at seventeen, the year I started college, because if I knew then what I know now, I'd be so brave! I'd join everything, try everything, and ask for forgiveness later."

"There are no regrets in life, just lessons."

—JENNIFER ANISTON, American actress, film director, and producer

This self—self-gratification—is where the rubber meets the road in terms of pleasure, passion, and panache—*unfettered gusto!*

It also oversees occupational wellness—not necessarily what we do for a paycheck, but our purpose, our calling. This is the self that drives a stake in the ground and lays claim to—defines—our life purpose.

Before we go any further, let's take a minute to define the difference between pleasure and passion, which are both important:

Pleasure is associated with enjoyment—it's pleasing, agreeable, even amusing—but it's tame compared with the sense of emotional abandon that comes when we're passionate about something. Most of us derive a great deal of pleasure from a wide variety of people, places, things, and experiences in our lives.

Some of life's simple pleasures include having our feet rubbed, soaking in a hot bath, having our hair brushed by another person, sleeping in freshly laundered sheets, being lulled by the sound of ocean waves, and enjoying the delectable taste of our favorite food.

Marley shared, "I used to be a sugar addict. Now I still enjoy an occasional dessert but in tiny portions, eaten very slowly. What I enjoy even more, though, is cold fruit—a chilled peach, some blueberries, a few strawberries, or a plum. I eat one bite at a time, closing my eyes to *savor* each bit and enjoy it to the fullest."

When was the last time you had to scrub under your fingernails because you planted something in the dirt in your garden or worked with clay?

When was the last time you checked the girth strap on a saddle and rode a horse?

When was the last time you kicked off your shoes and ran barefoot in the rain, tossing your head back to catch drops in your mouth?

Doing things that are pleasurable heightens our capacity for joy.

Passion is the drive behind our purpose, the force, the enthusiasm. It's the internal *oomph* we apply to a person, place, thing, or experience—a tremendous mental and emotional investment.

....

"One person with passion is better than forty people merely interested."

—E. M. FORSTER, English novelist, short-story writer, and essayist

....

When we're passionate about something, we'll go to the mat for it. Most of us are passionate—truly passionate—about a select few people, places, things, and experiences in our life.

What occurs in the space between a person and the object of their pleasure or passion is vastly different depending on the lens through which it's viewed:

- When the object (person, place, thing, or experience) is viewed through the lens of *pleasure*, the space is pleasant and engaging.
- When it's observed through the lens of *passion*, the space practically sizzles like an electric current.

What is it that you love to do?
What excites and energizes you?
What are you really good at?
What are your proudest achievements?
What can you lose yourself in?
How would you like others to remember you?

Many times, the answers to these questions hint at an aspect of your life purpose. If you're not sure of the answers, it's time to do a personal gap analysis. Take a close look at your *actual* life (where you are) and your *potential* life (where you want to be). Think of the distance between the two as a road that's under construction.

What we believe about ourselves is what we become.

Taking an active role in occupational wellness can remove the ruts of life and build a smooth surface that takes us to destinations we really want to visit, rather than keeping us in the slow lane of inactivity, drifting without purpose or direction.

STICK OUT YOUR TONGUE AND SAY AAH!

How's your occupational wellness? For some this can mean needing to find a job, for others it can mean finding work-life balance, and for nearly everyone it means finding healthy ways to reduce stress. Because what we do in exchange for a paycheck utilizes so much of our time, it's vital to our well-being that we do what we enjoy, and enjoy what we do. This enhances personal satisfaction and enriches our life.

On Ben's way to celebrate his father's eightieth birthday, he stopped by our healing studio and shared that he was heading to his dad's office to surprise him.

"His office? Your father still works?" I asked in wide-eyed astonishment.

"Oh, gosh, yes!" he replied. "He's still a practicing dentist. He retired when he was sixty-seven and found that he missed it too much, so, after six months, he reopened his practice. He's one of the fortunate people who absolutely love what they do."

Unfortunately, for some there's a fine line between enjoying their job and workaholism. A workaholic is a person with a compulsive and unrelenting need to work. They're intelligent, ambitious, successful people who are prisoners of their own success.

Justin, a thirty-five-year-old executive at a high-pressure investment firm, works sixty to seventy hours per week. Even on vacation, he often slips away from the rest of his family to go online, check messages, and answer e-mails and phone calls. Until recently, he saw nothing abnormal about his behavior; in fact, everyone at his job works like that.

Chad, age thirty-two, shared this story: "I've lost my wife, my daughters, most of my friends, and my driver's license because 'it's all about me.' I did so well, so fast, in the corporate world, money and opportunities were thrown at me hand over fist. I began to believe the publicity, that I was a 'golden boy'—untouchable. I didn't think the rules applied to me, so I betrayed confidences and marital vows and drank to cover up how that felt. I believed I was bulletproof and rode that wave until it crashed, taking everything I held dear."

Rita, an attorney, gets by on four to six hours of sleep per night, or even as little as an hour if she's preparing for a trial. She's accessible to her clients from 4:00 a.m. to midnight, seven days a week, via cell phone, air phone, e-mail, or her cherished iPhone, which has become like an appendage.

....

"American Average Work Hours:

- At least 134 countries have laws setting the maximum length of the workweek; the United States does not.

- In the United States, 85.8 percent of males and 66.5 percent of females work more than 40 hours per week.
- According to the International Labor Organization (ILO), 'Americans work 137 more hours per year than Japanese workers, 260 more hours per year than British workers, and 499 more hours per year than French workers.'
- According to data from the US Bureau of Labor Statistics, the average productivity per American worker has increased by 400 percent since 1950. One way to look at that is that it should take only one-quarter the work hours, or 11 hours per week, to afford the same standard of living as a worker in 1950 (or our standard of living should be 4 times higher). Is that the case? Obviously not. Someone is profiting; it's just not the average American worker."

—G. E. MILLER, 20SomethingFinance.com

Rita's husband Sam, an attorney who left a successful practice to be a stay-at-home dad to their two children, said, "At her best, she's decisive, persistent, self-motivated, passionate, and committed—hence the long work hours. At her worst, she can be demanding, impatient, intolerant of flaws, and emotionally distant."

Success is subjective. Like beauty, it's in the eye of the beholder.

I think my friend Sam defined it best when he said, "It all comes down to the capacity for love, which trumps all else in this world."

Occupational wellness means that we bring the unhealthy aspects of our career or life purpose to light—take them out of our baggage—for examination so we can find the mind-body correlation and work through them in a healthy and productive way, offloading baggage and increasing joy.

Occupational wellness means that we intentionally set aside our busyness and schedule time to play the piano, read a book, take a walk like we used to, play with a puppy, lie on our back in the yard and watch the clouds dance across the sky, learn how to make something, go out to a restaurant with a friend, skip stones on a lake, visit a museum, or sit under a tree to experience silence again.

In taking an active role, we come to understand and value the best use of our gifts, skills, and talents in order to make a contribution to our life and to the lives of those in our sphere of influence. It means being engaged in what we do and integrating a job well done into a lifestyle that's balanced, satisfying, and rewarding.

ZERO IN ON YOUR PURPOSE, MISSION, AND PATH

Purpose

Depending on the type of session we're having, I may well ask an adult client to tell me what their purpose in life is. I never cease to be amazed at the number of people who look back at me with a "deer in the headlights" look.

Women especially have trouble answering this question. As mothers, workers, home-makers, artists, social networkers, lovers, chauffeurs, spiritual guides, etc., they find that their purpose can sometimes get buried—even lost.

My next question is "Do you *know* what your purpose in life is?" At this point, I often receive a version of this answer: "I haven't found my purpose yet."

The bad news is, if you're waiting to "find" your life purpose, you can stop looking now, because you're never going to "find" it.

The good news is you don't find your purpose; you *determine* it. It's a choice, a conscious decision that you make. For example, I have determined that my purpose is to be a mindful agent of heart-based change—body, mind, and spirit.

....

"You do not have to go out looking for your calling. It will be quite apparent to you once you have 'gotten yourself out of the way.' The very immediacy of the task, placed where you all but trip over it, will make it indisputably yours and no one else's."

—MAHATMA GANDHI, Indian political and spiritual leader

....

It's my perspective that knowing one's life purpose—and living it—is vital to dynamic participation in the world and to joy.

As we learned earlier, passion is different from purpose. Passion is what *fuels* our purpose; it's the *drive* behind it.

In his book, *To Reach the Clouds*, Philippe Petit—a French high-wire artist who gained fame for his high-wire walk between the Twin Towers in New York City on August 7, 1974—said, "Passion is something that knows no bounds."

The drive behind my purpose is compassion.

Mission

The natural outcome or result of a person's purpose—in my case, to be a mindful agent of heart-based change—is the person's mission. In other words, if I'm authentically living my purpose, people will naturally experience change, be it physical, mental, emotional, or spiritual.

This means that my mission is to effect change that's positive, uplifting, constructive, and healing—heart-based change.

Path

Our path is the vehicle by which we accomplish our purpose and mission. Once we've determined our purpose and the natural outcome (our mission), we must choose a path.

At this point, you might think that the path through which we accomplish our purpose must be what we do for a living—our career. It may well be, but that's not necessarily the case.

When a client goes through the Life Harmony program, part of that experience includes determining their life purpose if they haven't already done so. Here are some wonderful examples of what many of my clients have arrived at:

Valerie, a financial advisor by day and hospice volunteer by night, said, "I determined my purpose to be an end-of-life caregiver to the terminally ill; to provide practical, emotional, and spiritual support as they make their end-of-life transition."

She went on to say, "It's been a steep learning curve. What I love most—and sometimes dislike most—is the interaction with people. Everyone reacts differently when dealing with death, whether it's their own or that of a loved one. Sometimes it brings out the best in them. Sometimes it brings out the worst. I've learned to practice levels of patience and compassion that have gone well beyond what I've known in the past."

Kimberly shared, "My purpose is to learn to be fully and authentically me; to find the person at the core of myself, claim her, and celebrate her!"

Carol works in a coffee shop next to the train station. She cheerfully serves bleary-eyed morning commuters before they head to the city. She shared, "My purpose is to live consciously and courageously, to resonate with love and compassion, to awaken the spirit within others, and to leave this world in peace."

Bonnie, a teacher, told me, "My purpose is to be a joy-filled guide. My mission is to discover, to inspire, and to restore joy in myself and in others. My path is to be a consistent beacon, lighting the way. And my passion—the drive behind my purpose—is to transition sadness."

I'm fortunate in that I love what I do, and I do what I love. My vocation (career) and my avocation (purpose) happen to be one and the same.

The purpose I have *determined* is not bound by geographic location; it's totally portable and can be accomplished from any vicinity. Additionally, I can be a mindful agent of heart-based change in any occupation: hairstylist, landscaper, astronaut, accountant, dentist, mechanic, corporate executive—there are no limits.

Currently, my path is transformational life coaching, which I do online with clients around the globe via Skype and FaceTime. This path provides me with the opportunity to be a mindful agent of heart-based change through my specific areas of interest—energy medicine, inner alchemy (personal transformation), and spiritual awareness.

....

"Understand that the right to choose your own path is a sacred privilege. Use it. Dwell in possibility."

—OPRAH WINFREY, American television host, actress, producer, and philanthropist

....

A person's purpose, mission, and path may change over time. For example, let's say that when your children are young and still at home, your purpose is to be the most amazing parent on the planet. Your mission—the outcome of that purpose—would be to have children who evolve into adults who appreciate life, put their best foot forward in everything they do, are responsible for their actions, contribute to society, and authentically live *their* purpose—not necessarily what *you* envisioned for them.

The vehicle for accomplishing that task (your path) is your everyday living. You're a role model—or, as Gandhi said, "My life is my teaching."

Once your grown children have left home, you may well change your focus and *determine* a different purpose. For example, you might decide that your purpose is humanitarian campaigning for organizations such as Amnesty International, Greenpeace, Sea Shepherd Conservation Society, Doctors Without Borders, Habitat for Humanity, or Conservation International. Perhaps you'll determine to promote world peace and friendship through the Peace Corps. The possibilities are endless.

DESTINY VERSUS FATE: THE DIFFERENCE REVEALED

We're in charge of our own destiny. We create our destiny with every choice we make. We can change it at any time.

Think of destiny as a horse that you're riding. Every pull of the reins and flick of the wrist (choices and decisions) guides the horse where you want it to go (creates your destiny).

Fate is different. Fate is what the horse becomes when you let go of the reins. The horse is no longer guided. Fate is something that *happens to you.*

In June 2008, Oprah Radio hosted Rabbi Shmuley as a guest. He said, "Believing in fate, instead of carving out your destiny, can leave you powerless." He went on to discuss how we can overcome fate by taking charge of our life.

Have you ever heard or used one of these common phrases: "Those are the cards I was dealt," or "That's just what life handed her," or "She really got the short end of the stick"? These are fate-based statements.

Rabbi Shmuley said, "We need to start thinking about our free will and freedom to make choices despite 'what life hands us.' Fate is not empowering, and belief in fate makes us feel like we're victims of our own nature or products of our environment. Destiny, on the other hand, is making the choice to avoid fate."

He went on to say, "Fate results from a belief that human beings are scripted and have no choice. Destiny is the product of a belief that we are always in control of our actions. What we become will be determined by what we do."

Destiny is a future place of unleashed, unlimited potential and possibility. We're not manipulated like puppets on a string.

"We are the creators of our own destiny. Be it through intention or ignorance, our successes and our failures have been brought on by none other than ourselves." These words of wisdom are shared by Enzo, the wise dog and narrator in Garth Stein's heartwarming book *The Art of Racing in the Rain.*

"It is our choices that show what we truly are, far more than our abilities." These now-famous words were spoken by professor Albus Dumbledore in J. K. Rowling's *Harry Potter and the Chamber of Secrets*. That statement is absolutely true. And every choice we make carries with it a resulting consequence. In fact, life is an ongoing series of choices and consequences.

I've had clients who say, "I feel like I've been painted into a corner." When we find ourselves in that position, nine times out of ten, we have but to look in our hand to see that we're the one who's holding the paintbrush. It took a series of choices to get painted into that corner; now it's going to take a series of different choices to get us out.

Barbara said, "I could try to take the easy way out and run away from my problems, but running away is only good for avoiding things. The trouble with this approach is that I'd end up avoiding myself, my life, and when it's all said and done, the problem's *still* going to be waiting there—unresolved."

My friend Sam wisely observed, "It's our very choices that mold our future to our own emotional and physical specifications."

WHATEVER YOU ARE NOT CHANGING, YOU ARE CHOOSING

In September 2007, I celebrated my fiftieth birthday. Holly, a teenage client, asked, "Gosh, Dr. B., now that you're *half a century old* [emphasis hers], what's the most important thing you've learned in your life?"

I went on a brief hermitage—took time away by myself—to think through my life. I asked myself questions like, "Where have I been?" "Where am I now?" "Where am I going?" And, by the way, "What is the most important thing that I've learned to date?"

In half a century of living, I've learned a great many things. But the one truth that keeps surfacing over and over again is clearly the most important thing that I've learned to date: *whatever you are not changing, you are choosing.*

What baggage are you carrying through life that weighs you down and makes the journey difficult and tiring?

Is it those extra pounds?

Are you punctually challenged—always running late?

Are you in a job you can barely tolerate?

Do you fail to keep your promises?

Do you bite your fingernails?

Are you staying in a relationship that's bankrupting your heart?

Do you continue to spend money you don't have?

Do you tell lies?

Are your spending habits out of control?

Are you still smoking?

The items we choose *not* to change are the same items we tuck into the unseen—but very real—suitcases we carry.

People tolerate in life what they subject themselves to. Remember, *whatever you are not changing, you are choosing.*

After a speaking engagement, a woman approached me and said, "I don't agree with your statement 'whatever you are not changing, you are choosing.'"

She went on to say, "I've recently been diagnosed with cancer, and I certainly didn't choose that."

I asked her if she was a smoker.

She responded, "I haven't smoked in ten years."

I asked her if she'd smoked prior to that time.

She looked a bit sheepish and said that she had, in fact, been a heavy smoker for over twenty years prior to quitting.

Did this woman choose to get cancer? Certainly not. But it's important to remember that there are some decisions we make in life that have the potential to catch up with us later. Just because we change a behavior doesn't mean the resulting consequences of previous actions automatically go away.

....

"Everybody, sooner or later, sits down to a banquet of consequences."

—ROBERT LOUIS STEVENSON, Scottish essayist, poet, and author

....

Another woman approached me after a different conference and shared that a drunk driver had killed her daughter. She went on to say that her daughter certainly hadn't chosen that.

There are many occasions in life when innocent people are affected by the negative fallout of another person's choices. The 9/11 terrorist attacks and the Columbine High School massacre are but two examples of this.

People make poor choices on a regular basis. That's part of the human condition. Some choices have individual ramifications; unfortunately, others are collective.

EIGHT LITTLE WORDS

I received an e-mail from a person who found my website and read the statement "whatever you are not changing, you are choosing" on the home page. She said, "That tagline at the top of your website stopped me in my tracks before I could even get to the rest of your site. I like it so much, I've been thinking about it ever since. It struck me like a punch in the gut–so hard, in fact, that I copied it out and put it on a kitchen cabinet for me to see, read, and remember. My kids are probably thinking, *Oh no—another one!*

"How many situations, choices, and thoughts could I filter through that phrase? And how the choices I make could look different in light of it—in the light of it—because I think it does call us to live in the light of our best intentions. Just eight little words, after all . . . "

Have you made the choice to step into your talents and gifts?

Soul Visioning: Clear the Past, Create Your Future, by Susan Wisehart, is a book written for those who are ready to go deeper and make a commitment to themselves. In it she teaches people how to clear the sabotaging beliefs and patterns that keep them on a treadmill of endless acquisition leading to nowhere. It's written for those who want to follow their soul's guidance to live a life of passion and purpose.

DON'T LOOK NOW, BUT THERE'S AN ELEPHANT IN THE ROOM

This self—self-gratification—oversees more than our occupation and life purpose; it also governs our sensuality and sexuality.

And while sex that both participants enjoy and embrace is incredibly pleasurable, healthy, and fulfilling, sexual frustration in a relationship is the elephant in the room. Many times, couples stop discussing it and look the other way because it can lead to arguments. However, left unresolved—tucked into our baggage—the problematic elephant gets very heavy to lug around and begins to invade other aspects of the relationship, even when no one's acknowledging it.

....

"One-third of the women around the world experience inhibited sexual desire, or low libido. As with male sexual dysfunction, female lack of interest in sexual activity can have a number of causes, both physical and psychological, that can produce feelings of shame, or complete emotional detachment during intercourse."

—RUTH WESTHEIMER (better known as Dr. Ruth), American sex therapist, media personality, and author

....

When we got to the section on sensuality and sexuality in the Life Harmony program, Gael blurted out, "We won't even go there!" Naturally, I asked her to explain.

"The best way I can explain is to say that I've spent so much of my adult life dealing with 'issues' that I've never really explored my sexuality. I didn't as a teenager, when most of my friends experimented, and as a young married woman, I was more interested in raising my children than being feminine. I was always the 'good girl.' As a single parent, and then meeting and marrying my second husband, I still was never interested in using my sexuality to entice or encourage.

"While I consider myself loyal, loving, and fully engaged in relationships, I wouldn't consider myself passionate. In some ways, my husband is the same, and I find that our level of intimacy has dwindled, for various reasons. And while he thinks it's because we're 'old,' I find his lack of interest sad and at times take personal responsibility for causing him to be disinterested.

"So my habit of downplaying my sexuality has played out exactly as I wrote the script, and now, at age fifty-eight, I feel I may have missed something wonderful."

IT'S WHAT'S INSIDE THE PACKAGE THAT COUNTS

The complex human design isn't just biological in nature. It includes emotional, intellectual, and spiritual components that work together to make up our human nature—and this includes our sexuality. Part of self-gratification's responsibility is to help us navigate these potentially treacherous waters.

Countless people have suffered because they've stuffed their sexual authenticity into their baggage in an effort to conform to familial or societal expectations.

Unfortunately, when it comes to sex, many of us carry heavy baggage that weighs us down. Some of the items tucked in our luggage can include unresolved, heartbreaking issues such as molestation, rape, intimacy, fertility, unrequited love, frigidity, or a feeling of needing to hide our sexual orientation or gender identity.

David shared, "I was raised in a small, narrow-minded, rural town by my father, a tough, emotionally inaccessible owner of a small trucking company. I've known since I was fifteen that I'm gay. After high school, I moved away from home to avoid having my family and friends find out. After years of hiding the truth, I couldn't stand it anymore. I called my dad and, during a two-hour conversation, gently told him that I'm gay. His reaction? For the first time in my life, he said, 'I love you.'"

Passive or active, what we do—or refrain from doing—with our gender identity and sexual orientation can impact our baggage. For some people, this occurs early on. For others, it happens later in life.

Connie, sixty-two, a mother of four, shared, "After three divorces and many other failed relationships with men, seven years ago I started my first relationship with a woman and my entire world changed. I got involved with someone I never expected to get involved with, and it was an awakening. I didn't fight it, because it was like, 'Now I understand why I had the issues I had early in life.' I had a great deal of difficulty connecting with men in relationships."

We express the direction of our sexual interest in our *sexual orientation*—our romantic, emotional, or enduring sexual attraction toward members of our own sex (homosexual orientation), or the opposite sex (heterosexual orientation).

"I've been with men all my life and had never met a woman I'd fallen in love with before," Bella shared. "But when I did, it didn't seem so strange. It didn't change who I am. I'm just a woman who fell in love with a woman."

There are many different sexual orientations: asexual, bisexual, heterosexual, homosexual, pansexual, and polysexual, to name a few.

....

"I'm a supporter of gay rights. And not a closet supporter, either. From the time I was a kid, I have never been able to understand attacks upon the gay community. There are so many qualities that make up a human being . . . by the time I get through with all the things that I really admire about people, what they do with their private parts is probably so low on the list that it is irrelevant."

—PAUL NEWMAN, American actor, film director, entrepreneur, and humanitarian

....

Helen, fifty-three, was married and dated only men for the first thirty-nine years of her life. But at forty, she had a fling with a woman and fell in love. She shared, "Life threw me a surprise party, and it's been the best relationship of my life!"

Gender identity refers to the internal sense of whether someone is male or female. Some people move in between; this is known as being "gender fluid."

Male and female are identities "assigned" at birth based on genitals; sex assignment is biological. However, there are many people who don't identify with the sex they were assigned. They feel it's a false or incomplete description of themselves—gender is emotional.

As a global community, we can choose whether to let differences regarding sexual orientation and gender identity go on dividing us into armed camps, or we can learn to work with them—and ultimately even celebrate them—by recognizing that each has its power, its authenticity, and even its sanctity.

THE INTIMATE DETAILS

Self-gratification, the maestro of pleasure and passion, orchestrates sensuality and sexuality. Many people confuse the terms "sensuality" and "sexuality," thinking they're synonymous. And while there are certainly areas of overlap, sensuality doesn't have to be associated with sexual intimacy, and sexuality isn't the only arena for sensual expression.

....

"Intimacy is being seen and known as the person you truly are."

—AMY BLOOM, social worker, psychotherapist, author, and
writer-in-residence at Wesleyan University

....

Sensuality is something much broader—it's enhancing and embracing our human experience through a conscious awareness of our senses. As a person who loves being in nature, I enjoy a sensual experience every time I go outside and engage my senses—connect—with nature: taking a deep breath of fresh air, smelling wildflowers, listening to birds calling to each other or the wind whispering in the leaves, feeling the bark of a fallen tree branch, or appreciating a star-studded night sky.

These forays in nature don't feed only the senses. Numerous studies show that people who are depressed, mentally ill, or just plain stressed out often find help from a walk along a sandy beach, in a park, or through a garden.

Reconnecting with nature triggers the release of endorphins, the body's natural pain-medication hormones. When they're released, endorphins make us feel better, improve our mood, increase pleasure, and minimize pain.

Drumming, whether alone or in a group, is another sensual experience. I play the bodhrán—a Celtic frame drum that's held close to the body. The curved rosewood frame, the ornate brass tacking, the tightly stretched head, all make for a rewarding tactile experience—the texture comes alive—as the hand inside the open end moves to control the pitch and timbre, while the other hand uses a smooth wood tipper to create the jovial beat of a celebratory jig or reel, or a deep, insistent, menacing boom that calls to mind ancient warfare.

Sensuality can include things of beauty, luxury, and refinement; an appreciation of simplicity; the awe-inspiring bounty of nature; the taste of food; a passion for creativity and the arts; aroma; and a deep connection to ourselves, to others, and to the universe.

"To be sensual, I think, is to respect and rejoice in the force of life, of life itself, and to be present in all that one does, from the effort of loving to the making of bread."

—JAMES BALDWIN, American novelist, writer, playwright, poet, essayist, and civil rights activist

Our senses—taste, touch, sight, hearing, and smell—are integral to sensuality, pleasure, and passion.

Kathy shared, "I have the urge to pay attention more to sensuous details: to the way the wind feels against the cheek; the smell of cilantro in the garden; the actual feel of the keyboard beneath the fingers. I want to pay more attention with my body and senses. That's a deep, soul-felt desire these days."

You can't see it, hear it, or touch it, but scent is powerful—our most powerful sense. The smell of things like crayons, jasmine, and burnt toast evokes memories that can transport us to the past and bring to mind people and places we might not otherwise recall.

Vivian shared, "I can remember as a very small child visiting my grandmother. While I was toddling around her garden, I flopped onto my bottom many times because I was just learning to walk. I remember being given numerous flowers and leaves to smell, feel, and look at, some even to taste. I can remember being told about the fairies that lived in the garden, so a strong sense of magic and mystery pervaded the experience for me.

"My grandmother moved shortly after this visit, and her next garden was mainly roses. The memory of exploring the first garden must have faded soon after that experience, as it wasn't until I was about twenty-four years old that I again smelled the flower of a morning, noon, and night bush and the scent of that flower brought the memory of my grandmother's magical garden flooding back."

Sensual perception also plays a role in who we find attractive. It may not be their drop-dead smile or dreamy eyes that draw us like a magnet to another person after all.

Remember the "va-va-voom!" effect used in cartoons, when a character's eyes pop way out of their head when they see someone they're attracted to? That's pheromones at work. In his article "The Smell of Love" that appeared in *Psychology Today*, F. Bryant Furlow tells us that human pheromones are naturally occurring chemical substances that trigger specific mating responses.

While pheromones have no smell or odor, they're sensed by an organ in the nasal passage—the vomeronasal organ—that sends a message to the hypothalamus and other emotional centers of the brain. These odorless compounds have a profound effect on human behavior, including attraction and the desire for sex.

Mood is demonstrably affected by what our senses experience. That's why many couples combine the sensual with the sexual experience to enhance their lovemaking. This may include candlelight, a scented bath, satin sheets, and romantic music. Sensuality is a key ingredient for richer sexual expression, gratification, and pleasure. And sexual pleasure comes with many emotional and physical health benefits.

Nadine, a fifty-one-year-old attorney, shared, "I don't feel sexy, and frankly, I'm just not in the mood. For the last six months, I've suffered from terrible hot flashes. My whole head feels like it's on fire, and sometimes even my hands burn. I wake up at night, and my bed is drenched in sweat. To be honest, I'd like nothing more than to lie naked on the cold linoleum kitchen floor, but I'm afraid I'll scare my teenage boys during their midnight food raids.

....

"The seven dwarfs of menopause—Itchy, Bitchy, Sweaty, Sleepy, Bloated, Forgetful, and Psycho."

—SUZANNE SOMERS, American actress, author, singer, businesswoman, and health spokesperson

....

"I have insomnia, am constantly on edge, have heart palpitations, am gaining weight, and basically feel depressed and fatigued most of the time. Sometimes I feel like I'm going through 'mental pause,' instead of menopause—I can't seem to remember anything. On the bright side, I hadn't had a period for four months, but just when I thought it was safe, bam—I got an exceptionally heavy flow."

HAVE SEX FOR BETTER HEALTH

Sex can improve cardiovascular health. When we feel sexually aroused, our heart and breathing rates increase. Our bodies do this in order to channel more blood to the genitals in preparation for the act of sex. But that's not the end of it. Our brain also sends a message to the adrenal glands telling them to increase the level of adrenaline in our bloodstream.

As things proceed from there, a rush of hormones gets released during the arousal and climax process, including adrenaline, oxytocin, noradrenaline, prolactin, DHEA, and testosterone, most all of which have cardio-protective effects, including:

Improved quality of sleep: this reaction is linked to oxytocin and the release of endorphins at orgasm, both of which can act like natural sedatives.

The benefits of exercise: muscles contract, heart rate increases, and our body releases calories and fat from storage to create more energy.

Pain relief: orgasm leads to the release of corticosteroids and endorphins that increase our pain threshold, providing short-term relief from conditions such as migraines, back pain, and arthritis.

Improved mood: endorphins make us feel euphoric and simultaneously relieve stress.

Enhanced sense of spirituality: many ancient traditions view sexuality as something sacred and spiritual. Sexual energy is unlike any other, and when we merge with this power during orgasm, some believe that we're connecting to the deepest parts of ourselves, our nonphysical aspects. Not only do we gain a deeper sense of ourselves, but we can experience an energy that feeds other areas of our lives.

Many who think of sex as a spiritual practice tell us they have a stronger sense of self and of their relationships.

Self-gratification governs both our occupational wellness and our sex life. If you're among the people who've slipped into the workaholic category, there are many costs of working so hard for so long, including that people tend to cut back on sleep and time with their families.

A recent survey found:

- Almost a third of people working more than forty-eight hours a week said that exhaustion was negatively affecting their married life.
- Nearly a third admitted that work-related tiredness was causing their sex life to suffer.
- Fourteen percent reported a loss of or reduced sex drive. They also complained that long hours and overwork led to arguments and tensions at home.
- Two out of five people working more than forty-eight hours per week blamed long hours for disagreements and said they felt guilty for not pulling their weight with domestic chores.

When we're confident in our pleasure and self-gratification, we're empowered.

When this self is healthy and in balance, there's an abundant return value to the heart. In this case, the dividends include driving our stake into the ground and *determining* our purpose. When this happens, all of the peripheral fluff falls away so that we can focus on the task at hand.

Busting through the baggage that weighs us down helps us to find pleasure and passion in life—helps us to thrive buoyantly, in joy.

In the following chapter, you'll find several keys—practical tips, tools, and exercises—to increase your sense of delight and offload baggage associated with self-gratification.

....

"True happiness is not attained through self-gratification, but through fidelity to a worthy purpose."

—HELEN KELLER, American lecturer, author, and activist

....

CHAPTER 6

Keys to Self-Gratification: Increase Your Sense of Delight

> "We do not believe in ourselves until someone reveals that deep inside us something is valuable, worth listening to, worthy of our trust, sacred to our touch. Once we believe in ourselves we can risk curiosity, wonder, spontaneous delight, or any experience that reveals the human spirit."
>
> —E. E. CUMMINGS, American poet, painter, essayist, author, and playwright

1. MIND-BODY CONNECTION

Self-gratification is associated with the reproductive system, integumentary system, urinary system, hip area, large intestine, appendix, lower vertebrae, and pelvis. If you're experiencing issues in any of these areas, it's time to make an appointment with your health care provider.

2. COLOR THERAPY

Orange is associated with self-gratification, pleasure, and occupational wellness. It enhances happiness, independence, and confidence. It's the color of molten lava. Think of the downy feathers on a robin's feathered breast, a mouthwatering tangerine, the velvet wings of a monarch butterfly, the impish grin of a jack-o'-lantern glowing on Halloween, or the life vest you wore in the boat at summer camp. Remember the taste of Orange Crush as the bubbles hit the back of your throat?

The *positive* properties of orange are expressed as joyful, enthusiastic, spontaneous, optimistic, sporting, good-humored, gregarious, and sensual.

The *negative* properties of orange are described as overindulgent, dependent, freeloading, deceptive, and superficial.

The *healing* properties of orange are warming and energizing and can address physical symptoms such as low vitality, poor appetite, indigestion, cramps/strained muscles, joint pains, and negative states of mind such as listlessness, boredom, sadness, and inhibition. Orange fosters sociability and helps us to assimilate new things and to unclog emotional energy that can get trapped in the lower abdomen.

When you need a boost in the areas of pleasure and self-gratification, indulge yourself with this color. The frequency of orange emboldens us to take in what we truly need from life and to let go of what no longer serves us.

The vibration of orange is energizing, exciting, and stimulating—what shade are you drawn to?

Vivid orange combines the drama of red and the cheerfulness of yellow. Pure orange is luminous, bright, glowing, and bold. Or maybe you prefer more muted and shaded tones that offer a bright but subtle glow that is restful, earthy, natural, and soothing.

What we do with our physical environment—our personal space—speaks to our heart and helps us to flourish:

- Accessorize with a piece of orange clothing or jewelry.
- Cheer up your kitchen with a bright orange cookie jar or ceramic teapot.
- Make a statement—paint a wall in your home deep apricot.
- Take advantage of the healing frequency of orange crystals, such as carnelian, sunstone, or moonstone that has a hint of peach or a shade of apricot.

3. DIET

In Chinese medicine, the kidneys store *jing*—our essence, our source of life. *Jing* affects everything from energy levels to immunity and sexual vitality. Using caffeine, tobacco, and alcohol can lessen *jing* and lower sexual desire. Improving our diet and lifestyle can enhance our *jing* and in turn enhance our sex life.

Foods that enhance *jing* include beans, peas, and lentils; whole grains like spelt, quinoa, and oats; and root veggies like carrots, yams, and parsnips.

Foods that boost our sense of delight include:

- **Sweet fruits**—melons, mangoes, strawberries, passion fruit, oranges, and coconut.
- **Honey**—a locally grown variety is preferable and can help reduce allergy symptoms.
- **Nuts**—almonds, walnuts, pecans, and cashews.
- **Spices**—cinnamon, vanilla, carob, sweet paprika, sesame seeds, and caraway seeds.
- **Supplements**—vitamin E helps to maintain reproductive health and enhances libido

4. AROMATHERAPY

The use of sandalwood, clary sage, sweet orange, patchouli, fennel, cardamom, elemi, or benzoin helps to eliminate fears associated with pleasure and self-gratification, including intimacy issues, hurt feelings, and fear of being controlled. These essential oils encourage warmth, sensuality, sensitivity, serenity, harmony, peace, unity, and insightfulness.

5. AFFIRMATIONS

When we encounter threats to our sense of pleasure, effective affirmations to speak out loud are:

I am relaxed, and my energy flows freely.
I live a life of honor and integrity.
I make healthy choices and decisions.
I move with grace and dignity.
I embrace my sexuality.
I nurture myself with pleasure.
I am alive with passion.
I greet each day with possibility.
I have the courage to take risks.
I function from a place of personal respect.

6. THE BUSINESS OF BEING

Establishing goals strengthens pleasure and self-gratification in the business world. For a moment, think of your life as a business and write the answers to the following questions:

- **Purpose:** Why are you here?
- **Mission:** If you're *authentically* living your purpose, what is the natural outcome, your mission?
- **Path:** By what means are you accomplishing your purpose?
- **Passion:** If there were a gauge on the level of your passion, would it be full, at the halfway mark, or near empty? If it's not topped off, how do you plan to refuel? Be specific.

7. BREATHWORK: 4-7-8 BREATHING

Whenever you recognize that you're hosting an unwanted, draining emotion related to issues of pleasure, self-gratification, or occupational wellness, stop what you're doing and focus on your breath. Breathe deeply, slowly, and steadily. Place a hand on your lower belly to ensure that you're breathing past your chest.

An effective breathing exercise to do is known as *4-7-8 breathing*, where the exhalation is twice as long as the inhalation. Here's how it's done:

- Inhale slowly and deeply through your nose while mentally counting to 4.
- Hold that breath for a mental count of 7.
- Exhale slowly through your mouth while mentally counting to 8.
- Pause briefly, without inhaling, and then start another round. This natural pause is therapeutic and relaxing.
- Once you've established a rhythm, identify a replacement attitude. Imagine that with each inhalation, you're breathing in the color orange and the feeling of that new attitude—increasing joy.
- When you exhale, imagine that you're releasing the toxins associated with the unwanted emotion—offloading baggage.
- Repeat for several minutes, drawing the orange breath and replacement feeling down into your lower belly to anchor the new feeling.

8. OCCUPATIONAL WELLNESS INVENTORY AND VITALITY CHECK

- Do you enjoy going to work most days?
- Is your workload manageable?
- Do you enjoy work-life balance?
- Do you relate well to your coworkers?
- Are you a team player?
- Attitudes are contagious. Is yours positive and uplifting?
- Do you carry your weight at work and make a fair contribution?
- Do you approach your manager with confidence when issues arise?

If you answered no to any of these questions, it may indicate an area of opportunity for you to improve the quality of your occupational wellness. Employers look at these types of efforts when making career-limiting or enhancing decisions regarding their staff.

On a scale of one to nine, where would you rate yourself in terms of how you feel about the current level of pleasure in your life, if one means life is hard (you're extremely stressed or overwhelmed) and nine means life is good (you're fully thriving, in the flow)?

Is there a difference between where you currently are and where you want to be? If so, write down how you'll close the gap. Be specific.

9. ACTION STEPS

To enhance your senses of pleasure and delight, enjoy the following activities:

- **Quick hits:** Turn on some music and dance, or do exaggerated hip movements with a Hula-Hoop. Indulge in a hot, aromatic bath, or embrace sensations such as different food tastes, touching different textures, or pampering your sense of smell with different scents.

- **With a little planning:** Take a water aerobics class or schedule a monthly massage. Inner-child work is beneficial to healing this self.

For those with an addiction, a twelve-step program can be incredibly valuable. Whatever thing we crave to fill our emptiness must pass the karmic litmus test:

> If it harms and diminishes us or another person, don't go there. If it
> fills and uplifts us or another person with love, go there.

Some people might argue that this is a subjective point of view. I disagree. We know when we're harming or uplifting ourselves or others. Only our justifications can muddy those waters.

Nancy shared, "As someone who struggles with addiction, it's important to look for positive affirmation in the right places. Expecting someone who doesn't know about addiction to provide any form of positive reinforcement is one of those 'slippery places.' Identifying what doesn't work is sometimes just as important as identifying what does work."

Sandi shared, "I'm trying to break myself of the habit of reaching for something external to settle myself. Instead I'm reaching for my 'inner grasshopper'—you know, the kung fu guy. When I do falter, I don't berate myself. I just remind myself that I didn't learn this habit in a day and it'll take more than a day for me to quit. I'm not asking myself to do the impossible, just to keep working at it and let it happen."

Kegel Exercises

Named after Dr. Arnold Kegel, this exercise is one of the best ways to strengthen pelvic muscles naturally while gaining tremendous benefit: stronger muscles (less chance of urine leakage); better support for your organs, especially the ones close to the pelvis; a stronger back and stomach; increased sexuality, stronger orgasms, and better sexual experiences; and improved self-image. Here's how it's done:

- Squeeze the muscles around your vagina and anus. These are the same muscles you use to hold in urine and feces. It's simply using those muscles except without the associated tasks. Just as you'd clench your fist, clench those muscles.
- When you start, do three to six sets of twenty-four one-second repetitions. One repetition is clenched muscles followed by released muscles. As you get used to doing Kegel exercises, increase the holds to two seconds, then three, and so on.

Since no one can see you doing them, you can do them *anywhere*. You'd be amazed at the number of women who make a practice of doing Kegel exercises while waiting in line—grocery shopping, clothes shopping, even at theme parks!

Examine Your Prescription Medication

If you have no appetite for intimacy, look at the medications you're taking. Some—certain birth control pills and antidepressants—can inhibit the desire to be physically intimate. Talk to your doctor about how your prescriptions may be affecting your hormones, brain chemicals, and physical desires. You might not be able to stop taking medication altogether, but your physician may be able to switch you to something that doesn't dampen your libido.

Whatever You Are Not Changing, You Are Choosing

Draw a line down the center of a piece of paper. On the top left, write "positive," and on the top right, write "negative." Below these headers, make a list of the negative and positive things that you're choosing. As you write each one, ask yourself, "Is this working for me?" If yes, why? If no, why? In either case, be specific.

Select one item on the negative side that you need to eliminate from the baggage you're carrying through life. Once you've made your decision, set your intent—establish your boundary—and then maintain it daily to ensure that it holds. Repeat this process every month until no items remain on the negative side of the list.

10. Personal Energy Signature

On a sheet of paper, draw a circle that represents your personal energy circle. Considering what you've learned about self-gratification, pleasure, and occupational wellness, on the inside of the circle, list the people, places, and things that are for this self's highest and best good—positive, uplifting, constructive, and healing.

On the outside of the circle, list the people, places, things, and actions you need to avoid to keep this self healthy and balanced. The examples on the following page will help you get started.

SELF-GRATIFICATION, PLEASURE, AND OCCUPATIONAL WELLNESS PERSONAL ENERGY SIGNATURE

Don't let the shadow side, self-denial, take over

Keep clear of people, places, or things that harm or diminish me

Incorporate the use of orange in my home or wardrobe

Determine my life's purpose, mission, and path and live it

Make choices that have positive consequences

Cultivate occupational wellness

Nurture my sense of pleasure

Increase my sense of delight with a new scent:
Body—fragrance
Space—aromatherapy

Give my pelvic-girdle area a good workout: buy a hula hoop and use it!

Make the time to connect with nature

Enhance my sense of delight

Do Kegel exercises

Treat myself to monthly bodywork, such as massage, reflexology, or cranial therapy

Function from a place of personal respect

Terminate relationships that bankrupt my heart

Leave a job I tolerate instead of enjoy

CHAPTER 7

Self #3: Self-Definition

Self-definition is responsible for personal power and social wellness; its purpose is to cultivate our inner landscape. When healthy, this self functions from a place of humble dignity. Corresponding to the solar plexus chakra, it resonates with the color yellow. An inspiring affirmation for this self is: *I am empowered*. The shadow side is self-importance.

❖ ❖ ❖

Heloise shared, "In high school, I wasn't smart enough to fit in with the nerds. Not pretty, outgoing, cruel, vapid—you name it—enough to fit in with the cool kids. Definitely not brave enough to fit in with the rebels, though that's where my heart was.

"I was the new girl in a small school where most of the kids had known each other since kindergarten. The new-new girl, who showed up a year after I did—stunningly gorgeous, exotic, sweet, and damaged—became my best friend and still is thirty-five years later. It was daunting to penetrate the formed cliques, so I didn't even attempt it.

"In college, I went to a small, religious school where many of the students already knew each other. I was an outsider. Again. I wasn't like them. Not as devout or catty or rich or breezily flirty with boys. I didn't have the clothes that were considered 'in style' in that circle.

"If you'd asked me then, 'Do you like being an outsider?' I'd have said no.

"But if you'd asked me, 'Do you want to be an insider?' I'd have said no way.

"Today, at fifty, I still don't feel like I'm a part of anything. Maybe it's because of the school situations; maybe it's just me. But it feels like I don't belong—like I live on the fringe."

Do you struggle with low self-esteem and feelings of unworthiness?

Is your life based on what you want or on the desires and opinions of others?

Are you easily persuaded to do things that you don't want to do?

Do you attract compatible people who nurture you, fill you with joy, and bring out your best?

This self—self-definition—is responsible for nurturing our sense of belonging and enables us to maintain and effectively use our personal power. Its clarion call is *carpe diem*—seize the day! The developmental stage begins somewhere between eighteen months and four years of age.

....

"The most common way people give up their power is by thinking they don't have any."

—ALICE WALKER, Pulitzer Prize–winning author and poet

....

This self signals us when to do—or refrain from doing—something. It's concerned with power, control, and freedom. As we continue to grow, this often translates to living authentically and to a sense of belonging.

When our senses of personal power and self-definition are in balance, we understand that the respect of human dignity begins with the celebration of personal dignity. We feel good-humored, hopeful, and spontaneous.

THE SHADOW SIDE: SELF-IMPORTANCE

When our senses of personal power and self-definition are out of balance, we can experience negative feelings such as powerlessness, fear, negativity, helplessness, inertia, and self-importance.

Vastly different than self-esteem (acknowledging and respecting one's personal value), self-importance can include being condescending to others because of a feeling of superiority, or making others appear wrong so you look right. Like a wolf in sheep's clothing, it can be disguised as altruism, compassion, or kindness. Self-importance includes narcissism—vanity, indifference to others, and an extreme concern about me, myself, and I.

Self-importance can manifest itself in a number of harmful ways that become items we tuck into our life's baggage. Some of them can include:

Physical: anorexia/bulimia, adrenal imbalances, pancreatitis, indigestion, intestinal tumors, stomach ulcers, cirrhosis, hepatitis, colon diseases, diabetes, and arthritis.

Mental: over-concern with body image, susceptibility to intimidation, trust issues, indecision, skepticism, pessimism, and slyness.

Emotional: fear of rejection, low self-esteem, oversensitivity to criticism, cowardliness, a tendency to be high-strung, and fear of one's "secrets" being found out.

Spiritual: lack of authenticity, lack of acceptance of one's purpose and place in the life stream.

Self-definition—the way we define ourselves—is determined in great part by how we view ourselves. This brings to mind the Panty Hose Incident:

For me to wear panty hose, someone has to get married or die, or I have to be giving a public presentation. No exceptions.

....

"Women want men, careers, money, children, friends, luxury, comfort, independence, freedom, respect, love, and a three-dollar panty hose that won't run."

—PHYLLIS DILLER, American actress and comedienne

....

Just before I was due to present at a women's conference, I used the restroom. While washing my hands, I glanced in the mirror to make sure my hair wasn't sticking out and I didn't have anything stuck in my teeth. I was in fact feeling pretty darn good about myself!

Adrenaline pumping, I made my way behind the curtain to where I would go out onstage to give my presentation. I passed several people with clipboards, ear microphones; they were red-faced and had great big, toothy smiles. I thought, *This is going to be fun!*

Through the curtain, I heard my name and a portion of my bio being delivered to the audience. I also heard people whispering frantically behind me. I stood a bit taller in my shoes as I listened to my own credentials—"Without further ado, ladies, please help me give a warm welcome to Laurie Buchanan"—followed by confidence-building applause.

I slipped between the curtains and into the spotlight. Stepping up to the lectern, I'd just started thanking the audience for inviting me as their guest speaker, when I felt a tug at the back of my waist, followed by the unmistakable sensation of my hemline hitting the backs of my knees.

I knew immediately that some kind soul had slipped an arm through the curtain and pulled my dress out of the back of my pantyhose. I was completely unaware that it had gotten caught when I visited the restroom.

Ego firmly back in its place, I continued on.

YOU—NOBODY DOES IT BETTER

Self-definition is also determined by our perception of how other people view us and how we believe they value us. It includes appearance and body image.

"People often say that 'beauty is in the eye of the beholder,' but I say that the most liberating thing about beauty is realizing you're the beholder. This empowers us to find beauty in places where others have not dared to look, including inside ourselves."

—SALMA HAYEK PINAULT, Mexican American film actress, director, and producer

A quick Internet search for the word "beauty" returns a bevy of links that lead to information on cosmetics, skin care, fragrances, hairstyles, tanning, plastic surgery, fashion trends, weight loss programs, diet pills, and exercise regimens.

Men, women, and teenagers alike are concerned—some obsessed—with physical attractiveness and perceived imperfections.

Unfortunately, many people gauge their beauty based on how they think other people perceive them. Emphasized by the media, this line of thinking is based on externals—on physical appearance. The cosmetics industry banks on people comparing themselves to airbrushed models and falling short.

Beauty isn't about meeting a prescribed set of criteria. Beauty is subjective; it's different for each person. But it can't be denied that inner beauty—a beautiful heart—makes a beautiful face.

The gemstones that shimmer in the crown of inner beauty include compassion, humor, intelligence, diplomacy, integrity, and trustworthiness. When these qualities are indwelling, the flow of beauty from the inside out is more effective than any work the most skilled of plastic surgeons can do.

Having spent a lot of time behind a camera, I've observed that the younger or older people are, the more they are themselves and don't try to appear different from who they are.

For her fortieth birthday, Stella received two tickets to see Kenny Chesney in concert in Las Vegas. She and Lily, her twelve-year-old daughter, flew off for a great weekend together. While waiting in line, they were selected by security and let in early.

"Lily, what does it feel like to be special?" Stella asked, smiling, as they sat waiting.

"No different, Mom. I always feel special."

The world would be a very different place if we all felt special each and every day.

In the booth behind me at a restaurant, two women were having a conversation. One of them said, "I tend to think too much about how other people perceive me. However, in recent months I've thought, be yourself. No one can tell you you're doing it wrong."

I wanted to stand up and cheer. Being yourself is a powerful experience to have. Being who we really are—a unique expression of source energy—frees us from being held hostage by the opinion of others. I've discovered that the longer I live, the easier it is to let go of what people think of me.

When we inhabit our own life—stop doing things based on the approval of others—we offload baggage and trade up to joy!

LIVING IN THE ZONE—IN HARMONY

Personal power and self-definition work hand in hand with social wellness—our ability to relate with the people around us in a pleasant, honest, and authentic manner. It includes using good verbal and nonverbal communication skills, respecting ourselves and others, and participating in a supportive structure of encouragement that includes friends and family.

Barbara shared, "For me, it seems to be that recognizing and exercising control of my own power is a decision. When I see it as a decision, rather than a reaction, it brings the power back into my court."

People who experience social wellness value living in harmony. They actively reach out to cultivate and nurture relationships that are based on mutual commitment, trust, and respect. This fosters a willingness to share thoughts and feelings. One of the hallmarks of social wellness is being inclusive, rather than exclusive, with our friendship.

During a Life Harmony session, I asked Celeste, "Do you feel that anything has been missing in your life? Is there an area where you feel some sort of lack? If so, what is it, and how might you fill the space?"

She responded, "Community. I've searched for a sense of community for over five years now. In doing the homework of last month's Life Harmony session, I had one of those aha moments when I realized that I don't belong to any groups. I've been hitting my head against the wall, waiting for something to create community.

"I'm still searching, but I find myself putting up roadblocks: too much travel so I can't schedule time in groups; don't want to be out in the evenings, when my husband is home; why get started with a group if we're retiring to some other location? The list goes on. I could fill this lack by joining a club, taking a class, or starting a circle. But I haven't."

In taking an active role, we come to understand and value that self-confidence strengthens our ease in being outgoing and in building a friendly rapport; it makes it easier to be open and approachable with others while maintaining healthy boundaries.

We all need relationships. The healthier our relationships, the better we feel toward other individuals and the global community as a whole.

WE ARE LIVING ART

Shades of color and contrast are important in a painting or a tapestry. They're what give it depth, capture our attention, and draw us in. A multitude of things contribute to the shades of color in our life; we are, after all, living art.

Jim Saw, art teacher at Palomar College in San Marcos, California tells us:

"***Hue*** is the traditional color name of a pigment.

Value is concerned with the light and dark properties of color.

Saturation is concerned with the intensity, or the brightness and dullness, of color."

In this body of work, I liken *hue* to our physical body, the package we reside in, *value* to what we think and feel, and *saturation* to our essence—spirit.

A fun and easy exercise that's helpful in revealing your colors is to write out the answers to the questions below. Your answers are part of how you define yourself; they'll give you a misty look at the current stage of your masterpiece.

I've shared my answers as an invitation for you to step into my life and get a glimpse of the colors I've chosen. You might find them useful to jump-start your own answers:

1. What are your top three priorities?

At the end of an interview for a magazine article on healers, I was asked what my top three priorities are. I thought for a moment and responded, "I'll answer that if I can give you four. Each of them is equally important to me:

- To live a life of simplicity.
- To forgive.
- To let go.
- To make a contribution that's positive, uplifting, constructive, and healing—daily, if possible."

What's at the top of your list?

2. What is, or was, your favorite subject in school?

I liked school but had to work at it. My worst subject was math. My favorite subjects were spelling, reading, and science. Fifth grade was by far my favorite school year. During that time, I was deciding between becoming a magician and becoming a mad scientist; I was fascinated with both.

....

> "No artist's work is so high, so noble, so grand, so enduring, so important for all time, as the making of character."
>
> —CHARLOTTE SAUNDERS CUSHMAN, American stage actress

....

Do you still gravitate toward the subject you loved in school, or have other interests replaced those?

3. Who are your favorite teachers, past and present?

Marriage and motherhood are the best teachers yet also the steepest-leaning cliffs that I've ever climbed. I married a sailor named Len. Actually, we eloped. After the initial shock wore off our parents, we got down to the interesting lessons that a marriage relationship can teach.

The first two that come to mind are:

What do you mean, "share?"

What do you mean, my way's not the only way?

Marriage is hard. A good marriage is *really* hard.

Three years into wedded bliss, along came our son, Evan.

Did I mention that marriage is hard? Parenting is harder. *Much* harder.

I can remember when we shared the news with my parents. My mom said, "Motherhood is the best and worst thing that will ever happen to you."

I said, "Mom, that's completely contradictory. How can that possibly be?"

With a wicked gleam in her eye and a knowing smile, she said, "Just you wait and see."

4. Who are your heroes?

My heroes include people from all walks of life who exude hope—a belief in a positive outcome. Their lives reflect their heart's desire, combined with active expectation.

My mother, Delle Hunter, was a physically small woman, yet she was the biggest person I've ever known. She had total focus, an attribute that deeply impressed me. She taught me by example that how we live impacts how we die. She lived a life of courage, beauty, and integrity; she died in the same manner.

When my mom was seven years old, she contracted polio. As a result, one of her legs was shorter than the other one. She never let it hold her back. When I was in grade school, she had an operation to lengthen her heel cord. It worked, to a degree. She never voiced any disappointment. My mother's cup was half-full, never half-empty. She was all about joy and love and passing it along.

Diagnosed with breast cancer at the age of forty-one, my mom had a mastectomy, followed by chemotherapy and radiation treatment. She never complained—even when I had to shave her head because huge chunks of hair had fallen out. She faced her challenges head-on and did what she had to do. Other than the fact that she'd lost her hair, you never would have known the agony of what she was going through. Life burned inside my mother; she glowed.

Which of your family members come to mind when you think of heroes?

My other heroes include Mother Teresa, Jane Goodall, and Anne Frank.

Mother Teresa left an exemplary, indelible fingerprint of compassion on the globe. She became a nun at age eighteen and devoted her life to working among the poorest of the poor in the slums of Calcutta, India. In 1950, she started the Missionaries of Charity, whose primary task is to love and provide practical help to people nobody's prepared to look after.

On a religious or spiritual front, who is your hero?

In her individual efforts, Jane Goodall has helped to make our planet a better place for people, animals, and the environment. Her book *Harvest for Hope: A Guide to Mindful Eating* is among my favorites.

Who's your hero when you think in terms of environmental stewardship?

Optimistic, patient, selfless, and strong, Anne Frank has been called the "human face of the Holocaust." The diary she kept when she was in hiding from the Nazis is a life-affirming record of her spirit and hope in the face of cruelty and danger.

When it comes to overcoming daunting obstacles, who is your hero?

I have tremendous regard for Amelia Earhart, Barbara Walters, and Rosa Parks.

American aviation pioneer and author Amelia Earhart was the first woman to receive the Distinguished Flying Cross award for becoming the first female pilot to fly solo across the Atlantic Ocean.

American broadcast journalist and author Barbara Walters began her career as a receptionist in an ad agency and then worked—hard—and eventually took the news world by storm in 1976, when she became the first female coanchor alongside Harry Reasoner on *ABC Evening News*.

Remembered as the black woman who refused to give up her seat on a bus to a white man, Rosa Parks stood up for her rights. She was arrested for believing she had the same rights as white people. She's remembered as saying, "The only tired I was, was tired of giving up."

When you think of people whose experience created opportunities for others, who's your hero?

When Susan Boyle appeared on the television show Britain's Got Talent, she didn't have any glitz and glamour. There wasn't anything astounding about her physical appearance. In fact, she appeared "ordinary." When she walked onstage, the audience began to snicker.

....

"To free us from the expectations of others, to give us back to ourselves—there lies the great, singular power of self-respect."

—JOAN DIDION, award-winning writer, playwright, screenwriter, essayist, novelist, and journalist

....

In his famously condescending style, the show's host asked the usual preperformance questions. To the audience's delight, she answered nervously. It was evident that everyone was looking forward to watching her fail. And then she sang, "I Dreamed a Dream."

As CNN reported later, "She wasn't painfully ordinary; she was amazingly extraordinary."

The audience immediately jumped to a standing ovation and stayed there until the end of the song. CNN went on to say, "Susan Boyle is a phenomenal role model for all of us, not just because of her talent or her courage or her perseverance or her supportive friends. She is a phenomenal role model for us because she is us, in all our awkward ordinariness and amazing extraordinariness."

When it comes to authenticity—living transparently—who is your hero?

Each of my heroes overcame challenges in the face of discouraging obstacles. They persevered even when the task seemed daunting—sometimes dangerous or even life threatening. Each of my heroes handed me a key to unleashed, unlimited potential and possibility.

5. To whom are you a hero?

You've heard the saying "never underestimate the power of one." It's true. Each of us has a sphere of influence. Whether we're a global citizen, like Mother Teresa, or a local citizen, what we think, say, and do has far-reaching and lasting ramifications.

My fifth-grade teacher, Mrs. Kline, gifted me with the book *The Swiss Family Robinson*, and with her determined but gentle understanding, she changed the trajectory of my life.

Sometimes we have no idea how one simple act can result in reverberating changes that undulate outward—and sometimes inward, too.

It's my perspective that each of us has an undeniable responsibility to ourselves and the rest of the world to be our personal best on any given day.

Similar to putting a hand in wet cement, we leave an impression long after we've left the scene. We exercise wisdom when we're mindful of our influence on others.

Who is looking up to you?

6. What's your favorite book?

Not because I agree or disagree with the content, but because of the engaging way she wove the story, my all-time-favorite book is *Atlas Shrugged*, written in 1957 by philosopher, author, and playwright Ayn Rand.

What's your all-time favorite book, the one you'd want along with you if you were stuck on a desert island?

"Literacy Statistics and Juvenile Court:

- When the State of Arizona projects how many prison beds it will need, it factors in the number of kids who read well in fourth grade.
- Fifteen percent of the population has specific reading disorders.
- Forty-six percent of American adults can't understand the label on their prescription medicine.
- Forty-four percent of American fourth-grade students can't read fluently, even when they read grade-level stories aloud under supportive testing conditions.
- Fifty percent of American adults are unable to read an eighth-grade-level book.
- Over 50 percent of NASA employees are dyslexic. They're deliberately sought after because they have superb problem-solving skills and excellent 3D and spatial awareness."

—RICHARD SUTZ, the Literacy Company

---

7. Who are your favorite authors?

I enjoy reading a wide range of genres, so my list is diverse. In the pure-enjoyment group, the top of the list reveals five authors: Barbara Delinsky, Maeve Binchy, Diana Gabaldon, Kristin Hannah, and Dorothea Benton Frank.

Who are your favorite fiction writers?

In the world of fantasy, I'm mesmerized by the works of writers such as Madeleine L'Engle, C. S. Lewis, and J. K. Rowling.

Who are your favorite fantasy authors?

Mary Oliver and Irish poet John O'Donohue are among my favorite poets. I keep their books on hand for my morning cup of tea.

Do you have a favorite poet?

When it comes to the category of spiritual awareness, there's simply not enough space in this book to list all of my favorite authors. So, in a brief thumbnail sketch, I'll list thirteen—a baker's dozen: Richard Bach, Gregg Braden, Oriah Mountain Dreamer, Wayne Dyer, Thich Nhat Hanh, Louise Hay, Jon Kabat-Zinn, His Holiness the Dalai Lama, Byron Katie, Don Miguel Ruiz, Eckhart Tolle, Doreen Virtue, and Susan Wisehart.

In the realm of personal growth and spiritual awareness, who are your favorite authors?

8. Who are your friends?

I'm nurtured by a small circle of friends who refer to ourselves as GNO—Girls' Night Out. I think a more accurate name would be *Bella Brigata,* meaning Delightful Gang. Funny thing is, we never go out. We gather in each other's kitchens for food, fun, and conversation. We pollinate each other's minds with original thoughts and creative ideas. We laugh, and sometimes we cry. We agree, and sometimes we disagree.

We come together in a simple manner: being our true selves—our authentic selves. The difference in our ages spans decades. We come from diverse backgrounds, have a wide variety of interests, and represent a spectrum of different spiritual traditions. We are women who celebrate, love, and support each other.

Who are your friends—the people who know the *real* you and still like you?

....

"A friend is one to whom one may pour out all the contents of one's heart—chaff and grain together—knowing that the gentlest of hands will take and sift it, keep what is worth keeping, and with a breath of kindness blow the rest away."

—MARY ANN EVANS, better known by her pen name George Eliot,
English novelist, journalist, and translator

....

9. Who is your family?

Peter shared, "I've finally come to the realization that, other than a blood relationship, I have very little in common with my family and I don't like being in their company.

"During a heated argument several years ago, my brother said, 'If we weren't brothers, I'd never spend time with you!' At the time, I thought it was a rash assessment and set out to prove him wrong.

"Over the years, I've traveled annually to spend time with him, to get to know him as an adult, to listen, and try to appreciate his ways. I've made it a practice to watch my projections and to see our relationship for what it is.

"My sense today is that we're familiar strangers who share few values, and it's difficult to agree on much. The sole thing that binds us is a document that states we were born of the same parents.

"I don't feel sadness or regret. Instead, a weight of self-imposed 'duty to like' has lifted, as I see us clearly as separate people, detached not only geographically but, more significantly, in our attitudes toward things we consider vitally important.

"My friends have become my family—people whom I'm not obligated to love and who aren't obligated to love me, but somehow the love is there, stronger than blood, because it's been created out of choice."

Are your family members blood-related, close friends, or both?

10. What are your areas of interest?

Environmental stewardship—living a green lifestyle—is important to me; this includes ecological pursuits such as recycling and sustainable living.

What eco-friendly activities are you involved in?

As an active listener, I thrive on learning and paying attention. I'm an avid proponent of humanitarian endeavors and animal rescue. I enjoy photography. I keep my personal energy signature "humming" with tai chi.

Do you engage in a mind-body-spirit exercise?

I'm fond of long-distance bicycle rides. I thrive on people watching, cultivating kindness, and the characteristics of a wabi-sabi lifestyle—simple yet full, functional, authentic, and imperfect.

How would you describe your lifestyle?

Another area of tremendous interest to me is the optical occurrence in certain gemstones such as moonstone, opal, and labradorite. It's known as *adularescence*—a distinctive shimmering or glow that appears to come from below the surface but is caused by diffraction of light.

This phenomenon is impossible in the absence of light. The shimmering takes place only when light is present. Similarly, it's my desire to live in a heart-based manner that radiates the presence of inner light—divine love.

> "People are like stained-glass windows. They sparkle and shine when the sun is out, but when the darkness sets in, their true beauty is revealed only if there is light from within."
>
> —ELISABETH KÜBLER-ROSS, Swiss-born psychiatrist, and pioneer
> in near-death studies

What's your favorite gemstone? Does it reflect your personality?

11. What are your favorite things?

I love to laugh! I take great pleasure in travel and spending time in nature. My favorite creatures on this planet are trees. A person can learn a lot by observing these woody giants. I've learned to be respectful of the earth and its natural resources. I enjoy many types of music, but to my ears, there's none more soothing or calming than the music a tree makes as the wind passes through its leaves.

What's your favorite type of tree?

I'm drawn to simplicity, efficiency, and order—a place for everything, and everything in its place. For me, outer order contributes to inner calm.

Do you remember the television show *The Odd Couple*? Are you more like Felix Unger (neat as a pin) or more like Oscar Madison (messy)?

I take great pleasure in watching a skein of geese fly across the sky, full moons, gratitude, and a good thunderstorm. I prefer quiet gatherings to loud, bold affairs. I enjoy lavender plants, climbing roses, and tulips. I love the heady smell of star jasmine blossoms.

What's your favorite flower?

I enjoy picnics and canoeing with our dogs. A firebug since childhood, I adore maintaining a campfire—poking at it and keeping it fed. I can get lost in the dancing flames for hours. I admire manners and nonviolent courage. A friend of solitude, I enjoy spending time by myself.

Do you enjoy spending time alone?

Garlic bread is high on the list of food indulgences that I treat myself to every so often. My other favorites are red licorice, Stilton cheese, crème brûlée, and kettle-style barbecue chips.

What's your favorite indulgence food?

UNITY IS BIRTHED BY INDIVIDUALS

Identification with groups is important because it helps us to connect with like-minded people and makes us aware of our inherent unity. When we're warmly included—validated—rather than tolerated or rejected, it gives us a sense of belonging, a sense that we're part of something bigger than we are.

....

"We don't need a melting pot in this country, folks. We need a salad bowl. In a salad bowl, you put in the different things. You want the vegetables—the lettuce, the cucumbers, the onions, the green peppers—to maintain their identity. You appreciate differences."

—JANE ELLIOTT, American teacher and antiracism activist

....

Birthed by individuals—you and me—groups are established by people who come together in unity. Each person has within him or her two orientations:

Our *vertical* orientation is our individual connection with divinity, whatever that means to each person.

Our *horizontal* orientation is how we connect with the people around us.

Our relationship with divinity and the way we interact with others—our vertical and horizontal orientations—are somewhat like crosshairs in a scope. Where they intersect is the seat of compassion, the key ingredient for unity at its best.

Identification with a group is vital to healthy self-definition. The worth of any group lies, in great part, in the behavior of its individual members. Every group has people who are positive, uplifting, constructive, and healing, and, of course, every group has people who are otherwise.

It's in setting aside our differences that we clear space for a common agenda and make it possible to forge ahead with solutions that create a better future for everyone.

As we grow up and begin to make our own choices, we choose to align ourselves with certain groups. This choice is born of one of our strongest desires as humans: validation.

Ingrid, an aspiring writer, shared, "I wish I weren't so shallow, but, sadly, honestly, I am. I wait for validation. I wait for recognition. I wait to be invited—by him, by her, by them, by the publishing world. While I wait, I sharpen the tools of my craft and I dream."

Some examples of group identifications include ethnicity, religious affiliation, type of education, employment status, political affiliation, relationship status, and zodiac sign, among many more. To conform to a group for the sake of acceptance is to shortchange oneself. The finest groups are made up of individuals at their compassion-filled, authentic best.

There are times in life when we encounter other individuals we don't care for. It's interesting to note that oftentimes the habits, attitudes, and behaviors of people we dislike are closely linked to our own subconscious or unresolved issues. Understanding this can be an eye-opening, humbling experience and a launching point for positive change.

Our social fabric is rich with diversity. When we come together in unity, we have a deep well to draw from. With an eye to the future, our combined efforts have tremendous potential for transformational thinking and solutions for future generations.

PUTTING A STAKE IN THE GROUND

While attending a "Reversing Panic Attacks" workshop facilitated by Belleruth Naparstek, I sat next to a striking woman whom I mentally calculated to be in her early eighties. She was so obviously comfortable in her own makeup-free, beautiful skin.

I asked her if she was attending the workshop alone or with someone else. She shared, "I've been married for fifty-six years, and while I'm aging as a natural result of living, my husband has chosen to become old. He's content to sit and do nothing, so I came by myself."

Those few sentences told me that she was true to herself and had a healthy sense of personal power—a building block of self-definition.

I remember when I was seven years old and in the throes of defining myself. A friend and I had gone fishing, and when she cast her hook, it accidentally caught my left ear. We ran to my dad, who discovered it had more than caught my ear; it had gone through—shanks and all—and he had to work it out carefully with a pair of needle-nose pliers.

My parents decided that I needed to have a tetanus shot. They took me kicking and screaming to the hospital, where I swung at and bit everything within my reach.

Once the process was over and we were back home, I went fuming to my room. I remember thinking how "mean" they were and that the process had taken place against my will (another building block of self-definition).

My vocabulary was that of any ordinary seven-year-old. I knew the word "suffocate," and I knew the word "smother." I decided to give my parents a piece of my mind. As I marched down the hall, I worked up a good head of steam.

I stood at the end of the hall, looking into the living room, with my shoulders squared, legs apart, and hands firmly on my hips, stating, "The next time either one of you tries to do anything to me against my will, I'll *smuffocate* you in your sleep!"

In my haste and anger to define myself, display my personal power, and establish future authority in this area, I got my words confused. I'm sure my parents had a difficult time containing their laughter as I marched back to my bedroom and slammed the door.

"Life isn't about finding yourself. Life is about creating yourself."

—GEORGE BERNARD SHAW, Irish literary critic, playwright, and essayist

It's important to have a healthy sense of self—to acknowledge and embrace personal value. However, when this becomes excessive, we function from ego, which can hold us captive in a limited perspective—one that a sense of entitlement often fortifies.

Our viewpoint on the world is a direct result of our thinking and inner beliefs. In the Talmud, we read, "We do not see things as they are. We see them as we are."

Thoughts and beliefs are an accumulation of learning (knowledge) and life experience (wisdom) from birth until now—the current place on our life's journey.

Our personality is governed by our mind, which is composed of three separate yet interdependent aspects:

- The *mental/thinking* aspect is cognitive; it's where thinking takes place. It pertains to perception, memory, judgment, and reasoning. It's where logic resides.
- The *emotional/feeling* aspect is an affective state of consciousness; it's where feeling takes place. It pertains to emotions such as joy, sorrow, fear, and hate. It's where passion resides.
- The *volition/will* aspect is the act of willing, choosing, or resolving; it's where preference is established and decisions take place. It's where choice resides.

"A man is but the product of his thoughts. What he thinks, he becomes."

—MAHATMA GANDHI, Indian political and spiritual leader

WHO'S AT THE WHEEL?

For a moment, let's think of our personality as a vehicle. It can have only one driver at a time—Ego or Spirit.

Ego

Anyone experiencing dysfunction with self-definition—too much or too little—has difficulty obtaining or maintaining personal power and encounters issues with ego.

Some of the characteristics of ego include arrogance, intolerance, self-absorption, impatience, resentment, cruelty, fear, blame, guilt, lack, conceit, craving approval, hatred, control of others, being judgmental, anger, selfishness, scarcity, vanity, greed, negativity, vengeance, entitlement, deceit, stubbornness, the need to receive "credit" for things, and that green-eyed monster—envy.

My friend Terrill Welch, author of *Leading Raspberry Jam Visions Women's Way: An Inside Track for Women Leaders,* said, "I think envy in its very first blush can be a motivator. If we can use it as a stepping-stone to our own growth and action, it can enhance our work and success. However, if we stand on its soft green head too long, we will sink into the mire of our own self-rejection."

When Ego has the steering wheel and is in control of our personality while we make choices and decisions, the outcome is usually not in our best interest.

Ego is short-lived. It's bound by time and space as we know it.

An example of working from a position of ego—specifically envy—took place in my town. The owner of a yoga studio had an amazing instructor working for her—so amazing, in fact, that the owner started working from a place of envy and fear, characteristics of ego.

....

"To fear is one thing. To let fear grab you by the tail and swing you around is another."

—KATHERINE PATERSON, American author and National Ambassador for
Young People's Literature

....

The owner became afraid that the instructor was even better than she herself was. As a result, she didn't promote the instructor's classes. In fact, she squelched them. As you can well imagine, this action had two impacts:

- It diminished the owner's income (a case of cutting off one's nose to spite one's face).
- It provided the amazing instructor with the opportunity to be mindful of the shifting circumstances. Being mindful—without being fearful—gave her the final push she needed to launch her own yoga studio.

When we approach life with a "guarding my rice bowl" attitude, there's only enough rice to feed one person—self.

The individual sitting at life's banquet with their arms wrapped protectively around their rice bowl is missing out on joy, conversation, and interaction with the other people at the party.

However, when we sit back in a relaxed position and share our time, talent, praise, and support, giving freely from our rice bowl, our life is enriched.

Since 2012, Dorothy, age sixty-five, has been the primary live-in caregiver for her mother and stepfather of thirty years. When her stepfather became gravely ill, her stepbrothers and sisters, in an attempt to "guard their rice bowl," forced Dorothy out of the home, fearing that "possession is nine-tenths of the law" and they might not end up with as much as they wanted.

Dorothy could have gone toe-to-toe with them in a battle, but she opted to view this as an opportunity, instead of a problem, and used it not only to clear material clutter from her life but to clear emotional and mental clutter as well.

She took a mindful inventory of the "stuff" in her parents' house and opted to leave it behind. She said, "I've come to realize that less really is more. With fewer things to tie me down, I can do more living."

In offloading baggage, Dorothy increased her joy.

Spirit

Spirit is the vital principle in humans. It's our very essence, our being, our soul.

Our inner self—the unseen part of us—is our compass, the light within. It is divine. The soul is concerned with the nature and purity of our motivation, not so much *what* we choose to do or not do, but *why* we do, or refrain from doing, something—our motivation, our intention.

The soul is what inspires us. Unlike the body and mind, which are interdependent, spirit is a different entity, separable from the body.

Soul is eternal. It's not bound by time and space as we know it.

The soul's purpose is to guide our personality, to help us determine and fulfill our life purpose—what some would call our *soul contract*.

"Soul is the bridge to God."

—CAROLINE MYSS, American medical intuitive, mystic, and *New York Times*
best-selling author

When Spirit/Soul is in the driver's seat as we make choices and decisions, the outcomes are for the highest and best good—positive, uplifting, constructive, and healing.

Some of the characteristics of soul include inspiration, creativity, love, generosity, dignity, empathy, acceptance, farsightedness, receptivity, patience, understanding, hope, laughter, harmony, kindness, honesty, respect, selflessness, honor, gratitude, compassion, humility, and joy.

In a Life Harmony session, Natalie determined that her purpose was to "be extraordinary." She said, "Being extraordinary isn't being a 'bigger' person. It's a soul-based life that keeps Spirit in the driver's seat. It's waking up in the morning and saying, 'Thy will be done through me.'"

You may have heard Gandhi's inspirational words "Be the change you wish to see in the world." This statement and Gandhi's actions launched a Be the Change movement, which continues to wash across the globe among individuals who share the desire to make a positive change. The movement challenges people everywhere to commit to doing at least one intentional positive act of change each day for the betterment of the planet and its people.

Self-definition determines the terrain we encounter during life's journey and our sense of belonging. When this self is healthy and in balance, there's an abundant return value to the heart. In this case, the dividends include not being held hostage by the opinions of others, and living authentically—being one's true self.

In the following chapter, you'll find several keys—practical tips, tools, and exercises—to cultivate your inner landscape and offload baggage associated with self-definition.

....

"Never be bullied into silence. Never allow yourself to be made a victim. Accept no one's definition of your life; define yourself."

—HARVEY FIERSTEIN, American actor and writer for stage and screen

....

CHAPTER 8

Keys to Self-Definition: Cultivate Your Inner Landscape

"Alchemy is the process of changing lead into gold. Inner alchemy (personal transformation) occurs when we clear our clutter—internal and external—and let go of things that no longer serve us well. This creates balance and space, a place that nurtures contentment, which I believe is true success."

—LAURIE BUCHANAN, holistic health practitioner and transformational life coach

1. MIND-BODY CONNECTION

Self-definition is associated with the digestive system, midspine, abdomen, spleen, adrenal glands, liver, gallbladder, kidneys, and pancreas. If you're experiencing issues in any of these areas, it's time to make an appointment with your health care provider.

2. COLOR THERAPY

Yellow is associated with self-definition, personal power, and social wellness.

It enhances awareness, wisdom, and clarity. It's the color of a shiny rain slicker. Think of the vibrant skin on a lemon or banana. It's the lively color of daffodil bonnets that herald spring, and the dazzling color of finches jockeying for position at the feeder on a warm summer day.

It's the flamboyant color of bumblebees showing off as they dart from blossom to blossom. It's the bursting color that greets you when you pull the husks from grill-roasted corn on the cob that then get buttered to the ears. Remember the vibrant color on the Beatles' Yellow Submarine album cover?

The *positive* properties of yellow are expressed as motivational, happy, radiant, social, lighthearted, mentally active, clear thinking, rational, and detached from negative emotions.

The *negative* properties of yellow are described as critical, argumentative, opinionated, evasive, and restless.

The *healing* properties of yellow are uplifting and supportive and can address physical symptoms that include intestinal and digestive issues, such as constipation, diarrhea, and flatulence; water retention; skin problems; all mental processes; and negative states of mind, such as depression, low self-esteem, short attention span, "exam nerves," and writer's block. Yellow increases awareness, perception, and understanding. It also stimulates the appetite.

When you need a boost in the areas of personal power and self-definition, indulge yourself with this color. Its frequency resonates with the solar plexus chakra, the well-spring of our power, the hub—the very heart—of our body's electrical system. It promotes vigor and improves memory. Yellow energy stirs feelings of well-being and positive thinking and triggers the outward expression of inner joy.

The vibration of yellow is energizing, uplifting, and stimulating. What shade are you drawn to?

Vivid yellow is closest to sunlight; it conveys hospitality and promotes deep feelings of vitality. Muted hues make a quiet background for busy lives, while shaded yellows' soft, glowing presence speaks of home, harvest, and abundance.

What we do with our physical environment—our personal space—speaks to our heart and helps us to flourish:

Accessorize with a piece of yellow clothing or jewelry.

Wake up your bathroom with a dazzling yellow shower curtain.

Fill a clear glass contemporary container or an antique mason jar with bright yellow lemon drops and use it as a focal point in your living room.

Take advantage of the healing frequency of yellow crystals, such as citrine, golden tiger eye, and imperial topaz.

3. DIET

Foods that boost our sense of vitality include:

- **Granola and grains**—quinoa, amaranth (complete-protein grains), pastas, breads, cereal, rice, flaxseed, and sunflower seeds.

- **Dairy**—milk, cheeses, and yogurt.
- **Spices**—ginger, mints (peppermint, spearmint, etc.), chamomile, turmeric, cumin, and fennel.
- **Supplements**—Acidophilus is a "friendly" bacteria that's naturally present in the digestive tract. It promotes health by suppressing the growth of potentially harmful bacteria, improving immune function, enhancing the protective barrier of the digestive tract, and helping to produce vitamin K.

Tip: If you don't have an allergy to nuts, eat a handful every day, but avoid salted and honey-roasted varieties.

4. AROMATHERAPY

The use of juniper, cedarwood, bergamot, coriander, grapefruit, black pepper, lime, hyssop, marjoram, or cardamom can help to eliminate fears associated with personal power and self-definition (e.g., fear of rejection; fears related to physical appearance, such as obesity, aging, and baldness) and fear that others will "discover our secrets." These essential oils encourage strength, balance, fortitude, persistence, confidence, protectiveness, and concentration.

5. AFFIRMATIONS

When we encounter threats to the way we define ourselves, effective affirmations to speak out loud are:

I am balanced and own my power.
I act with self-esteem.
I am able to handle a crisis.
I have a strong sense of self.
I choose to fill my world with joy.
I trust my gut instinct.
I have the courage to take risks.
I am authentic; I am accepted.
I am motivated by confidence.
I function from a place of humble dignity.

6. THE BUSINESS OF BEING

A clearly defined mission statement can strengthen personal power and self-definition in the business world. For a moment, think of your life as a business and write the answer to the following question:

- Have you crafted a clear, concise, and articulate mission statement? It is, after all, the banner that you fly. As an example, my mission is to be a positive, uplifting, constructive, and healing influence in the lives of those I touch.

7. BREATHWORK—SOFT BELLY

Whenever you recognize that you're hosting an unwanted, draining emotion related to issues of personal power, self-definition, or social wellness, stop what you're doing and focus on your breath. Breathe deeply, slowly, and steadily. Place a hand on your lower belly to ensure that you're breathing past your chest.

An effective breathing exercise to do is known as *soft belly*. Here's how it's done:

- Set a kitchen timer. When you start, set the timer for five to ten minutes and gradually add time as you do soft belly more often.
- Sit quietly in a comfortable chair. It helps to have objects in the room that comfort you—something from nature, or from your spiritual tradition.
- Close your eyes, then inhale through your nose and exhale through your mouth. Let your stomach be "soft" as you breathe, expanding on the inhalation and relaxing on the exhalation.
- Mentally say "soft" on the inhalation and "belly" on the exhalation. Remind your stomach to be soft, and repeat the phrase "soft . . . belly . . . soft . . . belly . . ."
- Once you've established a rhythm, identify a replacement attitude. Imagine that with each inhalation ("soft"), you're breathing in the color yellow and the feeling of that new attitude—increasing joy.
- When you exhale ("belly"), imagine that you're releasing the toxins associated with the unwanted emotion—offloading baggage.

- Repeat for several minutes, drawing the yellow breath and replacement feeling down into your lower belly to anchor the new feeling.
- When the timer rings, open your eyes and return your attention to the room.

8. SOCIAL WELLNESS INVENTORY AND VITALITY CHECK

- Do you have a network of close friends and/or family?
- Do you contribute time or money to the well-being of your local community (community projects, volunteerism)?
- Are you able to balance your own needs with the needs of others?
- Do you live in harmony with others?
- Are you free from the pressure to live up to a social image?
- Do you see spending time with others as an energetic investment?
- Do you interact with people from different cultures, backgrounds, and spiritual traditions?
- Do you actively plan time to be with family and friends?

If you answered no to any of these questions, it may indicate an area of opportunity for you to improve the quality of your social wellness.

On a scale of one to nine where do you rate yourself in terms of social connectedness—the current quality of your social relationships—if one represents being disconnected (lonely, alone, conflicted, withdrawn) and nine represents being connected (loved and cared for, harmonious)?

Is there a difference between where you currently are and where you want to be? If so, write down how you'll close the gap. Be specific.

9. ACTION STEPS

To enhance your sense of personal power and cultivate your inner landscape, enjoy the following activities:

- **Quick hits:** Put on some '60s music and do the twist or some sit-ups. Work on a puzzle, read a book that engages your mind, go outside and get some sunshine.

- **With a little planning:** Take a calculated risk. As author Frederick B. Wilcox said, "Progress always involves risks. You can't steal second and keep your foot on first!" When you meet with success, take more risks. Incorporate vigorous exercise, such as running, belly dancing, aerobics, or martial arts. Take some classes. Psychotherapy can be effective in helping people to release or contain anger, work on shame issues, strengthen the will, and encourage autonomy.

Your Favorites

- Make a list of your favorite teachers—people who provided you with tools for success.
- Make a list of your favorite authors—people who engaged your heart and mind with well-crafted words.
- Make a list of people you admire because of what they've done—contributed to humanity.
- Heroes are people who inspire. Everyone's actions have an effect, whether they make history or not. To whom are *you* a hero?

Friends

Make a list of your true friends—people with whom you are transparent because they accept you for who you are. They tell you the truth, even at risk of hurting your feelings. Their influence is positive, uplifting, constructive, and healing. They encourage you to grow.

Interests

Make a list of the people, places, and things you're interested in.

Favorite Things

Make a list of your favorite things.

Group Identification

Make a list of the groups that you identify with:

- Which groups were you born into?
- Which groups did you elect to become part of?
- Has there ever been a group that you disassociated with because you no longer wanted to be identified with it?
- If so, what was the group and why did you disassociate with it?

Influence

Who has the steering wheel of your personality when you make most of your decisions: Ego or Spirit?

Rice Bowl

Make a list of the areas in your life where you're "guarding your rice bowl," where you exclude, rather than include, because of fear.

Self-Defining Moment

Think back to a self-defining moment and write it down. Be specific.

Power Moment

Think of a time when you asserted your personal power and write it down. Be specific.

Power Quiz

- What was the greatest moment of the greatest thing that you've ever been part of?

- On a scale of one to nine, where do you rate yourself on the quality of your current energy experience, if one represents low (weak, ineffectual) and nine is reminiscent of the energy behind your greatest moment (drive, passion, effort, elation)?

Physicists tell us that we live in a world filled with possibilities driven by probabilities that are affected by observation and attention.

If you haven't thought about the energy behind your greatest moment and its relationship to the energy you're expending today, then you're not using what you observed there to affect your current probability and possibility.

It's been said that, "if you always do what you always did, then you'll always get what you always got." That's true no matter how you slice it—both positively and negatively.

If you develop a habit of relating the energy of your greatest moment to the energy of your current moment, then you'll find yourself leveraging power.

Be the Change

- Paula travels a lot. She's made it her practice to stand up every suitcase that comes down the conveyor belt she's waiting at so they're easier for others to grab.
- When Theresa brings her trashcans in from the curb, she brings her neighbor's bins in, too.
- When Jodi borrowed her manager's van, the gas tank was nearly empty. She filled it up and ran it through the car wash before returning it.
- The woman in the parking lot next to Rita finished unloading her groceries at the same time. When Rita returned her shopping cart to the corral, she returned the other woman's as well.
- When Sandra and her husband take their evening walk, they carry bags along and pick up litter.

In thinking about your home, friends, school, job, and community—the spheres of influence you move in—what can you do to "be the change"?

10. PERSONAL ENERGY SIGNATURE

On a sheet of paper, draw a circle that represents your personal energy circle. Considering what you've learned about personal power, self-definition, and social wellness, on the inside of the circle, list the people, places, and things that are for this self's highest and best good—positive, uplifting, constructive, and healing.

On the outside of the circle, list the people, places, things, and actions you need to avoid to keep this self healthy and balanced. The examples on the following page will help you get started.

SELF-GRATIFICATION, PERSONAL POWER, AND SOCIAL WELLNESS
PERSONAL ENERGY SIGNATURE

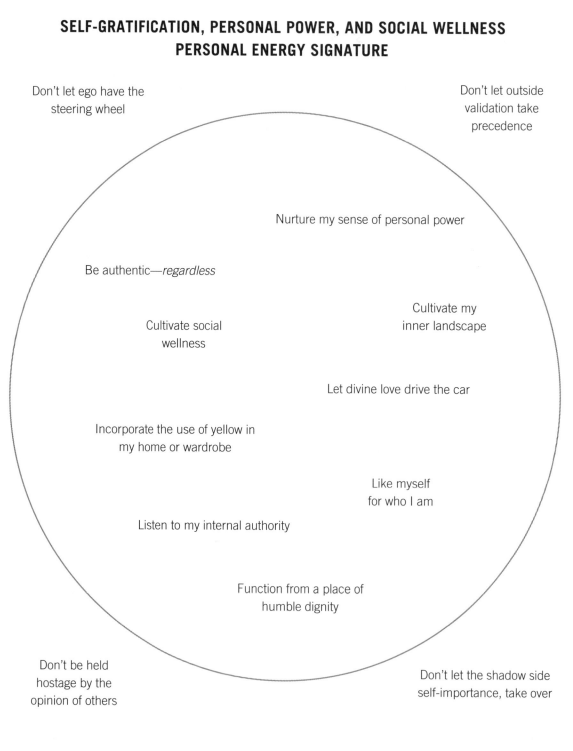

Don't let ego have the steering wheel

Don't let outside validation take precedence

Nurture my sense of personal power

Be authentic—*regardless*

Cultivate my inner landscape

Cultivate social wellness

Let divine love drive the car

Incorporate the use of yellow in my home or wardrobe

Like myself for who I am

Listen to my internal authority

Function from a place of humble dignity

Don't be held hostage by the opinion of others

Don't let the shadow side self-importance, take over

CHAPTER 9

Self #4: Self-Acceptance

Self-acceptance is responsible for love and emotional wellness; its purpose is to develop our emotional empowerment. When healthy, this self functions from a place of compassion and forgiveness. Corresponding to the heart chakra, it resonates with the color green. An inspiring affirmation for this self is: *I am loved*. The shadow side is self-rejection.

❖ ❖ ❖

LaToya shared, "When someone wrongs me, I'm not quick to let it go and chalk it up to humans' making mistakes, because, honestly, some people do some blatantly stupid things on purpose. I don't lie around gritting my teeth and thinking of them in my downtime, either, nor do they get swept under the carpet. They simply get pushed out of my memory.

"You may not understand this. You may not grasp how I possess the ability to completely ignore someone based on their egregious actions. There are people—family members, in particular—who just can't understand that I have nothing to prove by being on cordial terms with individuals that I can't stand.

"I don't feel the need to be on speaking terms with everybody in the interest of appearing mature or secure. I've seen all the hype floating around about forgiveness and how the refusal to do so means that the other person is 'winning.' Sometimes forgiveness just isn't possible.

"I'm not against forgiveness. I just don't think some people deserve to be forgiven as much as they deserve to be forgotten and marked 'nonexistent.'"

Do you sabotage relationships with distrust, anger, or a sense that you'll lose your independence if you rely too much on others?

Do you struggle with commitment, experience frequent fights or misunderstandings with your loved ones, and always keep yourself "on guard" to keep from getting hurt?

When you have a conflict with someone else, do you consider *their* pain?

Have you forgiven those who've hurt or offended you, or are you harboring resentment—withholding forgiveness?

This self—self-acceptance—validates our sense of worth and provides emotional empowerment. The developmental stage begins somewhere between four and seven years of age.

This self is concerned with unconditional love, generosity, and self-esteem. As we continue to grow, this often translates to forgiveness, letting go, and compassion.

When our senses of love and self-acceptance are in balance, we enjoy qualities from the constructive side of this self. These include hope, trust, harmony, understanding, self-esteem, compassion, and love.

THE SHADOW SIDE: SELF-REJECTION

When our senses of love and self-acceptance are out of balance, we can experience feelings of self-rejection. Many addictions are fueled, in part, by a self-critical component.

Feelings of unworthiness are at the forefront of self-rejection. When we allow the opinion of others to hold us hostage, our personal value is based on what other people think. This can keep us on a continuous, gut-wrenching roller-coaster ride. Praise and criticism trigger our actions. When we receive praise, our self-esteem skyrockets; when it's withheld or we're criticized, it plummets.

Self-rejection also includes the fear of outside rejection. When someone rejects—emotionally wounds—us, we become fearful that it could happen again. If it does, we build defenses and become emotionally guarded, or sometimes even emotionally impenetrable.

Self-rejection can manifest itself in a number of harmful ways that become items we tuck into our life's baggage. Depending on their size and impact, we may slip them into a tote that we keep within arm's reach, for handy retrieval, or stuff them into a large suitcase that comes around on the baggage carousel only occasionally. These can include:

Physical: heart conditions, asthma, allergies, lung and breast cancers, problems with the thoracic spine, pneumonia, upper-back and shoulder issues.

Mental: possessive, jealous, reckless, greedy, deceitful, cruel, and addictive behavior.

Emotional: loneliness, resentment, bitterness, self-centeredness, and the anguish of inconsolable grief.

Spiritual: unwillingness to forgive, and a lack of compassion.

Jocelyn, age forty-eight, shared, "Accepting myself isn't something I do easily. I was taught from an early age that I wasn't important. That lesson was reinforced by continuous emotional abuse—not surprising when you understand that I come from an alcoholic, dysfunctional family.

"That wobbly beginning has affected my ability to express my true feelings in a productive way, even with my husband. I find that I still hold back my feelings from a fear of producing more conflict. I'm careful not to make waves and find myself flinching at the slightest sound. In many areas I go into 'freeze mode' because I couldn't fight or flee when I was growing up. I haven't been able to shake that habit."

Love and self-acceptance work hand in hand with emotional wellness. More than just handling stress, it includes anger management, healthy personal expression, and working through self-esteem issues. It entails paying attention to all of our thoughts, feelings, and behaviors, whether they're positive or negative.

....

"No man can think clearly when his fists are clenched."

—GEORGE JEAN NATHAN, American drama critic and editor

....

OUR PERSPECTIVE CREATES OUR WORLD

Dogs and many other animals experience life through their nose—their sense of smell. Humans experience life through perspective—what we think and how we feel.

Our thoughts and feelings impact the way we perceive people, places, and things and correlate directly to what's in our baggage and how we respond to life's ups and downs. In fact, our perspective creates our world.

Dana's mother-in-law, Kate, frequently demeans her. Kate seemingly stops at nothing to hurt Dana, even ridiculing Dana's children—her own grandchildren.

Dana obliges by becoming outraged at and devastated by each attack. What she expects is love and acceptance from a woman who releases only venom. And every time it happens, Dana feels the sting as sharply as she did the first time. Dana and I role played and practiced establishing a verbal boundary. With me playing her mother-in-law, I encouraged her to calmly express specific examples of disrespect, how they made Dana feel, and let me (the mother-in-law) know that disrespect to her and her children would no longer be tolerated. Needless to say, Dana was nervous at the prospect of executing the boundary.

When it played out in real life, Dana's mother-in-law was slack-jawed at the examples she couldn't refute, and apologized saying she hadn't realized she'd been wielding that type of negative behavior. Dana said the value of her *chutzpah* skyrocketed in her mother-in-law's eyes that day.

Being emotionally well doesn't mean that we'll never encounter negative feelings. It means that when we do, we acknowledge them, rather than deny them, and cope with stress in healthy ways.

Everyone has coping mechanisms. Some of them are beneficial, while others are detrimental.

Emotional wellness means that we bring the unhealthy aspects of our feelings to light—take them out of our baggage—for examination so we can work through them in a productive way, offloading baggage and increasing joy.

In taking an active role in our emotional wellness, we come to appreciate the value inherent in not taking things personally and in setting internal boundaries, and we come to understand that when we clear internal clutter—emotional baggage—we create space for joy.

My friend Nancy said, "Clearing internal clutter is a journey not for the faint of heart but rather for a warrior—one who is willing to explore, to find the secret key, and to steadfastly turn it."

COPING WITH GRIEF

This self—self-acceptance—oversees grief. It resides in our heart center, the seat of our emotions.

....

"While grief can result from a variety of situations, ranging from divorce and separation to traumatic injury or illness, probably the most difficult and heart-wrenching circumstance to deal with is the loss of a loved one through death.

"According to US government statistics, approximately 36 percent of the population is grieving at any given time. Grief associated with this type of loss is devastating for family and friends. This type of grief is a profound and all too often devastating experience for family members who are left behind. If left unchecked, grief can quickly turn into deep depression and other serious psychological disorders."

—THERAVIVE, grief counseling

....

Kimberly shared, "It took me three years after our son died before I freely came to a sense of willingness to move on. Until I felt that, I only trusted myself to be as I was moved to be—whichever way the wind blew.

"I lost my marriage at the same time. That's another kind of grief, losing a beloved one while they're still alive."

Alex shared, "I lost my sixteen-year-old, firstborn daughter to suicide fifteen years ago. Loss has come up sharply as a fundamental thread of what I call 'my life.' I grieved my daughter, but I was also grieving 'my life.' I didn't fight anything during the grief. Fighting never leads to peace.

"For a long while, the world was simply the footprint of where she had walked, the absence of her light and being."

....

"Many people don't need professional help after the loss of a loved one, but of those who do need help with their grief, only 10 percent will seek it."

—NATIONAL INSTITUTE OF MENTAL HEALTH

....

Patricia, whose partner of ten years was killed in a car accident, shared, "Grief plays tricks with time. The past three months have passed in the blink of an eye, and they've lasted forever. I never thought I'd last three weeks, let alone three months; at times the pain was so unbearable, I wanted to scream. So I did. And I go to a grief support group. It does help to be around people who understand this journey, to hear how others are handling their loss.

"'Loss.' What an odd way to describe death, as if the person is simply misplaced, like a ring, and will soon be found."

Patricia's coping mechanisms are healthy—screaming and attending a grief support group. Even though she's suffered a tremendous blow, her approach has forward momentum.

Depending on the amount of life luggage we carry and what the contents are, sometimes the journey to emotional wellness involves seeking support from a mental health professional who's trained to help us express our emotions in a constructive manner, to help us make informed decisions, and to guide us in unpacking our emotional baggage so that it never has to be stowed away and carried again.

THE HEART OF THE MATTER

Our heart is the seat of our emotion—the way we feel.

Research from the Institute of HeartMath shows that "a change of heart changes everything."

When we experience sustained positive emotions—like care, compassion, gratitude, and patience—our body produces dehydroepiandrosterone (DHEA), which our adrenal glands secrete. DHEA is known as the vitality hormone; it accelerates renewal and improves our health.

....

"Different than the aura or subtle energy around us, the electromagnetic field of the heart extends somewhere between three and eight feet in diameter around the body. The frequency of this field is tangible and measurable, changing based on our emotional state."

—HEARTHMATH INSTITUTE

....

When we experience sustained negative emotions—like anger, bitterness, worry, or fear—our body produces cortisol, which contributes to suboptimal performance, accelerates aging, and is degenerative to health.

We don't always have a choice about the circumstances in which we find ourselves, but we do always have a choice about how we respond to them.

Alyssa shared, "I'd like to learn to react less and respond more. There's a blurry boundary between reacting and responding. I—the slightly battered-by-life human that I am—tend to react, while my true presence, who lives, breathes, and whispers wisdom, prefers to respond."

....

"Laurie Buchanan has a quote that is central to her work; it is *'Whatever you are not changing, you are choosing.'* And even though some circumstances in our life seem unchangeable, what we can change is our attitude toward the situation, circumstance. Sometimes it is our attitude that brings the pain in. I welcome changes that will bring even more joy and healing into my life. May I, may you, may all embrace the choice."

—AUDREY DENECKE, senior leadership coach

....

THE NUT DOESN'T FALL VERY FAR FROM THE TREE—OR DOES IT?

Our emotional diet is important because we experience the world through the way we feel. Healthy or not, many of us continue to emulate the *physical* diet we learned from our parents or other caregivers. Likewise, many of us continue to follow the *emotional* diet we learned from them as well.

You either have or had parents, whether biological, adopted, or foster. Self-acceptance is determined, in great part, by that parent-child relationship.

You may be an only child or one of many. You may be the youngest or the oldest or fall somewhere in between.

Some people had amazing childhoods, while others had experiences that were less than stellar.

Self-esteem—our sense of worth—fosters self-acceptance. It's feeling lovable and capable. Self-esteem is both gleaned from those around us (by being loved and valued) and earned (by becoming a capable, growing person). Both components are equally important.

When we don't have self-esteem, we feel unworthy. Unworthiness stems from complex negative memories and emotions.

BUILDING BLOCKS: A THREE-STEP PROGRESSION TO WHOLENESS

In my work, I've observed and become familiar with a three-step progression:

> *Self-esteem* is acknowledging and embracing our personal value—who we are and what we do. It's recognizing the inaccurate message that can permeate our consciousness. It's being diligent about authenticating the truth, or nontruth, behind the messages. Once we do this, it's much easier to take the second step.

> *Self-acceptance* is when we fully accept our authentic self. It's knowing that we're not responsible for whether or not anyone loves us. Rather, it's understanding that what matters is that we love ourselves and that we know how to love others. When we do this, a heart space is created for us to flow into the third step.

> *Self-confidence* is not arrogance that's oftentimes associated with overconfidence. Rather, it's an assured self-possession, one that allows us to move forward with dignity, poise, and grace.

To change self-image and improve low self-esteem, you must release limiting beliefs and embrace beliefs that empower.

DOES YOUR CAREER DEFINE YOU?

I once learned of a person who equated his personal value with what he did for a living. When he lost his job, he could no longer accept himself; he couldn't move forward in self-confidence. He felt as if when his livelihood was removed, his value was removed, too. He perceived the termination of his career as an end-of-life event.

When people limit their identification to what they do for a living, it can be extremely detrimental, especially if they lose their job or retire. They view the loss of their career as the loss of themselves personally—the loss of their identity, their validation. They believe they've lost their sense of purpose and that they don't have anything left to contribute.

It's our state of mind, rather than our circumstances, that so often makes the ultimate difference. When we're properly equipped, we can embrace whatever comes our way (illness, financial loss, solitude, and so on), instead of being overwhelmed by it. We can welcome adversity—invite it to sit for a spell—so that we can take the opportunity to learn from it. Once we have grasped the lesson on offer, we can acknowledge the learning, ease our embrace, and send it on its way. As a result, we're a better person for the visit, a better person individually and collectively, a better person locally and globally.

That isn't to say that while we're sitting with and learning from adversity we shouldn't take realistic, tangible action steps. Sometimes adversity is a natural result of our choices and consequences—the law of cause and effect. Regardless, it's an opportunity to learn.

THE CORNER OF LONELY STREET AND HEARTBREAK HOTEL

Being alone and being lonely aren't synonymous; they're not the same thing. Many people, including me, enjoy being alone; we're content and comfortable being by ourselves.

Loneliness is a feeling that intimacy, understanding, friendship, and acceptance are missing from one's life. It's a feeling of isolation or separation from others, of being unhappy with the emotional and social relationships that we don't have, or even with the ones that we do have.

A person can be surrounded by people and still feel lonely. Loneliness can be about the number of friends or people in a person's life, but it can also be about whether or not we feel connected to people.

Caitlin, a successful real estate agent, shared, "One December I gave a huge party for all of the people—buyers and sellers—I'd closed transactions with during the year. I was surrounded by at least one hundred people, all smiling and laughing, yet I experienced a profound sense of loneliness."

"Don't surrender your loneliness
So quickly.
Let it cut more deep.
Let it ferment and season you
As few human
Or even divine ingredients can."

—HAFEZ, fourteenth-century Persian poet

At some point on our life path, many of us have found, or will find, another person to whom we're attracted and want to establish a relationship. Yet partnering in any form—intimate or platonic—isn't easy. It requires that we understand and work toward satisfying our partner's needs, and in that process, our own needs must also be met.

"Remember that the best relationship is one in which your love for each other exceeds your need for each other."

—HIS HOLINESS THE DALAI LAMA, paramount leader of Tibetan Buddhism

Because these two separate yet intertwined processes are taking place simultaneously, building and maintaining relationships of any type is difficult, but the rewards can be well worth the effort.

Many of us skip important steps in creating the love relationship that we long for by forgetting the fundamental rule: in order to experience authentic, mature love with another person, we must first love ourselves.

World-renowned expert on the mind-body connection Joan Borysenko said, "We can only love others to the degree [to which] we have opened our hearts to ourselves."

SELF-LOVE: A KEY TO HEALING

Self-love is one of the most important keys to healing body, mind, and spirit. "When I accept myself without criticism or blame, I allow myself to heal." This is one of the powerful affirmations that Belleruth Naparstek expresses on her *A Meditation to Help with Anger & Forgiveness* guided-imagery CD.

Equally powerful are Eckhart Tolle's words "You are here to enable the Divine purpose of the Universe to unfold. That is how important you are."

Self-love doesn't come about until after we enter the sacred heart space of self-acceptance.

Our heart is the seat of our emotions, what we feel. True love is healthy, respectful, and nurturing, whether it's for ourselves or for another person. It's positive, uplifting, constructive, and healing to those in our sphere of influence, including the person we look at in the mirror every single morning—ourselves.

Each and every person is vital. Each of us has tremendous value and purpose. We are, in fact, sacred. That should be enough right there to boost our self-acceptance and enhance our self-love.

....

"It took me a long time not to judge myself through someone else's eyes."

—SALLY FIELD, American actress

....

When self-love is intact, we experience joy. Different from happiness—which fluctuates based on external circumstances—joy is inexplicable peace that comes from within.

A joy-filled life is a life in which one's roots in self-love run deep, a life that incorporates a variety of activities and healthful practices that support a person's overall well-being, practices that aren't seen as inconvenient or something to tick off a to-do list. Rather, it's a way of living—a lifestyle—complimented by healthy choices that foster our highest and best good in every area.

HAPPINESS AND JOY: UNDERSTANDING THE DIFFERENCE

Many people use the words "joy" and "happiness" interchangeably, when in fact they're different. Let's establish the difference.

Happiness is a feeling. It goes up and down—fluctuates—based on external circumstances. It's temporary, fleeting at best.

For instance, we check the mailbox and find a notice from the IRS that states we owe a considerable sum in back taxes. Most people's happiness level would plunge at this news. On the flip side, if we check the mailbox and find an unexpected refund check from the IRS—in any amount—our happiness level soars.

Happiness can also be a result of manufactured merriment, such as going to the circus, watching a funny movie, or attending a birthday party.

When our perspective is governed from the inside out, the external pressures fall away and we experience joy.

Joy is a state of being. It's inexplicable peace. Joy is internal, and when nurtured and encouraged, it becomes resident—abiding—regardless of external circumstances. Cultivating and maintaining joy eases the struggle that exists along life's path.

....

"A woman recently asked me, 'What are the blocks to my happiness?' I said, 'The belief that you have blocks.'"

—WAYNE DYER, American self-help advocate, lecturer, and author

....

Viktor Frankl is a perfect example of someone who attained inexplicable peace. As a Vienna Jew, he was interned by the Germans for more than three years, but being confined within the narrow boundaries of a concentration camp didn't rob him of his joy. In nine separate passages throughout his book, *Man's Search for Meaning*, he wrote of joy.

There are people who suffer tremendous personal devastation yet retain a state of joy—inexplicable peace that defies explanation.

THE LINK BETWEEN MONEY AND HAPPINESS

Does the amount of money people accumulate have anything to do with their level of happiness?

In his 2008 book, *The Geography of Bliss: One Grump's Search for the Happiest Places in the World*, Eric Weiner wrote, "Recent research into happiness reveals that money does indeed buy happiness, up to a point. That point, though, is surprisingly low: about $15,000 a year. After that, the link between economic growth and happiness evaporates."

Sibyl shared, "My husband was thrilled with his $3,000 bonus until he learned that someone else got $7,000. Now all he thinks about is *Why not me?* His green-eyed jealousy has turned to resentment, and it's eating him alive."

It's been said that the greatest enemy of happiness is envy.

Envy is an emotion that occurs when we feel as if we lack another person's qualities, achievements, or possessions and desire them for ourselves.

Self-acceptance and envy are mutually exclusive. When we have true self-acceptance, we don't envy what another person has, is, or accomplishes.

Many would agree that joy is a spiritual practice. It stems from an awareness of abundance—inner wealth. It grows out of faith, grace, gratitude, and love. It's the deep satisfaction we appreciate when we're able to serve others and be glad for their good fortune.

If we remain a passive participant in our life, waiting for joy to find us, our life will be unfilled and the wait will be endless. If, however, we're active participants, we're choosing to cultivate joy.

CULTIVATING JOY WITH THE WRITE STUFF

Gratitude unlocks the fullness of life.

Dr. Michelle L. McClellan, licensed clinical psychologist, is a proponent of journaling, which, she says, "is an age-old introspective technique that assists individuals in their personal growth. Writing is a time-honored process that enhances and speeds the process of change."

In his article "Rx for Life: Gratitude," which appeared on Beliefnet in November 2000, Gregg Easterbrook wrote, "Consider that recent academic studies have shown that people who describe themselves as feeling grateful to others and either to God or to creation in general tend to have higher vitality and more optimism, suffer less stress, and experience fewer episodes of clinical depression than the population as a whole."

In an experiment conducted by Robert Emmons, a psychology professor at the University of California, Davis, college students who kept a "gratitude journal"—a weekly record of things they felt grateful for—achieved better physical health, were more optimistic, felt less lonely, exercised more regularly, and described themselves as happier than a control group of students who kept no journals but had the same overall measures of health, optimism, and exercise when the experiment began.

The practice of gratitude isn't a denial of life's difficulties. One of the best ways to respond to a difficult situation is by acknowledging it as such and then saying, "Yes, this is terrible, yet I'm grateful for . . ."

By making gratitude a regular part of our daily experience, we set the stage for connecting more deeply with our higher self.

IT'S ALL IN YOUR HEAD

Researchers at the University of North Carolina in 2000 determined that a positive mental state—such as one brought on by humor—increases open-mindedness, creativity, the capacity to adapt to change, and broad thinking.

....

"The average preschooler laughs or smiles four hundred times a day. That number drops to only fifteen times a day by the time people reach age thirty-five."

—VARSHA TIBREWAL, Camellia Institute of Technology

....

Experts also speculate that a sense of humor goes hand in hand with higher levels of "emotional intelligence," which determines people's ability to handle their feelings and understand the emotional states of others.

Scientists speculate that humor stimulates the brain's reward center in the same ways sex and chocolate do. In turn, this reward center secretes two hormones into the brain: dopamine and serotonin. Also known as happiness molecules, these are anti-stress chemicals associated with the feeling of happiness. As we grow older, the body's production of these chemicals decreases, so laughing becomes even more important.

Laughter decreases blood pressure, normalizes heart rate, and increases appetite. To top it off, it's a great workout that helps the lungs breathe better and keeps muscles in the diaphragm, abdomen, respiratory tract, face, legs, and back healthy.

"It takes ten minutes on a rowing machine for a person's heart rate to reach the level it would after just one minute of hearty laughter."

—WILLIAM FRY, laughter research pioneer

As a holistic health practitioner, I can share this fact with certainty: of the 206 bones in the human body, the most important one is the funny bone.

Laughter is indeed the best medicine.

NONFORGIVENESS: A SELF-IMPOSED PRISON

When someone we love and trust hurts us—whether through a lie, rejection, a betrayal, an insult, or abuse—it can be extremely difficult to overcome. Forgiveness begins when we're ready to release the feelings associated with being a victim.

Erin shared, "I was in a self-imposed prison; the bars that held me captive were anger and hatred. The single key that unlocked the door and set me free was forgiveness. Not condoning what the other person did, but rather forgiving it. Not pretending that it didn't happen, but acknowledging it."

In their article "Helping Clients Heal: Does Forgiveness Make a Difference?," which appeared in the December 2005 publication of *Professional Psychology: Research and Practice,* professors Nathaniel Wade, Donna Bailey, and Philip Shaffer of Iowa State University wrote that "broken trust, broken hearts, and broken spirits are all potential issues facing clients who've been hurt by others."

With that in mind, they posed the question, "If that's the case, is it then the counselor's responsibility to bring up the issue of forgiveness?"

In a survey of 381 members of the American Mental Health Counselors

Association, almost every counselor agreed that it was appropriate for therapists to raise the issue of forgiveness (95 percent), and just over half (51 percent) reported that it was the counselor's responsibility to raise forgiveness as an issue in appropriate situations.

In her book *Remembering the Future*, Colette Baron-Reid wrote, "To despise another person is to hate ourselves, and to love and support someone else reflects back onto us."

One of the most destructive and debilitating emotions we can harbor is chronic anger. It can negatively affect and disrupt every aspect of our being—body, mind, and spirit.

There's a time and place for anger. For instance, the hormones that are associated with anger stimulate action and are what motivates us to act when we see an injustice. However, uncontrolled, chronic anger—hostility—gets people in trouble and can lead to physical aggression.

Chronic anger can be based in a deep mistrust of other people. Oftentimes formed during childhood, such mistrust leads to defensive thought patterns, the idea that *this person has it in for me.* Many people drag this baggage along with them throughout life.

"When you hold resentment toward another, you are bound to that person or condition by an emotional link that is stronger than steel. Forgiveness is the only way to dissolve that link and get free."

—CATHERINE PONDER, Unity minister and inspirational author

A colleague of mine shared, "When I was training to be a counselor, I learned that the underlying emotion of anger is pain. This was such an eye-opener for me. If we can get to the pain underlying the anger, we can begin to heal the fuse and defuse potentially explosive situations by dealing with the actual cause.

"The thoughts I have are that anger can feel easier than allowing the experience of pain. Anger can almost feel 'attractive' in comparison, especially if a person is feeling disempowered, then a shot of rage can seem quite seductive. I'm imagining someone who's not used to admitting sensitivity; such a person would far rather see others feeling sensitive."

Many times anger stems from withholding forgiveness.

—ANN LANDERS, American advice columnist

On her CD *The Power of Your Spoken Word*, Louise Hay says, "Cancer is a disease of resentment that eventually eats away at the physical body."

She goes on to say, "All dis-ease comes from a state of nonforgiveness, and therapy usually revolves around forgiveness, letting go of the past—moving from forgiveness into understanding."

Aimee shared, "My son, Drew, was killed in a car accident at the age of twenty-four. I almost lost my mind with grief over it all. His father was absolutely inconsolable, and my brother, Drew's favorite uncle, was speechless with fury.

"Our son was a passenger in his friend's car on an early spring evening. They were just being guys—radio on, seat belts on, no one was drinking, though other nights they probably did. Kids don't know that they're mortal.

"Drew was in the front seat, and somehow, without any reason we were able to discover, Drew's friend lost control of his car and it flipped over and landed against a tree. My son was unconscious when the paramedics took him to the hospital. When his father and I arrived at the hospital, the doctor told us that Drew wouldn't live.

"He regained consciousness under deep sedation for just a few minutes. He was able only to mumble. I don't really remember what he said; my husband said that Drew said, 'I love you both.' I'll never really know, but I'm glad he heard that.

"Drew and Jack had been best friends since elementary school. They were in and out of each other's homes, classes, cars, and apartments. Jack wasn't hurt. He didn't even break a bone—nothing. He walked away from the accident unscathed. But did he really?

"While his father and I were so grief stricken we couldn't breathe or talk at first, we came to know after a few months that Jack was suicidally depressed about having 'killed his friend.' It would be a lie to say that angry thoughts didn't enter our heads sometimes.

"As time wore on, we of course went through Drew's things. There was so much of Jack in his life, and we both came to realize, after some counseling, that this young man was equally a victim in the accident. While he'd waited to be cut out of the car, he'd watched his friend start to die beside him. Can you imagine what was going through his head? I can't, but I saw it in his eyes.

"We talked to our therapist, we raged against the unfairness of it, and then one weekend when we were talking, my husband and I both realized that loving Drew meant loving his friend. This could've easily gone the other way and our son [could have] been 'at fault.'

"They were young, happy, and carefree. No one meant for it to happen, and we agreed that to have Jack suffer without forgiveness was to kill him, too. We called his parents and agreed to meet at their house. We expressed our love for Drew and our grief over losing him. Jack was pale and nearly fetal with pain.

"I saw our son in his face and, without any conscious decision, walked over and put my arms around him and said, 'It was an accident. It should never have happened, but you're not going to be sacrificed in this. You didn't mean for it to happen; it was a senseless accident. You are and always will be a part of our lives. If you can accept our forgiveness, we want you to know that you're part of this family.'

"His mother cried, my husband cried, and Jack was in shock. Suddenly, he started sobbing. He was literally gasping for breath; he told us how sorry he was and that he would do all that he could to represent Drew in all he did in life.

"I don't know if this is how we would've reacted with a stranger; I only know that we were finally able to sleep. And slowly, ever so slowly, we started to move forward. Jack comes over from time to time. We invite him for Drew's birthday, and we always remember his, too.

"I don't think that life's always fair. I think that terrible, senseless things happen. I hate that our son died. There are still days when I get in the car, drive to an empty parking lot, roll the windows up, and scream and scream.

"Our son should be here, but he's not. He's gone. And my husband and I just couldn't add Jack to the list of casualties in this tragedy.

"Forgiveness helped us all to heal."

It's my perspective that the place to start—the place to launch joy, hope, positive aspirations, and healing—begins with forgiveness. Until that bit of housekeeping has been taken care of, everything else is futile.

All of us at one time will have someone to forgive.

All of us at one time will need forgiveness ourselves.

It's important to understand that forgiving is not the same as condoning.

Sometimes the person or people we need to forgive are still living; sometimes they're no longer alive. I've found the following tangible exercise to be effective in either case. It's also helpful in working with overwhelming sorrow or grief.

"Healing can't take place without forgiveness."

—JOAN BORYSENKO, PhD, licensed clinical psychologist, and cofounder and former director of the Mind-Body Clinical Programs at the BethIsrael Deaconess Medical Center, Harvard Medical School

THE ASHES EXERCISE

By hand, write out all of the details of the experience. Don't use a computer. There's something tremendously therapeutic and liberating about writing this out by hand.

In story form, as if you're a reporting journalist, write out the who, what, when, where, why, and how of it. In detail, write about how you think and how you feel as it relates to the matter. Capture on paper how it's impacted your life on every level—body, mind, and spirit.

Once you have everything written out—this may take a few days—wait for either a new moon (which represents new beginnings) or the full moon (which represents closure). Only you'll know which is right for you.

Regardless, on the date you select, roll the pages in scroll fashion into a long, cylindrical tube. Then use a lighter and hold the paper over a large, fireproof container (a metal pot for cooking spaghetti noodles is ideal). As you're burning the paper, state out loud:

"By burning these remembrances, I lovingly forgive and release them
from my life. I am no longer held hostage by this negative energy.
I nurture my highest and best good with things that are positive,
uplifting, constructive, and healing. In offloading this baggage, I have
created space for joy. Thank you. And so it is."

Once the ashes have cooled, gather them and mix them with soil. Using a ceramic pot inside your home, or the ground outside, plant bulbs or a beautiful plant—a visual reminder of your commitment to release negative energy and to move forward. Each of us has to find our own way through the many layers of forgiveness. I hope the ashes exercise helps you.

THE BERMUDA TRIANGLE: DEPRESSION, ANXIETY, AND STRESS— YOU CAN GET LOST IN IT

Three other emotions that are important to define and talk about in the context of self-acceptance are depression, anxiety, and stress. Pretend for a moment that we're standing on a giant timeline:

Depression

Depression is behind us on the timeline. It belongs to the past.

It's usually about something we lost or perceive that we lost. It takes a great deal of energy to dwell in the past. For many, this is a place where anger and resentment reside. What's more, stressing or worrying about the past won't change anything that's already occurred. That's impossible.

What's done is done; it is what it is.

Can you think of a moment in your life that brought you pain or sadness? Was it a poor decision? Someone who hurt you? The loss of someone you love? If only that moment hadn't happened. But it did.

Do you know anyone who lives in the past with such intensity that it drives their very decision-making? Rather than releasing the past, they embrace it. They choose to keep the wound open; some even use it as leverage for manipulation, or as a convenient excuse for their current state of affairs.

When the sweetness of life leaves, it's time to go within and allow ourselves to relieve the pent-up feelings that we've been holding in, to empty our baggage: childhood problems, prejudices, assumptions, interpretations, and projections.

A helpful way of doing this is to make a release statement. You can say these words quietly to yourself, speak them aloud, write them down, or create a mantra. Whatever you choose will be right for you.

"I release and let go of [fill in the blank] with love."

Anxiety

Anxiety is in front of us on the timeline. It belongs to the future.

It's about uncertainty, the unknown, the what-ifs. Like the past, it also takes a great deal of energy to dwell in the future. For many, this is a place where fear resides.

There's not a single person in the history of mankind who has changed a future outcome through worry.

The only way to change a future outcome is if we can make a *realistic* plan of action and see it through. If it's something that you can't create a *realistic* action plan for, then you don't own it; it doesn't belong to you, and you must let it go. You can use a release statement here as well.

"I release and let go of [fill in the blank] with love."

According to the National Institute of Mental Health:

- Anxiety disorders affect about forty million American adults ages eighteen years and older. That's about 18 percent of the population in a given year.
- Anxiety disorders are the number-one mental health problem in America, surpassing even depression in numbers.
- Women suffer from anxiety and stress almost twice as much as men.
- Anxiety is the most common mental health issue facing seniors.
- Anxiety disorders cost the US workplace $46.6 billion annually; 88 percent of this figure is from lost productivity.

Stress

Stress occurs where we currently stand on the timeline.

It happens when we focus on the past or the future, instead of the present moment. It's been estimated that up to 90 percent of all illness is stress related. The effects of stress substantially reduce efficiency and accuracy not only in performing physical tasks, but also in the areas of abstract planning, decision-making, and creativity.

Prolonged stress leads to tiredness and irritability, a weakening of the immune system, and the development of physical illness. Stressing or worrying about what lies ahead is an exercise in futility.

There's an old saying, "Worry is like sitting in a rocking chair. It gives you something to do but doesn't get you anywhere."

Simply put, the past is over and the future has yet to be written. We have the gift of the present moment in which to live.

You've heard the Latin phrase *carpe diem,* "seize the day." Now is the time. Now is the day.

We can't reshape the past, and none of us has a guaranteed future; they're tenuous places to live. Dwelling in either one of them leads to limited satisfaction, feeds control issues, and fans the flames of discontent.

Your time is now. Live in the moment.

DO YOU KNOW WHO YOU ARE?

There are times during a session when I ask a client to tell me who they are. I preface this by saying, "I don't want to know whose mother, wife, or daughter you are, what you do for a living, what group(s) you identify with, where you live, what you collect, or what you drive. Take away all of those trimmings and tell me who you are."

When asked this way, the question usually causes a long, thought-filled, inward examination.

The question—who are you?—is important for each of us to be able to answer for ourselves.

....

"All my life, I always wanted to be somebody. Now I see that I should have been more specific."

—LILY TOMLIN, American actress, comedian, writer, and producer

....

I remember Olivia, who thought quietly about this question for the longest time. Eventually, tears slowly began to roll down her cheeks, but she was smiling. When she finally answered, she said, "I am enough."

That was the most powerful, profound answer I'd ever received. This is the place that we all need to be—*I am enough!*

When we let outside factors determine our personal value, we're at the mercy of upheaval. The classroom of life has an ever-changing terrain. As such, our internal foothold must be strong and secure, one that allows us to stay the course.

Self-acceptance is at the very heart of our humanness, governing our sense of worth—the quality that allows us to embrace our personal value and sanction our feelings.

Emotionally painful events such as separation, divorce, betrayal, grief through death, abandonment, and emotional abuse affect our core, the place where our inner child resides.

When we're confident in love and self-acceptance, we're empowered.

When this self is healthy and in balance, there's an abundant return value to the heart. In this case, the dividends include tangibles such as self-confidence, calm, joy, laughter, and emotional wellness. These in turn pave the way for delightful moments of synchronicity—unexpected events that occur in a meaningful manner on life's journey.

In the following chapter, you'll find several keys—practical tips, tools, and exercises—to enhance your sense of emotional empowerment and offload baggage associated with self-acceptance.

....

"There is overwhelming evidence that the higher the level of self-acceptance, the more likely one will treat others with respect, kindness, and generosity. People who do not experience self-love have little or no capacity to love others."

—NATHANIEL BRANDEN, Canadian-born psychotherapist and writer

....

CHAPTER 10

Keys to Self-Acceptance:
Develop Your Emotional Empowerment

"You take your life in your own hands, and what happens?
A terrible thing—no one to blame."

—ERICA JONG, American author, poet, and essayist

1. MIND-BODY CONNECTION

Self-acceptance is associated with the heart, circulatory system, thymus gland, lungs, diaphragm, breasts, ribs, shoulders, and arms. If you're experiencing issues in any of these areas, it's time to make an appointment with your health care provider.

2. COLOR THERAPY

Green is associated with self-acceptance, love, and emotional wellness.

It enhances love, peace, and inner balance. It's the color of growth. Think of freshly mown grass that springs back after a barefoot step, the vibrant green of newly beached seaweed, a wedge of lime hugging the rim of a glass, moss-covered rocks in a stream, freshly snapped sugar peas, the dusty green of pistachios peeking out from their split shells, or new leaves unfurling as they herald spring.

The *positive* properties of green are expressed as warm, sympathetic, compassionate, soothing, relaxed, fair-minded, and consistent.

The *negative* properties of green are described as envious, mean, bitter, inflexible, and jaded.

The *healing* properties of green are described as calming and soothing and can address physical symptoms that include headaches; heart and kidney problems; flu; and negative states of mind such as irritability, spite, fear of emotional involvement, and claustrophobia.

When you need a boost in the areas of love and self-acceptance, indulge yourself with this color. Its frequency revitalizes the heart chakra, the center energy station in a system of seven. It encourages us to love ourselves just as we are. Love, the most powerful energy of all, helps us to heal emotional wounds through unconditional acceptance and understanding. It's here—the place of the heart—where we become balanced and peaceful beings.

The vibration of green is calming, soothing, and relaxing. What shade are you drawn to?

Pure green is strongly associated with nature, new beginnings, and a sense of renewal; it's the most neutral color in the spectrum. The more muted tones are calm, restful, and soothing. Or maybe you prefer the deeper shaded variants, which project trust and order, encouraging contemplation, serenity, and repose.

Regardless of the hue, green reminds us to listen with our hearts and encourages us to fulfill our heart's desire. Archangel Raphael—known as Heaven's Physician—is associated with the color green. It's no wonder this color is often used in healing circles.

What we do with our physical environment—our personal space—speaks to our heart and helps us to flourish:

- Accessorize with a piece of green clothing or jewelry.
- Make a serene statement in your work area by adding stalks of bamboo; it helps to bring calm to chaos.
- Do you enjoy antiques? Add a few pieces of soft green Depression glass or an emerald-green seltzer bottle to your collection.
- Take advantage of the healing frequency of green crystals, such as green aventurine, malachite, green jade, or emerald.

Zipped in the Pod!

Green is my favorite color. I associate it with sacred space—space for transformation to occur; space to find new direction. When people ask me to pray for them or their loved ones, I explain that I'd be happy to hold heartlight—sacred space—for them.

The visualization I use is a sugar snap pea. In my mind's eye, I unzip the pod, scoop out the peas, and place the person inside. Carefully, I rezip the pod and envision it as a "station," somewhat like an incubator, of vivid green, pulsing with vital energy that's working for the person's highest and best good—body, mind, and spirit.

3. DIET

Foods that boost our sense of emotional empowerment include:

- **Dark leafy vegetables**—spinach, kale, and dandelion greens
- **Air vegetables**—broccoli, cauliflower, cabbage, celery, and squash
- **Liquids**—green teas
- **Spices**—basil, sage, thyme, cilantro, and parsley
- **Supplements**—CoQ10 is an antioxidant that helps maintain heart health. If you suffer from either premenstrual syndrome (PMS) or premenstrual dysphoric disorder (PMDD) irritability, you may want to consider vitamin B_6—an antistress vitamin. You can take 50 to 100 milligrams a day to get on a more even keel.

4. AROMATHERAPY

The use of rose maroc, bergamot, Melissa, ylang-ylang, mandarin, rosemary, lime, tangerine, geranium, jasmine, or lavender helps to eliminate fears associated with love and self-acceptance (e.g., fear of loneliness, commitment, and following one's heart; fear of the inability to protect oneself emotionally, or the inability to forgive others or oneself). These essential oils encourage optimism, openness, sensitivity, harmony, awareness, profundity, inspiration, and joy.

5. AFFIRMATIONS

When we encounter threats to our sense of emotional well-being, effective affirmations to speak out loud are:

I am worthy of love.
I act with emotional strength.
I build healthy relationships.

I follow my heart.

I model inspiration, hope, and trust.

I am peaceful and balanced.

I project calm and joy.

I accept myself and others.

I embrace positive emotions.

I function from a place of compassion and forgiveness.

6. THE BUSINESS OF BEING

Love and self-acceptance in the business world relate to stakeholders (investors/clients) and the strength of those relationships. For a moment, think of your life as a business and write the answers to the following questions:

- Who are the "investors" in your life (the people who love you, the people who are up close and personal)?
- Are they for your highest and best good (positive, uplifting, constructive, and healing)?
- Do some of the people who are currently in your sphere of influence belong outside, or vice versa?

7. BREATHWORK: SITALI BREATHING

Whenever you recognize that you're hosting unwanted, draining emotion related to love, self-acceptance, or emotional wellness, stop what you're doing and focus on your breath. Breathe deeply, slowly, and steadily. Place a hand on your lower belly to ensure that you're breathing past your chest.

An effective breathing exercise to do is known as *sitali breathing*—*sitali* means "cool breathing." It's a yoga breathing method that lowers the fire energy principle. Here's how it's done:

- Make an "O" shape with your mouth, and then roll your tongue in the shape of an upright taco shell.
- Inhale slowly and deeply through your tongue.
- Close your mouth.

- Exhale completely through your nose.
- Once you've established a rhythm, identify a replacement attitude. Imagine that with each inhalation, you're breathing in the color green and the feeling of the new attitude—increasing joy.
- When you exhale, imagine that you're releasing the toxins associated with the unwanted emotion—offloading baggage
- Repeat this process for three minutes as needed throughout the day, drawing the green breath and replacement feeling through your heart area and down into your lower belly, to anchor the new feeling.

8. EMOTIONAL WELLNESS INVENTORY AND VITALITY CHECK

- Do you have an optimistic approach to life?
- Do you adjust well to change?
- Are you aware of your coping mechanisms?
- Do you accept your true thoughts and feelings?
- Do you express your feelings freely?
- Do you manage your feelings effectively?
- Are you able to make effective decisions with minimum stress and worry?
- Do you accept your mistakes and learn from them?
- Do you seek personal growth opportunities?

If you answered no to any of these questions, it may indicate an area of opportunity for you to improve the quality of your emotional wellness.

On a scale of one to nine, where do you rate yourself on the current quality of your emotional experience, if one represents negative feelings (sad/depressed, anxious/overwhelmed, irritable/angry) and nine represents positive feelings (happy/joyful, calm/peaceful, loving/enthusiastic/excited)?

Is there a difference between where you currently are and where you want to be? If so, write down how you'll close the gap. Be specific.

9. ACTION STEPS

To enhance your senses of love and emotional empowerment, try these activities:

- **Quick hits:** Do some push-ups. Work with your arms—reaching out, taking in, hug yourself. Engage in self-discovery by journaling on a regular basis.

- **With a little planning:** Carve out time to examine your assumptions about relationships. Gift yourself with emotional release by forgiving yourself and others. Let go of grief. Delight yourself by spending time in nature. Invest quality time with family and friends. Participate in codependency work if it applies to you.

Giving and Receiving Forgiveness

How has giving forgiveness—or the lack thereof—played a role in your personal health and wellness?

How has receiving forgiveness—or the lack thereof—played a role in your personal health and wellness?

Parental/Caretaker Input

Make a list of the long-term positive and negative input your parents or primary caretaker had on you.

If you're a parent, which of these same contributions are you, in turn, making to your own children?

Random Acts of Kindness

The main characteristic of this self—acceptance—is love. With that in mind, explore the Random Acts of Kindness website at www.actsofkindness.org to get some ideas of positive action steps you can take in your community; then select one and do it.

Pay It Forward

Never underestimate the influence you have on others. Our individual ripple effect is the power of one generating hope and change in others for a better world. And, like ripples in a pond when a pebble's tossed in, compassion is powerful and has far-reaching, positive ramifications that bring about a tremendous sense of joy.

With love as the focus of this self, read the book by Catherine Ryan Hyde, see the movie, or visit the Pay It Forward Foundation online at www.payitforwardfoundation.org and then go out and *pay it forward*.

JOY JOURNAL

Get a notebook, any size. It can be a simple spiral-bound notebook or a blank book meant specifically for journaling. At the end of the day, simply jot down anything you can think of that felt like a blessing to you. Maybe it was some encouraging words that you heard, or a song that lifted you up. Possibly the sun shone and that energized you. Perhaps your spirits lifted when you saw a hawk flying overhead. A daily entry of something you're grateful for—large or small—is one of the most effective ways to cultivate joy.

Laugh!

You've heard it said that laugher is the best medicine. In a study of thirty-five patients in a rehabilitation hospital, 74 percent agreed with the statement "sometimes laughing works as well as a pain pill." These patients had a broad range of conditions, such as spinal cord injuries, traumatic brain injuries, arthritis, limb amputations, and other neurological or musculoskeletal disorders.

With that in mind, rent comedies—movies that make you laugh. One of my favorites is *Something's Gotta Give*, with Diane Keaton, Jack Nicholson, Keanu Reeves, and Amanda Peet. When I saw it, I laughed so hard that I cried.

Ashes Exercise

Dallas Willard, a philosophy professor and author of *The Divine Conspiracy: Rediscovering Our Hidden Life in God*, offers a telling definition of anger: "It is a feeling that seizes us in our body and immediately impels us toward interfering with, and possibly even harming, those who have thwarted our will and interfered with our life. It is frequently used to make others around us change their course of action. In so doing, it thwarts their will, resulting in anger on their part. My anger feeds off your anger, and back again."

If you're holding on to an unhealthy emotion—anger or otherwise—that stems from a specific incident or a series of incidents, do the ashes exercise described in the previous chapter and let it go.

Release Statement

As described in the previous chapter, create a release statement for depression (past), anxiety (future), or stress (present)—whichever is relevant to your situation.

Let Go of Your Problems

My friend Sheila Glazov, author of *What Color Is Your Brain? A Fun and Fascinating Approach to Understanding Yourself and Others*, shared this story about letting go of stress:

> "While traveling to Palm Springs, California, many years ago, my mother was seated next to a handsome gentleman in the first-class section of the aircraft. Right after takeoff, her seatmate stretched his left arm out in front of his body and rhythmically began to open and close his fist.
>
> "My 'blue brain' mother became concerned and thought he was not feeling well. She inquired, 'Excuse me, are you feeling okay?'
>
> "He responded, 'I'm fine, thank you. I'm just letting go of my problems and negative thoughts.'
>
> "'Splendid,' my mother said.
>
> "When her 'yellow brain' began to worry, Mother would practice his relaxing technique to reduce her stress and remove troublesome thoughts."

What a simple activity and metaphorical solution:

- Unclench your problems.
- Fan your fingers apart to free yourself of detrimental thoughts.
- Release and relax!

When using this technique, I've found that a release statement is effective here as well. "I release and let go of [fill in the blank] with love."

Who Are You?

When I take away all of the extraneous fluff, I'm an extension of source energy, an expression of divine love. When you remove all of the trimmings, what's left? *Who are you?*

Define Love

I believe that love is a person's divinity in action. Write your personal definition of love.

10. PERSONAL ENERGY SIGNATURE

On a sheet of paper, draw a circle that represents your personal energy circle. Considering what you've learned about self-acceptance, love, and emotional wellness, on the inside of the circle, list the people, places, and things that are for this self's highest and best good—positive, uplifting, constructive, and healing.

On the outside of the circle, list the people, places, things, and actions you need to avoid to keep this self healthy and balanced. The examples on the following page will help you get started.

SELF-ACCEPTANCE, LOVE, AND EMOTIONAL WELLNESS
PERSONAL ENERGY SIGNATURE

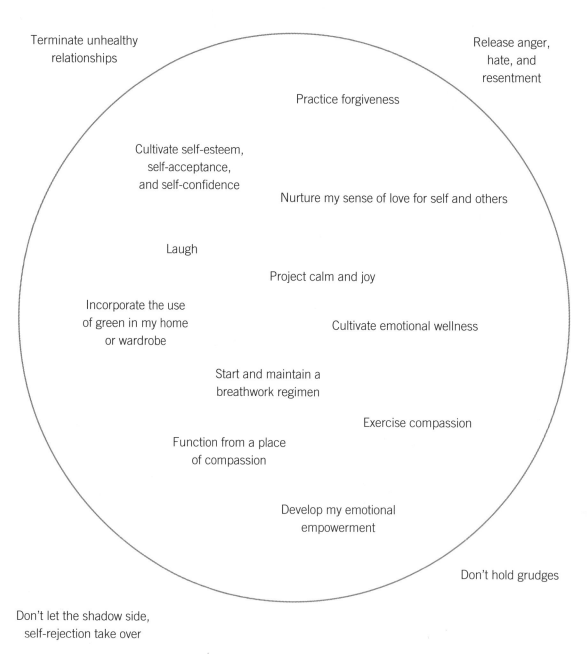

Terminate unhealthy relationships

Release anger, hate, and resentment

Practice forgiveness

Cultivate self-esteem, self-acceptance, and self-confidence

Nurture my sense of love for self and others

Laugh

Project calm and joy

Incorporate the use of green in my home or wardrobe

Cultivate emotional wellness

Start and maintain a breathwork regimen

Exercise compassion

Function from a place of compassion

Develop my emotional empowerment

Don't hold grudges

Don't let the shadow side, self-rejection take over

CHAPTER 11

Self #5: Self-Expression

Self-expression is responsible for creativity and environmental wellness; its purpose is to unleash our creative flair. When healthy, this self functions from a place of original thought. Corresponding to the throat chakra, it resonates with the color blue. An inspiring affirmation for this self is: *I am creative*. The shadow side is self-repression.

❖ ❖ ❖

Having recently relocated from another state, Joyce shared with me during her first visit, "It's important for you to know that I'm a liar. I had two best friends, whom I adored. That came to an end because of my lies. My promotion at work was based on lies—well, not lies exactly, just embellishments. Even my therapist felt it necessary for me to see him only once a month because of all my 'progress.' If only he knew!

"The problem is that I look good on the outside—I present myself well. But let me tell you, my life is a house of cards that's just collapsed around me. It's two weeks until my wedding. Everything about me is made up, except for the one truth that I can't tell [my fiancé]: *the woman you love is a complete fabrication.*

"Only people who don't believe in themselves try to be someone else. Eventually someone will come along whose reality exceeds the fiction I created that he fell in love with."

Do you tend to embellish or stretch the truth?

Do you lend momentum to gossip, rumors, or lies by passing them along?

Are you transparent? Do you live authentically?

Are you as good as your word? Do you follow through on what you say?

This self—self-expression—empowers us to speak our truth and to express our creativity. The developmental stage begins somewhere between seven and twelve years of age.

This self is concerned with communication: conveying ourselves honestly and creatively. As we continue to grow, this often translates into our having the courage to speak about what's getting in our way, the ability to "voice our choice," and unleashing our creative potential.

We may never pick up a paintbrush or sculpt a masterpiece, but each one of us—without exception—is an artist in our own way.

When our senses of creativity and self-expression are in balance, we enjoy qualities from the constructive side of this self. These include honesty, tactfulness, original thought, and creative ideas.

THE SHADOW SIDE: SELF-REPRESSION

When our senses of creativity and self-expression are out of balance, we can experience feelings of self-repression.

Different from being modest, timid, or reserved, self-repression is akin to censorship—intentional restriction—of self. It can include painful shyness, extreme introversion, and tremendous social unease.

It's the polar opposite of self-assertion. Self-repression is holding oneself in the background and remaining as inconspicuous as possible, shrinking away from exposure and interaction with other people.

The origin of self-repression is oftentimes insecurity.

Self-expression through writing and other types of art created by people who live with self-repression are oftentimes exquisite. However, self-repressed people encounter difficulty when promoting their own work, so many times it remains hidden.

Self-repression can manifest itself in a number of harmful ways that become items we tuck into our life's baggage. Depending on their size and impact, we may slip them into a tote that we keep within arm's reach, for handy retrieval, or stuff them into a larger suitcase that comes around on the baggage carousel only occasionally. These can include:

> *Physical:* swollen throat glands, sore throat, laryngitis, mouth ulcers, voice problems, gum or tooth problems, issues with the temporomandibular joints (TMJ), and thyroid dysfunctions.

> *Mental:* creative blockage, overambition, criticality, instability, indecision, and lack of judgment.

> *Emotional:* stress, addictive behaviors, lack of self-expression, and lack of personal authority.

Spiritual: lack of faith, lack of strength of will, and failure to follow one's dream.

Lenore refers to herself in the third person when discussing something she doesn't like, and in the first person otherwise.

She shared, "I don't know who I am, but I know who I'd like to be. The person who I am is in tremendous debt because she can't stop using her charge card. I guess you could say she's a 'spendaholic.' Her house is filled with boxes and bags of things that she can't bring herself to part with. She's gotten caught up in the world of having to have in order to be. She takes in every stray pet she finds because that's her tangible source of love. It also contributes to the filth in her home that she doesn't clean because she no longer cares.

....

"The US Department of Energy reports that one-quarter of people with two-car garages have so much stuff in there that they can't park a car. If you rent a storage facility to store your excess belonging, you're contributing to a $154 billion industry—bigger than the Hollywood film business."

—THE TINY LIFE

....

"The person I'd like to be is someone who's responsible with her finances. I'd like to stop buying things I don't want or need—my house looks like Stuff Mart. I want to be someone who cares about my personal appearance and does something about my weight. I want to come home to a clean house that I can invite people to without feeling embarrassed. I want to make friends—human friends—and find good homes for all but one of the animals I've rescued."

....

"Live more by owning less."

—JOSHUA BECKER, author of *Simplify: 7 Guiding Principles to Help Anyone Declutter Their Home and Life*

....

Some of the "stuff" we have is for "special" occasions. I have a few pieces of my mom's Depression glass, some green and some pink; they're lovely. In the past I used them only for special occasions, but when I realized that breathing—everyday living—is a special occasion, I started using them, along with everything else that I had set aside as "special," on a regular basis.

What "special" things have you set aside that you can weave into your everyday living?

Prior to making a purchase, I usually ask myself, "Am I going to have to dust or iron this?" If the answer's yes, then I'm more likely to take a pass.

....

Of Mice and Men . . . and Pack Rats

Is it a collection or clutter? Is it treasure or excessive acquisition? It seems the answer is in the mind of the beholder.

"The overwhelming desire to acquire, save, and compulsively collect—hoard—can be attributed to a 'unique pattern of brain function abnormalities.'

"Some women declare that men are the worst culprits, feeling that males suffer from 'just in case' syndrome—'you never know when I might need this.'

"Some men, on the other hand, say that women are the worst culprits, feeling that females suffer from 'too much is never enough' syndrome—'I know I have three other pairs of black shoes, but this pair has just the right height heel for the outfit I'm going to wear.'

"Research has shown the inability to discard doesn't play favorites; it can equally affect both men and women."

—OBSESSIVE-COMPULSIVE DISORDERS PROGRAM, University of California, San Diego

....

Over time, I've come to learn that experiential purchases—like taking a friend out to dinner—provide far greater pleasure than material purchases. A side bonus is that the pleasant memories of experience are long lasting and don't take up any space.

My friend Sandi made me laugh when she shared, "Being an Air Force brat taught me to leave things behind when they no longer applied to the present. That includes dead goldfish, ex-husbands, and really bad hair!"

THE NEED TO BE HEARD

Self-expression is the seat of communication—the desire to convey personal feelings, ideas, beliefs, and concerns to others. It's the human longing to be heard. This need is deeply anchored in our connection with others.

Healthy self-expression is the ability to convey our thoughts, opinions, beliefs, and convictions in an effective way. It's also the skill to disagree with others, voice views that are unpopular, and stand up for what we believe is right in a positive, nondestructive way.

....

"I know that you believe you understand what you think I said, but I'm not sure you realize that what you heard is not what I meant."

—ROBERT MCCLOSKEY, American author and illustrator of children's books

....

We've all encountered a "lump in our throat" when we didn't know what to say in a given situation. We may even have stuffed down our emotions. The mind-body connection of not speaking out can result in laryngitis.

Anita shares, "I have two children, ten years apart in age. My daughter, Courtney, is fifteen. My son, Dylan, is five. When it was time for Courtney to go to preschool, I worked very hard jumping through difficult administrative hoops for her acceptance and the funding to make it happen. When the time came, their father—my common-law husband, Max—reneged on his commitment, saying that we couldn't afford it, and pulled the plug.

"I had laryngitis, couldn't speak a word, for a month. With Dylan, I'm experiencing déjà vu. I'm currently jumping through the same hoops, and I haven't been able to speak for weeks. I feel a sense of dread, like I'm waiting for the other shoe to drop.

"In reading Louise Hay's book *Heal Your Body A-Z: The Mental Causes for Physical Illnesses and the Way to Overcome Them*, I found the probable causes for issues with the throat: 'Holding in angry words.' 'Feeling unable to express the self.' 'The inability to speak up for oneself.' And 'swallowed anger.' Oh my gosh, that's been true both times!"

What we say is an audible extension of what we think.

People who are adept in healthy self-expression exercise front-end consideration before speaking. They express themselves without being overly defensive, arrogant, or aggressive. Not interrupting, they show respect for the other person by letting them finish what they're saying before they speak.

When I'm in a conversation, I look at the other person and take in what they're saying. Giving them visual clues, I utilize soft expressions of agreement—nod my head, smile, softly say "uh-huh"—to let them know that I'm listening.

In their article "The Contribution of Emotional Intelligence to Individual and Organizational Effectiveness," Geetu Orme and Reuven Bar-On write, "When self-expression is discouraged or restricted, the potential for innovative ideas and creative ways of approaching challenges is limited. Moreover, depression and anxiety can also stem from a lack of self-expression.

"The ability to control emotions is an important component of effective and non-destructive self-expression.

"Action and reaction, ebb and flow, trial and error, change—this is the rhythm of living. Out of our overconfidence, fear; out of our fear, clearer vision, fresh hope. And out of hope, progress."

—BRUCE BARTON, American author, advertising executive, and politician

---

"People who are effective in controlling their emotions are typically calm, rarely impatient or impulsive, and work well under pressure. Good impulse control is an important ability that allows us time to listen, be empathetic, and accurately read social cues. All of these are keys to emotional and social intelligence."

MARCH TO THE BEAT OF YOUR OWN DRUM

The grace of universal rhythms is expressed in the phases of the moon, the ebb and flow of the tides, the earth's rotation, and the changing of the seasons.

As rhythm pervades the universe, so it does the human body. Our internal body clock governs our daily, or circadian, rhythm—the master timekeeper. It governs when things should and shouldn't occur.

Years ago, it was thought that the brain controlled the body's many functions. Today we know that the brain is the conductor of a large timekeeping orchestra of peripheral clocks widespread throughout the body.

Somewhat like a drum, each of us is home to sacred rhythms.

It's natural for the heart to open and close rhythmically thousands of times throughout the day. The pulsing of blood as it flows through our veins is another human rhythm. But the most life-affirming rhythm in our body is breathing.

Mindful breathing encourages a relaxed and focused state of mind. Its steady and slow rhythm calms the emotions and slows the heart rate, allowing the body to make peace with any tension it harbors within.

Tonglen is an active practice of loving-kindness, a breathing meditation of intentional sending and taking.

Tonglen: The Practice of Taking and Giving

"I happened to be present one of the first times Tibetan meditation master Chögyam Trungpa sprang this bizarre-sounding practice on an unsuspecting Western audience. One student of yoga had raised his hand and asked, with some bewilderment, why it wouldn't be better to imagine breathing in love and light and breathing out all negative impurities.

"Trungpa replied, 'Well, then you'd just be like a polluting factory, taking in all these good resources and spewing out your gray cloud on everyone else.'"

—MARC IAN BARASCH, author, film and television writer-producer, magazine editor, and environmental activist

---

Performed by Tibetan Buddhists and as part of other spiritual traditions, *tonglen* is a positive, uplifting, constructive, and healing way to care for other people. The heart of this practice is compassion, to breathe in another person's pain—physical, mental, emotional, or spiritual—and breathe out strength, joy, and peace of mind, whatever gives relief.

Tonglen can be done for people individually—for example, a person who's ill—or it can be done for people collectively, such as a group of people in a geographic area who've been struck by a natural disaster.

Tonglen can be done anywhere, anytime. It can be formal—in a brick-and-mortar facility, with other practitioners—or it can be done while you're driving, washing the dishes, or in bed.

When the Dalai Lama was touring the United States, he recommended the practice of *tonglen*. He made it very simple. "*Tonglen* is giving and taking. As you inhale, take on the suffering of others. As you exhale, give out to them all your gifts, virtues, and positive qualities."

Rhythm is a carrier of intention and information. Audible rhythms, such as speech, are expressions of vibration. Vibration is what triggers and gives momentum to earthquakes, tidal waves, and avalanches—some of nature's most powerful phenomena.

The word *om*—the most important mantra in yoga—represents primordial vibration, the heartbeat of the earth.

Each breath has a beginning (birth), a middle (turning point), and an end (death). It's said that *om* resides in the turning point. When spoken, it invokes unleashed, unlimited potential and possibility.

Like ripples in a pond when a pebble's thrown in, our personal rhythm flows outward.

The vibration of everything we do and think affects the people in our lives. Their reaction in turn affects others.

Our personal rhythm is powerful. With it we have the capacity to change the world in a variety of positive ways.

What's the ripple effect of your personal rhythm?

YES TALK: THE POWER OF POSITIVE STATEMENTS

You may have heard the famous quote by Epictetus, Roman (Greek-born) slave and philosopher: "We have two ears and one mouth so we may listen more and talk less." To me, that means when we speak, it should add value.

What we voice has the capability of transforming negative emotions and evoking particular emotional responses.

My friend Dawn says, "Our words create our world." For that reason, I suggest to my clients to voice only what they want to, and to refrain from stating what they don't want to say.

Instead of making statements like "don't slam the door," "don't forget your lunch," and "don't talk to me like that," state your desired outcome instead—say what you want.

"Shut the door quietly, please." "Remember your lunch." "Speak to me with respect."

Research shows that the brain processes positive statements and negative statements differently; it processes negative statements more quickly. An example would be saying, "Don't touch that" to a child looking at a freshly frosted cake. The first thing he's going to do is touch the frosting.

It's easier for our brains to remember negative statements than to remember positive ones. When you think about that in terms of relationships—especially parenting—it can be overwhelming. Many parents use "no," "stop it," and "don't" on a regular basis.

When we voice what we want—the positive end result of what we're asking for—we're providing those in our sphere of influence with tools for success.

....

"Attitudes are contagious. Are yours worth catching?"

—DENNIS AND WENDY MANNERING, keynote speakers for
corporate leadership training and seminars

....

We see constructive differences in behavior when we use subtle differences in our communication. "Remember to stop for milk," instead of "don't forget the milk." These types of encouraging statements help develop neural pathways in the brain for positive thinking. They also make us feel better about our interaction with the people whose lives we touch.

LISTEN BETWEEN THE LINES

People who are clear, concise, and articulate in their oral and written communication—self-expression—have the ability to transfer knowledge. They make good teachers because they can readily move facts, ideas, and concepts from their head into someone else's; because they're good at helping people to remain attentive and listen, not just hear. Doing so with ease—in a way that is painless for the recipient, the student—is the hallmark of a good teacher.

In my academic pursuits, I've been on the receiving end of a large amount of information. And while I was able to grasp it, in some cases it was difficult. The teacher relaying the information may have known the subject fully but didn't transfer it well. As a result, the knowledge was a challenge for me to receive.

I've also been on the receiving end of information presented by excellent teachers who made learning enjoyable. They knew their subject well, were enthusiastic and creative in their delivery, and were also good listeners.

Hearing and listening are vastly different. One of the benchmarks of great communicators is their ability to listen not just to what's being said, but to what's *not* being said as well. They listen between the lines.

Hearing is passive. We hear dogs bark, tires squeal, trash cans being rolled out to the curb on garbage pickup day, birds chirp, a train whistle wail mournfully, church bells ring, and the furnace rumble when it comes to life in the morning. In a conversation, people who are hearing instead of listening are oftentimes busy formulating their own response.

Listening is active. It's something we invest in. When we invest in something, we typically expect a return. When we invest in listening, the dividend is an expanded capacity for compassion.

DO YOU SWEAR TO TELL THE TRUTH AND NOTHING BUT THE TRUTH?

Truth doesn't change based on who's looking at it.

Truth is objective. If something is true, it's true for everyone. For example: the world is round, two plus two equals four, and the effects of gravity are real.

....

"If you tell the truth, you don't have to remember anything."

—MARK TWAIN, American author and humorist

....

There's no such thing as subjective truth. Subjective truth is opinion, the reflection of a person's perspective that is greatly influenced by the baggage they carry. "This meal is delicious," "flying is enjoyable," and "that piece of art is beautiful," are all examples of perspective—not necessarily true for everyone.

The Manual of Life: Understanding Character, by Parvesh Singla, defines honesty as, "the human quality of communicating and acting truthfully related to truth as a value. Superficially, honesty means simply stating facts and views as one truly believes them to be. It includes . . . honesty [both] to others and to oneself about one's own motives and inner reality. Honesty, at times, has the ability to cause misfortune to the person who displays it."

This line of thinking leads to many questions:

What positive consequences does telling the truth create? According to Dr. Abraham Kryger, of the Monterey Preventive Medical Clinic, "[t]here are numerous positive benefits that accrue from telling the truth. These benefits include:

- Greater success/personal expertise
- An increased sense of grounding/confidence
- Less anxiety/worry/guilt
- Increased ability to deal with crises/breakdowns
- Improved problem-solving abilities
- Improved interpersonal relationships
- Greater emotional health/control of one's emotions"

Investing in the truth has a high rate of return. Let's compare it with deceit.

"Bidden or unbidden, God is present." If we *really* believed this famous Latin writing attributed to Desiderius Erasmus, we'd think it would lessen the instance of lying. Apparently not.

In 2007, the *Washington Post* ran an article by Dan Zak titled "The Truth About Lying." He opens with, "We are liars and lie catchers, and the sport runs from the banal to the breathtaking, from personal to public. Right now, someone somewhere is lying about 'having plans tonight.' Meanwhile, someone else is discovering that his or her spouse has methodically concealed an affair."

....

"Please don't lie to me, unless you're absolutely sure I'll never find out the truth."

—ASHLEIGH BRILLIANT, author and syndicated cartoonist

....

In the same article, Robert Feldman, a social psychologist at the University of Massachusetts, was quoted as saying, "Experiments have found that ordinary people tell about two lies every ten minutes, with some people getting in as many as a dozen falsehoods in that period."

In his 2008 article, "Bonsai: The True Art of Deception," Russell Marchant defines deception as "the act of convincing another person to believe information that is not true, or not the whole truth, as in certain types of half truths."

Do you know people who simply can't resist enlarging things—making normal people into heroes and heroines and imbuing everything with extra drama? Exaggerating on our résumé to get a job we really want or need, fibbing to spare people pain . . .

In his article "Why Don't We Catch Liars?" psychologist Paul Ekman says there are seven reasons why people lie:

1. To avoid punishment
2. To get a reward
3. To protect others
4. To escape an awkward social situation
5. To enhance our egos
6. To control information
7. To fulfill our job description

Is lying worth it? It's difficult to trust someone we catch lying. It's even harder for the person who told the lie to reestablish broken trust. It's challenging to work with someone who tells lies; it's downright arduous to live with a liar.

Once trust is broken, its restoration is a long, hard process.

Can lies hurt others? Small lies cause small trust issues. The person on the receiving end of deceit starts to wonder, *If she'd lie to me about something so insignificant, what else is she lying about?*

Lies can, and do, cause cracks and fissures in relationships. If more lies are told, more trust issues come up, causing the fissures to grow, weakening the foundation of the relationship.

What are the negative consequences of lies? For the recipient, the negative consequences include emotional hurt and distrust. For the liar, the consequences can include the dissolution of the relationship and potential estrangement, being separated from those they hurt.

Are there negative consequences to physical health for liars? Remember the old adage "Oh, what a tangled web we weave when we first practice to deceive"? The mental effort of "double bookkeeping" is extremely stressful.

The American Institute of Stress (AIS) tells us that "75 to 90 percent of all visits to primary care physicians are for stress related problems." With this in mind, we can safely deduce that there are indeed negative consequences to the physical health of liars.

Are lies more believable than the truth? According to a group of experts whom *JET* magazine asked, the answer is yes. They said, "Oftentimes people want to believe what makes them feel good, no matter what the facts are."

Do men and women tell the same amount of lies? In his book, *Lies! Lies! Lies! The Psychology of Deceit*, Charles Ford said, "women have been socialized to become accommodating. Thus, they tend to read and accept what the person is *trying* to communicate, rather than what he or she is *actually* communicating.

"The need to please another person takes precedence over accuracy. . . . [W]omen tell just as many lies as do men, but women's lies seem to support other people. . . . [W]omen seem to achieve some of their supportiveness through deceit; men are less supportive in those ways but also more truthful."

It's all about honesty. In telling the truth, sometimes a little bit of discomfort can save a whole lot of pain down the road.

I HEARD IT THROUGH THE GRAPEVINE

The definition of gossip is varied, even among social psychologists. The most widely used definition is "any conversation between two or more people about another person who is not there." However, some people narrow the definition of gossip further.

....

"Gossip accounts for 55 percent of men's conversation time and 67 percent of women's—a much smaller gap between the two sexes than usually thought."

—SOCIAL ISSUES RESEARCH CENTRE, Oxford, UK

....

University of Surrey Psychology Professor Nicholas Emler, PhD, suggests, "Gossip must include information about someone whom both gossipers know personally, so talk about celebrities is a sort of pseudo-gossip."

And yet others take a much broader view. Researcher Robin Dunbar, PhD, of the University of Liverpool, said, "I consider any kind of talk about social or personal topics—really, any social chatter—to be gossip."

Some social psychologists believe that gossip must include an opinion or evaluative dimension, so simply posing a question such as "Did you hear that [such-and-such people] are dating?" is gossip only if the tone or something else in the conversation suggests the speaker's opinion of So-and-So's relationship.

Regardless of the definition, gossip seems to be everywhere.

Eric Foster, a psychologist and researcher at Temple University's Institute for Survey Research, said, "It's like breathing; it's so much a part of our day that we don't even realize we're doing it."

Sarah Wert, PhD and social psychologist, is a research associate at Yale University. She said, "I've always been interested in morality and moral decisions, and gossip is something that people make a moral decision about all the time—many times a day, every day."

Numerous studies have sought to determine the how and why of the human pastime of gossip. The common denominator in these studies is the distinction between gossip and rumor. It's easy to get them confused, but there is a difference:

Gossip is talk about other people, usually assumed to be based on facts.

Rumor can be about either events or people and is much more speculative.

And while gossip certainly has a negative connotation, surprising evidence from a number of studies shows that gossip isn't all bad. Yes, it can be used to hurt others, but these studies reveal that it's also the glue that binds groups of people together and helps them to learn the rules of their social worlds.

Sara Wert said, "Despite gossip's reputation for triviality, our need to chatter about one another in fact may be the evolutionary spur that pushed humanity to develop language."

In either case—gossip or rumor—it boils down to motivation. *Why* do we pass along certain information?

CAN YOU KEEP A SECRET?

Protecting confidences entrusted to our care is another task overseen by this aspect of self—self-expression. This is the self that steps up to the plate when we're invited into someone's intimate sphere. It's here that we're to bring our unreserved presence.

"How can we expect another to keep our secret if we cannot keep it ourselves?"

—DUC DE LA ROCHEFOUCAULD, French author

My friend Sandi is one of the most levelheaded and funniest people I know. She said, "If someone has struggled to unburden themselves to us, we should at least have the moral responsibility to keep that confidence to ourselves.

"If someone has ever betrayed a matter you entrusted to them and them alone, you'll remember how that betrayal not only shocked and hurt you, but also undermined the faith and trust you placed in them.

"If it doesn't involve a matter of public safety, such confidences we're gifted—or burdened—with should stay with us, and the matter should end there.

"However, if a friend should confide that she has six bodies buried under the rosebushes and is thinking about adding number seven, for goodness' sake, use your common sense!"

What does your track record indicate? Do you protect or betray confidences?

WELLNESS THROUGH CREATIVITY

Creativity is more than the capacity to be inventive or innovative. It's more than the ability to create great works of art, music, or dance. Creativity is an inherent tool that's needed for wellness.

We *all* have the ability to be creative, and its successful use generates feelings of pleasure and self-esteem that are beneficial to health. Denial of creativity is a serious issue that has harmful outcomes, particularly as it relates to the incidence of depression.

Sue said, "Creativity—she's full of nothing but ideas. She waltzes in, slaps one on you, and then leaves you to put it all together!"

Dr. Andrew Weil said, "Our bodies do know how to heal themselves. That they stay in tune and in balance as self-correcting systems most of our lives is truly miraculous. When this natural harmony is forgotten, all that the strongest drug, the well-placed acupuncture needle, the gentlest homeopathic remedy, or the wisest counsel can do is suggest a healing path to the body and encourage it to follow that path."

Artistic expression is one such path to reactivating the healing response. It's a healing modality whether the art illuminates and expresses the depth of love and joy or pain and fear.

. . . .

"I'm convinced that we all have great creative potential within us. To begin to connect with it, we first have to define it. Let me offer a definition: creativity is the ability to see the ordinary as extraordinary.

"Seeing the ordinary as extraordinary is something we've all done. We've all had those moments when we've looked at a landscape, a person, or an idea and for an instant, or a month, or the rest of our lives, felt its true uniqueness.

"I don't know about you, but to me those moments are like falling in love. Falling in love—I realize this isn't a very businesslike metaphor, but indulge me for a moment. Because maybe, at the base of it, that's what creativity really is: just falling in love with the world."

—DEWITT JONES, professional photographer, photojournalist, and film director

. . . .

Art helps us to know ourselves better. Art can lift us up and make the world fresher for a moment. It can make us laugh out loud, or it can make us weep. We can become immersed in a beautiful painting or awed by the grace and strength of bodies painted in the air with dance that seems more like magic than movement.

What makes someone an artist? To me, the creative spirit within a singer, writer, painter, dancer, or other type of artist won't let them rest until they create. An idea comes, or even the hint of an idea, and they're off and running in the depths of their imagination. It's a lovely place to work, and the world is extremely blessed by art and artistry of so many different kinds.

In addition to being effective and healing on a stand-alone basis, art therapists often work with physicians, mental health professionals, hospitals, and psychiatric clinics. We owe a lot to educators and psychiatrists for the emergence of art therapy as a distinct profession.

Psychiatrists began to utilize art therapy early in the twentieth century, as educators began to document the positive impact of creative expression on the emotional and cognitive development of children.

Why are fine art and performing art so effective at promoting wellness? In life, uncertainty is scary and disorienting, but in creativity, a state of the unknown is necessary and magical.

....

"Well done is better than well said."

—BENJAMIN FRANKLIN, American scientist, inventor,
statesman, printer, and philosopher

....

Creative expression helps us transform what we know about ourselves in the world. It helps us to articulate our feelings and perceptions through words, music, and images. It validates our unique presence on earth.

Working in a male-dominated field, Angela, an electrical engineer, uses an interesting mental technique to slow herself down when she's working on an invention that requires more endurance than intuition.

She shared, "When I have a job that takes a lot of effort—slow, meticulous effort—I pretend I'm in jail. If I'm in jail, time is of no consequence. In other words, if it takes a week, it takes a week. What else have I got to do? I'm going to be here for twenty years. See? It's a mental trick. Otherwise I'd say, 'My God, it's not working!' and then I'd make mistakes. Using this mental technique [means] time is of absolutely no consequence and my creativity flows."

Artist Donna Jill Witty mixes careful planning with spontaneity. When she began to push herself to explore the depth and brilliance of color, she made exciting changes to her whole creative process.

She shared, "I don't necessarily paint something the way it looks; I focus on the way it *feels*. I aim to paint the softness of the velvet or the hardness of the rock. When I can feel it intuitively, I know I have it right on the canvas."

Through drawing, painting, sculpture, collage, writing, theater, music, or movement, we become engaged with and tap into many dimensions of our life experience.

Self-expression through creativity also facilitates cognitive rehabilitation by promoting improved concentration, problem solving, visual perception, and motor planning skills; it both enhances our lives and contributes to our emotional vitality and health, including the development of positive social and other life skills.

ART: AN EXPRESSION OF WHAT WE FEEL

In his book, *Unlocking Your Creative Power*, Peter Jacoby tells us that, based on his creativity workshops, the funnest times involve three simple elements:

> **Letting go:** abandoning control to one degree or another; the degree of fun rises in direct proportion with the degree to which you let go.

> **Emotional risk:** allowing yourself to feel. (*Who cares if no one else thinks it looks like a tree? It's fun to paint like this!*)

> **Sharing:** including others in the letting-go and emotional risk process.

....

"In art the hand can never execute anything higher than the heart can inspire."
—RALPH WALDO EMERSON, American poet, lecturer, and essayist

....

Rhonda shared, "With all that I have going on, sometimes I feel that my creativity is buried under a pile of life experiences and obligations. It's refreshing to look under the pile now and then and see that the creative self has not given up waiting for a chance to flourish and dance again."

It's been said that art is the record of an extraordinary experience. The inner unseen experience is the art; it's what we feel.

Think for a moment. What is it that you're drawn to? What do you do that helps you to flourish when you're actively engaged in it?

Perhaps it's cooking, gardening, sewing, painting, singing, dancing, performing music, writing, taking photographs, scrapbooking, landscaping, weaving, quilting, sculpting, building, or woodworking.

If you don't already know, find out what it is and then indulge yourself in it. Unleash it and watch yourself begin to blossom!

SPACE: THE NEW FRONTIER

Creativity and self-expression work hand in hand with environmental wellness—our personal contributions to sustaining a clean and safe ecosystem that supports life on an individual and collective basis.

The world around us has a large influence on each of us, whether it's our personal, local, or global environment. The way we care for our personal space contributes to how we feel, whether it's at home, at work, or in our vehicle. When our personal surroundings and possessions are clean, organized, and cared for, we experience a greater sense of comfort and less anxiety.

In our more than thirty years of marriage, the continuing bone of contention that my husband and I pick is that I'm a minimalist and he's a maximalist: I throw. He saves. The physical space in our home impacts each of us personally. During one discussion, he asked, "Just exactly why is it that you need to have empty space around you?"

I answered, "Because it appeals to my *Zen*sibilities." I meant to say "sensibilities," but the word I blurted out fit so much better. For me, it's about more than being content; it's the enjoyment of very little with an awareness and deep appreciation of how less is truly more.

My home office is *my* home office. And while I'm normally a loving and generous person, I don't share *my* office space. In fact, I'm rather territorial about it.

I keep very few things in my work area: a friendly, worn desk of Southern yellow pine that hugs the windowsill, top cleared except for my laptop; an oak tree that stands sentinel outside the window; a colorful piece of artwork; and a single candle that I light, the flame encouraging me to press on.

My creative muse is *wabi-sabi*, a practice designed to trim away or eliminate inessentials. The intersection of *wabi* ("minimal") and *sabi* ("functional") is the platform for my creativity—space. Space to move at my own pace, space to invest my time the way I want, space for inspiration and quiet solitude.

The facilitator at a color therapy workshop I attended said, "When we give ourselves space, we find our direction."

Zing! As you can imagine, that statement resonated with my very core. She went on to say, "Right-sizing the space in our lives gives us the freedom to live large."

Environmental wellness also includes being respectful of the earth and her natural resources. By understanding the impact of our interaction with nature, we can choose to live in harmony with our planet and to minimize the negative impact our individual and collective actions have on the environment. Examples of environmental threats include land, air, water, and noise pollution, ultraviolet radiation in the ozone layer, and chemicals.

WE AFFECT EARTH, AND EARTH AFFECTS US

The wellness of the earth and the way it expresses itself are closely related to the wellness of humanity and the way we express ourselves.

When I was in junior high school, my friend Pam would invite groups of us over to enjoy her swimming pool. I fondly remember her mother launching each swim-fest by saying, "Now, girls, don't pee in the pool. If you've got to go, come in and use the bathroom."

The earth is like a giant swimming pool. What we do in it—how we express ourselves in living—affects everyone, us included.

The Hopi Indians have a saying, "We are the ones we've been waiting for!"

The mantle of responsibility is on our shoulders. When we "pee in the pool"—through industrial waste, oil spills, radioactive dumping, local and global pollution—we negatively affect ourselves and future generations.

The connection between caring for the environment and caring for our own self-expressive power is essential. If we ignore this connection, we miss something vital. When we nurture this connection—manage our negative impact on the planet—we simultaneously embrace our link with each other. The interconnection between Earth and humanity is constant and has the potential to be a perpetual cycle of healing.

Environmental wellness means that we bring the unhealthy aspects of our surroundings to light—take them out of our baggage—for examination so we can work through them in a healthy and productive way, offloading baggage and increasing joy.

When this self is healthy and in balance, there's an abundant return value to the heart. In this case, the dividends include tangibles such as inspiration, a sense of creativity, confidence in the way we express ourselves, authentic living, and the expression of truth.

In the following chapter, you'll find several keys—practical tips, tools, and exercises—to unleash your creative flair and offload baggage associated with self-expression.

CHAPTER 12

Keys to Self-Expression: Unleash Your Creative Flair

"This world is but a canvas to our imagination."

—HENRY DAVID THOREAU, American author, poet, naturalist, and philosopher

1. MIND-BODY CONNECTION

Self-expression is associated with the throat, thyroid, parathyroid, hypothalamus, trachea, esophagus, neck vertebrae, mouth, teeth, and gums. If you're experiencing issues in any of these areas, it's time to make an appointment with your health care provider.

2. COLOR THERAPY

Blue is associated with self-expression, creativity, and environmental wellness.

It enhances knowledge, relaxation, and health. It's the color of a cloudless summer sky. Think of your favorite faded denim jacket, robin's eggs in a nest, an exquisite piece of turquoise, or the shimmering, inviting water in a swimming pool on a hot day.

The *positive* properties of blue are expressed as peaceful, calming, tactful, sincere, trustworthy, fluent, introspective, and responsible.

The *negative* properties of blue are described as tongue-tied, cold, withdrawn, manipulative, and disloyal.

The *healing* properties of blue are cooling and protective and can address physical symptoms such as high blood pressure, migraine, fever, cuts, stings/burns, and negative states of mind such as timidity, fatigue, distrust, indecision, fear of speaking up, and confrontation. Blue decreases respiration and is ideal for sleep and overactivity.

When you need a boost in the areas of creativity and self-expression, indulge yourself with this color. The frequency of blue resonates with the throat chakra. It creates a calm throat center from which to speak our truth. Blue stimulates calm, open, and clear communication, ingredients that are vital to working with others peacefully.

The vibration of blue is calming and cooling. What shade are you drawn to?

Clear blue cools and calms. Or maybe you enjoy the muted hues that recall a spring sky after the rain, or shaded tones that exude comfort and rest.

What we do with our physical environment—our personal space—speaks to our heart and helps us to flourish:

- Accessorize with a piece of blue clothing or jewelry.
- Place chunky blue candles on a multitiered candleholder, which can add soft light to your space.
- Buy blue sheets—they'll gently encourage you to sleep at night.
- Take advantage of the healing frequency of blue crystals, such as aquamarine, chrysocolla, or blue topaz.

3. DIET

Foods that boost our sense of verbal and creative expression include:

- **Liquids in general**—water, fruit juices, and herbal teas.
- **Tart or tangy fruits**—lemons, limes, grapefruit, or kiwi.
- **Other tree-growing fruits**—apples, pears, plums, peaches, and apricots.
- **Spices**—salt and lemongrass.
- **Supplements**—Vitamin C supports throat health and a healthy immune system. It can't be made or stored by the body, so supplementing with vitamin C is essential.

4. AROMATHERAPY

The use of chamomile, linden blossom, cypress, petitgrain, basil, peppermint, hyssop, rosewood, or rosemary helps to eliminate fears associated with creativity and self-expression and boosts our confidence in expressing ourselves fully and truthfully. These essential oils encourage awakening, creativity, fulfillment, encouragement, direction, clarity, balance, and harmony.

5. AFFIRMATIONS

When we encounter threats to our sense of authentic expression, effective affirmations to speak out loud are:

> It is safe to speak my mind. I voice my choice.
> I express myself truthfully.
> I am clear, concise, and articulate.
> I live creatively.
> I keep my word to myself and others.
> I am a good listener.
> I exercise the benefit of the doubt.
> I embrace personal expression.
> I nurture my inner resources.
> I function from a place of original thought.

6. THE BUSINESS OF BEING

Creativity and self-expression in the business world relate to marketing strategy—public relations, brand recognition, and graphic identity. For a moment, think of your life as a business and write the answers to the following questions:

- How do you present yourself?
- How does the world see you?
- How do you want the world to see you?
- If there's a difference between how the world sees you and how you want the world to see you, what action steps are required on your part to bring the two perspectives closer or to make them the same?

7. BREATHWORK: FOUR-SQUARE BREATHING

Whenever you recognize that you're hosting unwanted, draining emotion related to creativity, self-expression, or environmental wellness, stop what you're doing and focus on your breath. Breathe deeply, slowly, and steadily. Place a hand on your lower belly to ensure that you're breathing past your chest.

An effective breathing exercise to do is known as *four-square breathing*. Here's how it's done:

- Breathe in slowly through your nose to the mental count of four.
- Hold the breath for a count of four.
- Exhale slowly through pursed lips to a count of four.
- Rest for a count of four (without taking any breaths).
- Once you've established a rhythm, identify a replacement attitude. Imagine that with each inhalation, you're breathing in the color blue and the feeling of that new attitude—increasing joy.
- When you exhale, imagine that you're releasing the toxins associated with the unwanted emotion—offloading baggage.
- Repeat for several minutes, drawing the blue breath and replacement feeling down into your lower belly to anchor the new feeling.

I discovered that for me, this breathwork exercise primes the pump and enhances the flow of creativity.

8. ENVIRONMENTAL WELLNESS INVENTORY AND VITALITY CHECK

- Do you recycle?
- Do you intentionally look for and purchase earth-friendly products?
- Have you ever planted a tree?
- Are you aware of the effects your daily habits have on the world around you?
- Do you walk, ride a bicycle, or take public transportation when you can?
- Do you keep your vehicle tuned up and in good repair?
- Have you turned your thermostat down a couple of degrees in the winter and your air-conditioning up a few degrees in the summer?

- Do you use energy-efficient windows, lighting, and appliances?
- Do you have water-saving toilets, faucets, and showerheads in your home?
- Have you calculated the size of your carbon footprint?

If you answered no to any of these questions, it may indicate an area of opportunity for you to improve the quality of your environmental wellness.

On a scale of one to nine, where do you rate yourself on your current ability to unleash your creative energy, if one represents low (dried-up, blocked, afraid of failure) and nine represents high (inspired, flowing, confident)?

Is there a difference between where you currently are and where you want to be? If so, write down how you'll close the gap. Be specific.

9. ACTION STEPS

To enhance your sense of creativity and unleash creative flair, try these exercises:

Quick hits: Gargle with salt water. Loosen your neck and shoulder muscles. Release your voice through singing, chanting, or toning. Scream into a pillow or let loose on drums. Read out loud, even if it's only to yourself.

With a little planning: Get involved in storytelling. Practice meaningful written communication through blogging or journaling, or establish a daily practice of "morning pages," as suggested by Julia Cameron, author of *The Artist's Way: A Spiritual Path to Higher Creativity.* Try something you've never done before: dancing, performing, cooking, hospitality, sign language, or painting—pick one and express yourself. There are as many ways to be creative as there are people.

Enough Is Enough

In the Zen notion of "knowing when enough is enough," Dr. Peter Renner, a practicing Zen lay monk, encourages us to ask ourselves these questions:

- What do I need to live a full life?
- What, in terms of things, relationships, and activities, is necessary to sustain body, mind, and heart?
- What is there that could be shed, given away, sold, recycled, or composted without causing suffering to self and others?
- What benefits might accrue from such shedding?
- Who'd be better off?
- What worries might be alleviated?

Clear Your Clutter

When was the last time you cleared your clutter?

It's easy! Focus on one closet or room at a time. You'll need boxes labeled as follows: GARBAGE, DONATE, RECYCLE, and SELL.

Don't keep things you don't use. A good rule of thumb is that if you haven't used something for eighteen months, you don't need it.

Donate clothes that no longer fit—they're nothing more than closet eye candy. Don't keep broken things because you might fix them "later." Recycle old magazines, catalogs, and newspapers.

Subtraction can be a bridge to gratitude.

Harness the Power of Vibration

Place the palm of your hand lightly over the divot in your throat, your voice box. Say the alphabet out loud, or sing a song and feel the vibration in your hand.

Yes Talk

Start the practice of positive statements. State your desired outcome—voice only what you want.

Identifying and Nurturing Your Muse

Pablo Picasso said, "Every child is an artist. The problem is how to remain an artist once he grows up." I think that half the battle is identifying and nurturing your muse.

- What inspires your creativity?
- What practical action steps can you take to cultivate it?

Creative Pulse

My friend Terrill Welch has a popular blog, *Creative Potager,* where she posts "sprout questions." In a post on creativity, she asked, "If your creativity had a pulse, what would be the rhythm of its beat?"

I responded, "The rhythm of my creativity is in harmony with my *Zen*sibility—deep, slow, quiet, and regular."

What's your creative rhythm?

Commitment Exercise

With a red face and clenched fists, Doreen shares, "I know *exactly* what I want to do with my life. That's not the problem. With my busy schedule, how am I supposed to find the time to actually *do* it?"

My friend and colleague, and author of *The Way Back Home*, Dr. Michelle L. McClellan, licensed clinical psychologist, challenged the audience with the following exercise when she came to speak to my clients on the topic of Writing the Soul—Journaling to Wholeness. It's an excellent example of actions speaking louder than words, and it really helped Doreen to shift her perspective:

- Get a spiral notebook with lined paper, and on the first page write down three things that you're totally committed to—things you'd absolutely go to the mat for.
- Each night before you go to bed, on a fresh sheet of paper behind the first page, make a list of ten things you did during that day.
- Do this each night for a month.
- At the end of the month, compare the list on the first page—the three items you're totally committed to—with the month's worth of lists containing ten items each.

This enlightening exercise reveals how many things you do that actually support the items you're committed to.

For example, someone might think they're completely and totally committed to writing a book. At the end of the month, they may find out that what they're really committed to is a spotlessly clean home. And while there's certainly nothing wrong with a spotlessly clean home, if they haven't worked on their book, they've discovered that they aren't quite as committed to writing as they thought they were.

Break Through the Creative Block

There are two types of creative people: those who believe in creative blocks and those who don't. If you believe in creative blocks, the best piece of advice is Nike's—*just do it!* A statue doesn't sculpt itself. A dance doesn't choreograph itself. A canvas doesn't paint itself. A book doesn't write itself. Music doesn't compose itself. Fashion doesn't design itself.

Whatever you're dreading the most, do it first and get it out of the way. It's like jumping into the deep end of the pool, rather than suffering the cold water inch by inch in the shallow end. Most people just need a little movement in the right direction; then the creative juices start flowing and momentum takes over.

And remember, taking a break is essential to the creative process. It's during the times when we least expect it—buying tickets for the theater, eating pizza with friends, sleeping, taking a walk in the park, squeezing melons in the vegetable aisle, brushing our teeth—that ideas strike like lightning.

Doing other things allows our brain to meander, seemingly on vacation, while our subconscious uses this downtime to create epiphanies—the ones that make us pull off the road, bolt out of bed, or stop mid conversation so we can jot down that perfect idea that suddenly appeared out of "nowhere."

10. PERSONAL ENERGY SIGNATURE

On a sheet of paper, draw a circle that represents your personal energy signature. Considering what you've learned about self-expression, creativity, and environmental wellness, on the inside of the circle, list the people, places, and things that are for this self's highest and best good—positive, uplifting, constructive, and healing.

On the outside of the circle, list the people, places, things, and actions you need to avoid to keep this self healthy and balanced. The examples on the following page will help you get started.

SELF-EXPRESSION, CREATIVITY, AND ENVIRONMENTAL WELLNESS PERSONAL ENERGY SIGNATURE

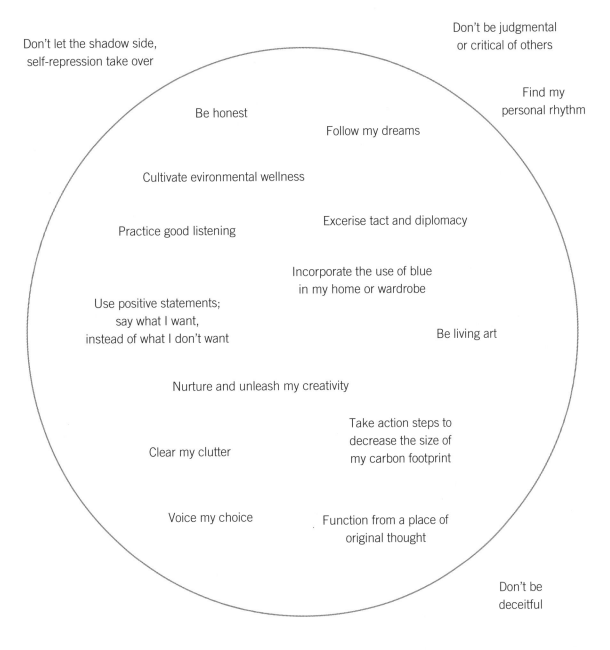

Don't let the shadow side, self-repression take over

Don't be judgmental or critical of others

Be honest

Follow my dreams

Find my personal rhythm

Cultivate evironmental wellness

Practice good listening

Excerise tact and diplomacy

Incorporate the use of blue in my home or wardrobe

Use positive statements; say what I want, instead of what I don't want

Be living art

Nurture and unleash my creativity

Clear my clutter

Take action steps to decrease the size of my carbon footprint

Voice my choice

Function from a place of original thought

Don't be deceitful

CHAPTER 13

Self #6: Self-Reflection

Self-reflection is responsible for intuition and intellectual wellness; its purpose is to boost our awareness. When healthy, this self functions from a place of endless possibilities. Corresponding to the brow chakra, it resonates with the color indigo. An inspiring affirmation for this self is: *I am insightful.* The shadow side is self-absorption.

❖ ❖ ❖

In a 2014 energy-medicine class, Monica raised her hand and asked, "Any other overthinkers in the house? Sometimes I just get into moods where I wonder a million what-ifs and think about how my life would be different if I'd done this or that, had these people in my life or not, had taken a different job or not.

"I try not to. I try to be content with my life and all the choices I've made so far, but I keep wondering, analyzing it, breaking it down to the gnat's whisker. It can be a very slippery slope, this overthinking."

Do you dwell more in the past or the future than you do in the present moment?

Do you tend to overintellectualize?

Do your trust your intuition or disregard your inner knowing?

Do you tend to feel helpless or lost when faced with judgment calls?

This self—self-reflection—is concerned with intellect, intuition, and evaluation; it's where our perception of time resides. The developmental stage begins sometime during adolescence.

Self-reflection is a process of examining and interpreting experience to gain new understanding. Exercised regularly, it develops higher-level thinking and problem solving. Purposeful reflection transforms experience into wisdom; it raises awareness.

When our senses of intuition and self-reflection are in balance, we enjoy qualities from the constructive side of this self. These include feeling connected to our senses of insight, clarity, discernment, and fulfillment of personal duty. We're open to unleashed, unlimited potential and possibility.

....

"Our genes dance with awareness . . . showing that our emotions and behavior have the power to shape our biology. This awareness can make a critical difference in health and longevity."

—NORMAN SHEALY, MD, PhD, founding president of the
American Holistic Medical Association

....

THE SHADOW SIDE: SELF-ABSORPTION

When our senses of intuition and self-reflection are out of balance, we can experience negative feelings such as self-absorption.

Self-absorption is an unrelenting preoccupation with one's own thoughts or feelings, to the exclusion of everything else. Self-absorbed people don't have a balanced view of the reality they share with those around them. They give themselves their undivided attention as they march down the street, yelling into their cell phone about the intimate details of *their* relationship, *their* job, *their* money, *their* dinner party, *their* workout, or *their* new hairstyle. They're oblivious to everyone and everything around them. They think and act as though the sun rises and sets for them. It is, after all, *their* universe.

Self-absorption can manifest itself in a number of harmful ways that become items we tuck into our life's baggage. Depending on their size and impact, we may slip them into a tote that we keep within arm's reach, for handy retrieval, or stuff them into a large suitcase that comes around on the baggage carousel only occasionally. These can include:

Physical: brain tumors, strokes, blindness, deafness, learning disabilities, seizures, panic, and spinal dysfunctions.

Mental: fear of truth; intolerance; close-mindedness; lack of discipline, memory, focus, or clarity; poor judgment or impracticality; inability to evaluate; mental illness, such as depression; and delusions or failure to separate reality from fantasy.

Emotional: frustration, nervousness, melancholy, and a feeling of being energetically or emotionally drained.

Spiritual: lack of wisdom, lack of confidence in the divine, and lack of willingness to ease up on the reins and rest in divine love.

Leigh shared, "Some days I'm the high queen of digression. I can start with a point of focus, and within a short span of time, I'm not only out of the county but completely off the map. I have, at times, felt like one of those little roaming pool vacs: you prime it, let it go in the swimming pool, and off it goes, mindlessly roaming, circling, and bouncing off the walls it dead-ends into."

Tracy shared, "One of the first things I learned about depression is that in our efforts to avoid pain, we block out joy as well. Understanding this was an aha moment for me!"

....

"Major depression affects approximately fifteen million American adults, or about 8 percent of the US population, age eighteen and older, in a given year. Approximately 80 percent of the people experiencing depression are not currently receiving any treatment. Depression is one of the most treatable illnesses: 80 to 90 percent find relief."

—DEPRESSION AND BIPOLAR SUPPORT ALLIANCE (DBSA)

....

Wanda shared, "Me, indecisive? Hmmm, I'm not sure. I might as well pick petals off a daisy. He loves me; he loves me not. I will go; I won't go. I like my job; I hate my job.

"I feel like I'm living on a roulette wheel. Sometimes I land on black; sometimes I land on red. It's not that I don't care. I do. I care a lot. I just don't have any idea which way is the best way. You see, it's got to be perfect. I don't want to fail by making the wrong choice, so instead I don't make any choice at all. It's safer that way. My fear of making the wrong choice is bigger than my fear of standing still."

Intuition and self-reflection work hand in hand with intellectual wellness—an eager curiosity and interest in learning new things about ourselves and the world in which we live.

They help us to utilize the things we've learned, to integrate the knowledge we have with the life that we live. We achieve this in a number of ways: taking classes, reading, learning a new skill, enjoying hobbies, utilizing our creativity, and appreciating the arts.

All of these pursuits stimulate the mind and keep us actively engaged with the world around us.

Intellectually healthy people are solution-oriented, rather than problem focused. They value mental growth and stimulation, are involved in intellectual and cultural activities, and are engaged in the exploration of new ideas and understanding.

As we develop our intellectual curiosity, we actively strive to stay abreast of current issues and ideas, and we welcome the opportunity for thoughts that are different from our own to challenge our mind.

Intellectual wellness means that we bring the unhealthy aspects of our mental activities to light—take them out of our baggage—for examination so we can work through them in a healthy and productive way, offloading baggage and increasing joy.

MISTY WATER-COLORED MEMORIES

Our three-pound brain is a wonder that houses both short and long-term memories. What we remember and what we forget helps to shape and inform our humanness. Much of what we put in the file cabinets of our mind depends on how often we're going to need that information.

....

"Memory is the diary that we all carry about with us."

—OSCAR WILDE, Irish poet, novelist, dramatist, and critic

....

We also tend to remember significant events in our lives—significant being self-defined (our choice) not event-defined (the size of what happened).

Maxi shared, "Some of the events I remember from my childhood 'didn't happen that way,' according to my parents and siblings. Well, they may not have happened to *them* that way, but they sure happened to me that way!"

Real or not, our perception is our reality. Chicken Little thought the sky was falling (perception), when in fact an acorn fell on her head (reality).

Maxi went on to say, "There are two instances in particular where I know precisely what happened. I can remember it in vivid, full-color detail. Yet my sister remembers it completely and totally differently.

"I know the difference between an acorn hitting me on the head and the sky falling. I don't know how in the world she can possibly remember it any differently. Then again, it no longer matters and probably never did."

Jenny shared, "Being conscious helps. For a very long time, I didn't want to look at my childhood, because it was so difficult and many of the difficulties were 'unspoken' and 'unknown.'

"I thought it was normal to have a mother with breakdowns and a father in shell shock. It wasn't until I was able to spend more time with others that I realized just how nutty it was, and to look back on it was unbearable. I was fortunate to discover a method that helped me not relive the events and to discover just how valuable my childhood really is."

During a self-reflection Life Harmony session, it's not uncommon for me to ask a client, "If you could go back in time to revisit a single, twenty-four-hour window of time, what twenty-four-hour window of time would it be? In this scenario, you wouldn't be able to change anything; you can only revisit it. However, you would have your current, full knowledge—your current age perspective.

"For instance, if I were to go back to a twenty-four-hour window of time when I was seven, I would be able to view it through the eyes of a fifty-eight-year-old woman, but I wouldn't be able to change a single thing, simply revisit it."

Katie shared, "I don't know the year, but I remember as a small child watching the interaction of my parents on a Christmas morning and standing in awe of their ingratitude. It made a huge impression on me. In looking back on it as an adult, I can see how that snapshot in time formed many of my thoughts about what I don't want to be like."

Jill shared, "It would be one of the days of the last vacation my family took to Powers Lake, Wisconsin. We rented a cottage there every summer, and my mom, dad, two brothers, two sisters, grandma, and aunts drove out together and stayed together.

"My dad took us to the lake to go swimming and fishing. We got to take turns sitting on his shoulders, and then he would tip us off his shoulders backward into the water; it was delightful. Sometimes we got to go out in a rowboat. At suppertime, we went across the street to the restaurant and had dinner overlooking the lake and then played the bowling machine.

"I can still smell the smells of that old cottage. I can walk to every nook and cranny in my mind. I can see the wet swimsuit hanging over the railing in the back while we sat and shucked corn. I can feel the breezes as they came in the screened porch and hear the click of the knitting needles and rocking chairs as the older ladies spun their crafts. It was such an idyllic time in my life and the life of our family.

"It makes me wonder what memories we made for our children and what memories they're making for theirs."

Wistfully, Alexis shared, "I would go back to the evening my dad came home from work and told my sister and me, ages nine and eleven, that he was leaving our family to marry a different woman. He didn't take off his coat, and my sister and I joked with him to 'take off your coat and stay awhile.' But he didn't take it off; he sat down and explained that he'd fallen in love with another woman and that he was going to live with her from now on.

"My sister and I cried in our room and finally fell asleep. It changed my whole life, being raised by my single, working mom, who was angry with my dad, not having a dad in my life to help in any way, watching my mom trying to find a new husband—unhappy, desperate, and bitter.

"I let her be a negative role model in some ways. I watched my mom continue through life as a victim, never moving through the tough time but stuck in it. It took me many years to realize that she's still stuck in it. She didn't change herself; she didn't forgive. She married an alcoholic, suffered, and then divorced again.

"I married an older man, probably looking for a father figure, and didn't take charge of my life, just like my mom. I was waiting for a man to complete me—not embracing my own life, myself, just getting through it in some ways, not loving myself and honoring myself, just like my mom still doesn't. Sadly, I'm still filling life with the needs of others."

What's your twenty-four-hour window of time, and why did you choose it?

Did the particular twenty-four-hour time period that you would revisit change the trajectory (positively or negatively) of your life in some way?

WHAT DOES IT MEAN TO ME THAT I EXIST?

Self-reflection plays a vital role in healthy human adaptation. It includes a sense of ownership of one's own thoughts and actions, emotional awareness, the ability to distinguish between fantasy and reality, and the integration of a range of different views of oneself and others.

Impaired self-reflection is a key aspect of many adult mental disorders.

"I'm so embarrassed. I want to crawl in a hole and die." These are the words that Evelyn tearfully shared with me about her adult son who'd just been diagnosed with bipolar disorder.

She was fearful about the stigmas, misconceptions, and prejudices people have about mental illness. It's for these very reasons that many people with mental health conditions don't seek treatment, or deny they have a problem. They don't want to face rejection or discrimination from their family, friends, or workplace.

These disorders can profoundly disrupt a person's thinking, feeling, moods, ability to relate to others, and capacity for coping with the demands of life. And mental illness can affect people of any age, race, religion, or income. It's not the result of personal weakness, lack of character, or poor upbringing.

There are many wonderful mental illness advocacy groups. I'm a member of the National Alliance on Mental Illness (NAMI). It's the leading grassroots advocacy organization in the United States dedicated solely to improving the quality of life of individuals living with mental illness and their families. If you or someone you know needs help, reach out to one of these groups.

People who wrestle with thoughts of suicide do so because feelings of hopelessness and utter despair overwhelm them. Any number of factors can trigger these feelings, but usually they're a response to extreme emotional pain, such as betrayal, inconsolable grief, or perceived failure. They can also be the product of prolonged negative life circumstances, such as abuse, poverty, poor health, disability, or neglect, or an outcome of a brain chemistry deficiency or mental illness. In all cases, suicidal people don't sense any hope of change or improvement; they feel desolate.

"When I was a little girl, I believed that if I looked up at the night sky and saw a purple star, everything would be okay. I never saw a purple star."

—SHARED BY A FIRST-TIME CLIENT AFTER HER FOURTH SUICIDE ATTEMPT

In his article "The Many Languages of Suicide," David Webb, suicide attempter and now suicidologist at Victoria University in Melbourne, Australia, wrote, "Contemplating suicide is like no other feeling. This life force within you that has taken you from birth to this present critical moment is losing its potency.

"Despite the joys and wonders of this extraordinary gift of life, you are thinking that it's not worth it. For whatever reason, life has become too difficult, too painful—and extinguishing this life force becomes a real possibility."

Webb adds, "With hindsight I can now say that at the core of my suicidal dilemma was the question 'What does it mean to me that I exist?' This question points to what is recognized as one of the key indicators of suicidality [the intention to take one's life]—hopelessness.

....

Suicide is everyone's business. If you or someone you know wrestles with suicidal thoughts, call a help line and speak with someone about how you're feeling. In the United States, you can call the National Suicide Prevention Lifeline at 1-800-273-TALK (8255).

....

"For me, hopelessness arises from an absence of meaningfulness. If I feel that my life is entirely without any meaning and purpose, and [there is] no hope of it ever being otherwise (i.e., helplessness), then suicide becomes a progressively more and more logical and attractive option. Why put up with this pain when there is absolutely no point?

"Spiritual self-inquiry saved my life. After four years of agonizing struggle and exhausted with desperation and failed therapies, I attended to the essential spiritual question of 'Who am I?'

"Almost immediately and almost effortlessly, I let go of my suicidality like a snake shedding a no-longer-useful skin.

"It took a while to physically recover from the wretched medications, but the real recovery of freedom from my suicidal psychache arrived and continues to this day."

Hearing first-person stories of suicidality not only empowers those who are suffering to speak up and reach out for help but can also guide us as a society toward a better understanding of the self that suicide seeks to destroy.

A deep inquiry into the aspects of self and the associated baggage must include spiritual, psychological, biological, and social needs. Suicide prevention is everyone's business.

A SHIFT IN PERSPECTIVE

Because each person carries different baggage, we see the same things in different ways. Our perspective is based on what's inside the luggage we're dragging around with us. The contents affect our judgment.

....

"Reality is what we take to be true.
What we take to be true is what we believe.
What we believe is based upon our perceptions.
What we perceive depends upon what we look for.
What we look for depends upon what we think.
What we think depends upon what we perceive.
What we perceive determines what we believe.
What we believe determines what we take to be true.
What we take to be true is our reality."

—GARY ZUKAV, spiritual teacher, New York Times best-selling author

....

Sound judgment is absolutely necessary to stay alive. Being judgmental—critical—is not. They are two very different things.

Have you ever gone to an art gallery to look at beautiful pieces of work? I find that I don't stand still in front of a piece; I move around and look at it from many different angles. I shift my perspective.

Have you ever experienced a noticeable emotional reaction to someone? That reaction can be due to a reflection of a beautiful aspect of our own essence. Or it can be recognition of a shadow—ours.

When I find myself judging a person, place, or thing, I make a point to move so I can observe from a different angle. I shift my perspective.

Self-reflection is driven by our perspective, our point of view, how we see things. Our thoughts shape our lives. As the Talmud says, "We don't see things as they are; we see them as we are."

Individually and collectively, our thoughts contribute to the healing, or the demise, of the planet.

Kaleen shared, "After spending many years buried in the depths of a damaged existence, it feels like I'm just now discovering that I was never really damaged in the first place. For many years I was taught to believe otherwise, and every thought and action was filtered through that perception. Now I'm surprised to learn the person that is me is very much alive and well. The perception was the only thing that was broken and damaged. I was just fine."

Tammy shared, "When I'm *disturbed*, I mentally take a step back to obtain a wider perspective. When I'm *confused*, I mentally take a step forward to narrow my focus and observe only what's directly in front of me."

....

"People think lights, sounds, and touch from the outer world constitute reality, but the brain constructs what it perceives based on past experience."

—DR. STEPHEN KOSSLYN, American psychologist, founding father of neuroscience study at Harvard, and current director of the Center for Advanced Study in the Behavioral Sciences at Stanford University

....

I applaud her ability to change lenses as necessary.

For my clients who would benefit from a change in perspective, I have them do the following exercise so they can physically see that there's always more than one way to look at something:

- Stand up and hold your dominant hand over your head, index finger pointed at the ceiling.
- Make a continuous clockwise circle about six inches in diameter.
- Maintain a clockwise direction.
- Slowly lower your hand while continuing a clockwise motion.
- Once the top of your index finger is just below your chin, take a look.
- Notice that your hand is now circling in a counterclockwise fashion.

When you started, your observation was from below. When you ended, your observation was from above, an aerial view. Your direction never changed. The only change was the way you viewed your hand—your perspective.

In my experience, shifting one's mental outlook (perspective) even slightly can significantly change the trajectory and reveal the sun coming up beyond the dark horizon.

French novelist Marcel Proust said, "The voyage of discovery is not in seeking new landscapes but in having new eyes." A shift in perspective is just that.

One day, at the end of each of my client sessions, I asked the question "What is life?" I received the following four responses:

"Life is our chance to be useful, to make a positive difference."

"Life is nothing but the echo of joy disappearing into the great chasm of misery."

"Life is people looking for similarly broken people. We communicate through damage."

"Life is a single skip for joy."

....

"Life is a state of mind."
— FROM THE CLOSING SCENE OF THE 1979 MOVIE *BEING THERE*

....

Each of us views life through a different lens. What we think is colored by the baggage we carry, and what we think is what we live. As Dr. Wayne Dyer says, "Change your thoughts, change your life."

In his blog, Korean monk Chong Go Sunim wrote, "There's only helping, not 'helping her.' There's only loving, not 'loving them.' There's only hating, not 'hating them.'"

This is a wonderful example of shifting one's perspective away from "the other."

At my healing studio, we were looking at our business model and asking ourselves, "What should we *add* to make things better?" We then turned the question around and asked, "What should we remove to make things better?"

In shifting our perspective, we decided to eliminate all displays and products that weren't against a wall. In doing so, we created dedicated space—sacred space—that's now available for ongoing yoga, tai chi, breathwork, movement meditation, and a spiritual-book club. The change has been positive, uplifting, constructive, and healing.

TIME AND TIME AGAIN

Self-reflection is the aspect of self that orchestrates our perception of time: its value, its speed, and our sense of it—where we are chronologically.

The Value of Time

One of the questions I ask myself when it comes to deciding how to use time is, "Is it worth the cost?" I am, after all, going to pay for it with my life.

We each have a certain number of heartbeats, a certain number of breaths. None of us knows our personal expiration date.

....

"The only reason for time is so that everything doesn't happen at once."

—ALBERT EINSTEIN, German-born theoretical physicist and Nobel Prize recipient

....

How we use our time is how we're either *spending* or *investing* our life.

Before engaging in activities such as watching reruns on television, staying in a job we can't stand, or remaining in a relationship that's bankrupting our heart, we can ask ourselves, "Is this worth exchanging my life for?"

Life! That's a pretty steep price to pay. That's why I opt for activities that are investments—something that yields a return, a dividend. It might be health from exercise, laughter from spending time with friends, fulfillment from writing, relaxation from a nap, or peace of mind from meditation.

Paul finally came to the conclusion that he can allow himself experiences for the mere joy of them. Before that, he felt guilty for doings things "for the joy of it." He said his mindset was such that he didn't deserve them and they would therefore be self-indulgent.

I shared with him that doing something for the mere joy of it—for one's self or others—is quite possibly one of the best returns on an investment of time that a person can receive.

The Speed of Time

I'm actively involved in a discussion group that poses thought-provoking questions. One of the questions I was asked was "What would you like to accept?"

After giving it some thought, I replied, "I have trouble accepting the speed at which time moves. I don't *think* it's moving faster than when I was a child; I *know* it's moving faster."

At a conference I attended where scientist, visionary, scholar, and author Gregg Braden and cofacilitator Howard Martin, executive vice president of strategic development at

HeartMath, were the keynote speakers, they, too, alluded to this phenomenon. They said, "Time is not going to slow down or return to what it's been. In fact, it may even speed up."

The Thief of Time: Procrastination

In the same discussion group, one of the participants, Robert, suggested that my feeling as if time moves rapidly is a result of procrastination. He said, "Postponing things causes people to play a harried game of catch-up, leaving them with the frazzled perception that time moves more quickly than it really does."

"Procrastination?"

It was like he'd thrown down the gauntlet. I told my husband that someone had *dared* suggest that I procrastinate.

"Procrastination is, hands down, our favorite form of self-sabotage."

—ALYCE P. CORNYN-SELBY, American manager and author

He laughed and said, "Whoever it is certainly doesn't know you very well."

My husband, Len's response went a long way toward smoothing my ruffled feathers, but did I let it go? No.

I contacted Robert and assured him that I don't procrastinate and, furthermore, that I use my time and resources wisely.

I said, "Procrastination isn't the problem. The problem is that I *feel* the future bearing down on me, like a train speeding on the tracks right behind me, and I'm running as fast as I can, just not fast enough. It's not a matter of time management."

It was at this point that the universe decided to remind me that what I was arguing about was of little to no consequence. I opened an e-mail from a friend, Tammy, who had no idea about the time conversation I was having. Her note said, "I just found this quote on a StoryPeople greeting card, and I know how much you'll love it. Enjoy!

"'Everything changed the day she figured out there was exactly enough time for the important things in her life.'"

The quote is by artist and storyteller Brian Andreas. It gave me a wonderful laugh and a whole new perspective on time.

Where We Are in Time

Chronos, or tick-tock time, is chronological, sequential, and linear in nature; it's governed by watches, clocks, and calendar pages.

We schedule our lives by it, making appointments and keeping deadlines. It can be more of a taskmaster than a friend. Many people speak of "never having enough of it" as we race against the clock.

Chronos time is symbolized by an infant who ushers in the new year and ends the annual calendar as an elderly, bent, and bearded man, Father Time—similar to the god Chronos in Greek mythology.

It's my perspective that there's more—much more—to it than that. I believe that the brow chakra (energy center), physically located at the carotid plexus, the lower portion of forehead and slightly above and between the eyebrows, is the gatekeeper to a time portal, a place where we can step out of *quantitative* time as we know it (*chronos*) and into *qualitative* time (*kairos*).

Kairos, or opportune time, is the word the ancient Greeks used to describe the right time, perfect time, supreme moment, or "now." Some might even call it *divine time*.

....

"*Kairos* time is full time, vital time, crucial time, decisive time . . . those rich special moments that break into the humdrum and change your life; those powerful dramatic moments when things seem to fall into place, a new perspective comes, and God seems to be speaking loud and clear. That is *kairos!*"

—FROM *SEIZING THE MOMENTS: MAKING THE MOST OF LIFE'S OPPORTUNITIES,*
BY JAMES W. MOORE

....

Kairos intersects with and brings transcending value to *chronos* time. It signifies an undetermined period of time (time in between) in which something special happens.

One doesn't catch up with *kairos* time; rather, one participates in it.

In one of my favorite books, *A Wrinkle in Time*, author Madeleine L'Engle suggests that *kairos* time can, and does, enter, penetrate, break through, or intersect with *chronos* time: the child at play, consumed in the moment; the painter held captive, mesmerized at an easel; the saint lifted up, removed, as it were, in prayer . . .

In her book *Close to the Bone: Life-Threatening Illness and the Search for Meaning,*

Jean Shinoda Bolen wrote, "When we participate in time and therefore lose our sense of time passing, we are in *kairos*; here we are totally absorbed in the present moment, which may actually stretch out over hours."

....

"Wild creatures live so close to life and death that they do not see either one of them as separate from themselves. They do not chase time or run from it. This is the psychology of the wild creatures: each day they rise new as dawn, and need no baggage on the tails, for they carry neither the mistakes of yesterday nor the hopes of tomorrow upon their shoulders. When evening tells them the day is over, they rest, and do not struggle to pull back the sun that has fallen into the sea."

—FROM THE CHILDREN'S BOOK *TIME OF THE WILD,* BY A. B. CURTISS

....

Throughout life, human beings are given multiple opportunities to seize high-impact moments. These *kairos* moments are rich with infinite potential and pregnant with unlimited possibilities.

In his book *Character Counts: Leadership Qualities in Washington, Wilberforce, Lincoln, and Solzhenitsyn*, Os Guinness wrote, "The hour is the God-given moment of destiny not to be shrunk from but seized with decisiveness, the floodtide of opportunity and demand in which the unseen waters of the future surge down to the present."

Throughout life, each of us is afforded opportunities to take a stand. Like a clarion call or cosmic gong proclaiming, *It's time!* these are the moments when we feel most alive, most in touch with our eternal purpose.

It's during these times—*kairos* time—that we need to step up to the plate and answer the call.

Oftentimes the weight of these opportunities takes us out of our comfort zone. It would be an understatement to say that *kairos* moments alter the trajectory of our lives.

To miscalculate *chronos* time is inconvenient.

To miscalculate *kairos* time is utterly regrettable.

I was six years old the first time I can remember experiencing *kairos* time. My family lived in sunny Southern California, and our home was just a few blocks from what we referred to as "the little store," which sat perched like a jewel on the watery hem of Lake Hodges, where I enjoyed many Tom Sawyer–esque adventures.

One day, after entering the little store, I veered off to the left and noticed a door beyond the counter that wasn't meant for customers. The shopkeeper must not have been watching as I let myself in.

Shutting the door quietly behind me, I discovered that I was in a large, unfurnished room. Once my eyes got used to the dim light, I noticed two unusual features. The first was what appeared to be a stage at the front. The second was that the windows were boarded, but one of the boards had come loose, allowing in what little light was in the room. And that's what captured my attention. Because of the way the board had slipped, the light entered as a shaft—like you sometimes see piercing a cloud-filled sky.

Approaching the light, I noticed little particles moving within the beam. I was captivated by what I saw, enough that I sat on the floor to watch the dust motes dance in the beam of light.

....

Dust motes are those small particles that we sometimes observe in a shaft of sunlight in an indoor or forested environment.

"In Aristotle's *De Anima*, we learn that many pre-Socratic philosophers, including Democritus and Pythagoras, believed that our soul is made up of dust motes. Their reasoning is sound. They thought that the soul must be the source of movement (our animation), and dust motes were the only things they observed moving without an apparent mover—seen always in movement, even in complete calm. They concluded, then, that dust motes have an internal principle of motion, and that our soul—internal principle of motion of the body—must be made out of dust motes."

—SENTENCIA LIBRI DE ANIMA, commentary on Aristotle's *De Anima*, by Thomas Aquinas, translated by Kenelm Foster, OP, and Sylvester Humphries, OP

....

I don't know how much time passed or was suspended, but I found myself in what I would refer to as an Old West saloon type of setting. There were cowboys playing cards at tables, dancehall girls in colorful regalia kicking it up onstage, and a piano player tickling the keys of an upright piano.

I must not have been visible to them, because no one looked at me, approached me, or spoke to me. I was simply a silent observer.

I don't remember traveling to or from that time. I assume—although I don't know—that I never left the geographic location; I simply left the current time.

Some might attribute this experience to a child's colorful imagination or a fanciful dream, but I assure you it was neither. Over the years, in talking with others about that occurrence, I've discovered that I'm not alone—many others have had a similar experience of transcending time.

"You don't have a soul. You *are* a soul. You have a body."

—C. S. LEWIS, British novelist, poet, academic, medievalist, literary critic, essayist, lay theologian, broadcaster, lecturer, and Christian apologist

---

When was the last time *you* were so caught up in *kairos* that you transcended *chronos* and found yourself at soul level?

DON'T MISS THE GORILLAS

Mindfulness is simple, but it's not easy.

Mindfulness is the openhearted energy of being aware in the present moment. It's the daily cultivation—practice—of touching life deeply.

To be mindful is to be present with, and sensitive to, the people we're with and the things we're doing, whether it's raking leaves, tying our shoes, or preparing a meal.

"Mindfulness means paying attention in a particular way: on purpose, in the present moment, and nonjudgmentally."

—JON KABAT-ZINN, professor of medicine emeritus and founding director of the Stress Reduction Clinic and the Center for Mindfulness in Medicine, Health Care, and Society at the University of Massachusetts Medical School

---

The following story is a paraphrased retelling of what took place in 2010, when my husband and I attended a fund-raising event at the Infinity Foundation in Highland Park, Illinois. The keynote speaker was scientist, teacher, and author Jon Kabat-Zinn.

People filled the facility to capacity for a lovely sit-down dinner. As we were finishing our meals, Jon Kabat-Zinn was introduced. He stood at a lectern and prepared us for a video he was going to show, by saying, "You're about to watch a brief basketball scrimmage. There are five people in white shirts and five people in black shirts. Please focus on the people in white shirts.

"When I turn off the video, I would like to know how many times the basketball was passed just between the people in the white shirts."

The lights dimmed, and he turned on the brief video clip. Each of us attentively watched the screen and counted the number of times only the people in the white shirts passed the ball to one another.

Once the clip was over, the lights came back on and Jon Kabat-Zinn asked, "By a show of hands, how many people think the number of times the ball was passed between the people in the white shirts was five?" A few people raised their hand. "How many people think six times?" Another small show of hands.

This questioning went on for a bit; each time, the number increased. At a certain point, there was a great show of hands. The majority of people in the room agreed that the people in the white shirts had passed the basketball this particular number of times.

Jon then asked, "How many of you saw something other than the scrimmage game while watching the video clip?" No one raised their hands.

"No, really," he said, "I won't call on you or anything like that, but if you saw something odd or strange during the video clip, simply raise your hand."

Again, no one responded.

"If you'd indulge me a moment longer, I'd like to replay the clip for you. This time, don't focus on the number of times the ball is passed between the people in the white shirts; simply enjoy the scrimmage."

The lights dimmed once again, and the video started playing. Within moments, a person wearing a gorilla costume entered the video clip from the right side of the screen, turned toward the camera, beat his chest Tarzan-style, then turned and continued walking until he was out of the frame.

The lights came back on, and Jon asked, "How many of you are so focused on something in your everyday living that you're missing out on the gorillas—the good stuff?

"Mindfulness points to being aware of, and paying attention to, the moment in which we find ourselves.

"Our past is gone, and our future isn't here yet. What exists between them is the present moment, the link that holds what was and what will be."

That brief teaching in mindfulness changed my life. Mindfulness is our capacity to be fully present in our own life, to be fully aware of what we're doing as we're doing it.

As we develop our awareness, an inner stillness grows naturally. In this case, stillness doesn't necessarily mean without motion; rather, it means to be free from inner tumult, to be tranquil. It was during just such a time of stillness that I was able to own the concept "I can do anything, just not everything." That awareness triggered a letting-go that brought with it tremendous peace and tranquility.

When we function from a place of tranquility, we're better able to embrace the world and better equipped to respond wisely and lovingly.

It's my perspective that mindfulness is more than paying attention; it's paying *intention*. Paying attention engages the mind.

Paying intention additionally engages the will.

....

"Ultimately, human intentionality is the most powerful evolutionary force on this planet."

—GEORGE B. LEONARD, journalist, editor and writer for *Look* magazine, and early leader of the human-potential movement

....

Intention is beautifully illustrated in a story that Barbara shared with me. She said, "I used to be part of a dinner book club where each month the group members would contribute a dish for dinner, and after what was always a wonderful meal, we discussed an agreed-upon book.

"One month, Debbie's food offering was a loaf of challah bread. As we were eating it and praising her efforts, she told us that as she kneaded the bread, she chanted our names; as she braided the bread, she said intentions for the well-being of each person who would later be partaking of the bread. I remember how honored I was when she told us this."

NOT-KNOWING IS NOT INFORMATION POVERTY

My friend Cassie shared, "I'm working on unknowing what I believe I know." Her comment brought to mind the wisdom of a Buddha-esque bumper sticker I saw that's stayed with me for decades. It said "don't believe everything you think."

There's tremendous interaction between knowing and not-knowing. Unfortunately, we live in a world that places more value on knowing, but they're both important. And just as the ability of knowing can be cultivated, so can the practice of not-knowing.

In his book *The Issue at Hand: Essays on Buddhist Mindfulness Practice*, author and Soto Zen priest Gil Fronsdal wrote, "The Zen practice of not-knowing is sometimes referred to as 'beginner's mind'—seeing with fresh, unbiased eyes; not being blinded to new possibilities or by preconceived ideas or judgments."

How can we cultivate the practice of not-knowing?

By adding "I don't know" to every thought, we open the door to examine ideas we embrace; the phrase invites us to question our line of thinking.

At its heart, Buddhism isn't about answering questions; it's about getting to the source that triggered the questions. When we're at the source, it eliminates the need to know.

Used regularly, "I don't know" becomes a healthy habit that evaluates the validity of our thoughts and beliefs. It creates a space for stillness in our mind. In turn, this stillness calms inner chaos.

Not-knowing doesn't mean that we don't know. It doesn't mean we have to overlook or ignore our understanding of a situation.

Not-knowing means not being limited by what we do know.

It's essential to clarify that the practice of not-knowing isn't the same thing as being bewildered or uncertain. Bewildered people are hesitant and somewhat lost, their mind paralyzed by indecision. Doubt and confusion are involuntary.

Provided by Gil Fronsdal, a practicing Buddhist of the Sōtō Zen and Vipassanā sects, here are some examples of how to use the practice of not-knowing: "If the judgment arises, 'this is a good meditation session' or 'this is a bad meditation session,' respond with 'I don't know.' Follow the thoughts 'I can't manage this,' 'I need...,' or 'I am...' with 'I don't know.' Like the bumper sticker that says 'Question authority,' the phrase 'I don't know' questions the authority of everything we think."

The practice of not-knowing is a conscious choice that brings greater peace. By holding lightly to what we know, we're ready for it to be different. Maybe things are this way, but maybe, just maybe, they're not . . .

The design of the human brain is beyond amazing. Divided into two hemispheres, the left side of the brain controls the right side of the body and mental activities such as math and science; the right side of the brain controls the left side of the body and oversees mental activities such as creativity and intuitive functioning.

....

"The mind is a flow of informational substances throughout the body. From bone marrow to immune cells to brain cells, you learn and change and grow through-out life. You're literally being given the opportunity to think new thoughts, change your mind, create the reality you experience moment to moment. . . .

If you have uplifting thoughts, you're building a very different brain than if you have negative ones."

—CANDACE PERT, PhD, neuroscientist and author

....

We humans filter what we see with our eyes through cortical processes in both hemispheres of the brain. But how do we see ourselves? We don't have the ability to look directly at ourselves like we do when looking at someone else. To see ourselves, we have to use something with a reflection—a mirror, a window, or water. We can see—and even admire—our reflection, but we can't look at ourselves directly. The outer self—the package in which we reside—is just that, a package. Self-reflection is about looking at the essence that resides *inside* the package.

If you were to paint a self-portrait of the real you, your authentic self, what would it look like? The purpose of this portrait isn't to capture any physical attributes, such as height, hair color, eye color, or body shape and size. Rather, it's meant to capture your thoughts, dreams, hopes, and aspirations and your psychological (mental and emotional) well-being, self-esteem, and coping skills.

It would capture your heart as it relates to humankind, your interconnectedness with every other living thing on this planet.

It would expose your ability to look at other living things as though they were you.

It would reflect your *humanness*—your humanity—even at its most wild.

Self-reflection blends inspiration and understanding. It provides clarity to our mind center, the avenue to wisdom.

When this self is healthy and in balance, there's an abundant return value to the heart. In this case, the dividends include the ability to look at things from more than one angle, to live in the present moment, to balance knowing and not-knowing, and to go inward and be at home—truly comfortable—with what we find.

A healthy mind center enlists courage for necessary change.

In the following chapter, you'll find several keys—practical tips, tools, and exercises—to boost your insight and offload baggage associated with self-reflection.

....

"Women need real moments of solitude and self-reflection to balance out how much of ourselves we give away."

—BARBARA DE ANGELIS, American author and personal growth and transformation expert

....

CHAPTER 14

Keys to Self-Reflection: Boost Your Insight

"You have to leave the city of your comfort and go into the wilderness of your intuition. What you'll discover will be wonderful. What you'll discover is yourself."

—ALAN ALDA, American actor, director, screenwriter, and author

1. MIND-BODY CONNECTION

Self-reflection is associated with the brain, pituitary gland, pineal, nervous system, eyes, ears, and nose. If you're experiencing issues in any of these areas, it's time to make an appointment with your health care provider.

2. COLOR THERAPY

Indigo is associated with self-reflection, intuition, and intellectual wellness.

It enhances imagination and understanding. Brooding and nocturnal, this mysterious color is a combination of deep blue and violet and holds the attributes of both of these colors. It's the color of ripe blueberries. Think of a deep-blue midnight sky, the breath-like movement of a nocturnal sea, the plumage of male indigo buntings in the summer, or the bottomless depths of a mountain lake.

The *positive* properties of indigo are expressed as visionary, wise, inspired, deep, intuitive, empathetic, broad-minded, and sensible.

The *negative* properties of indigo are described as fearful, arrogant, deluded, isolated, and overly idealistic.

The *healing* properties of indigo are sedative and can address physical symptoms such as hearing, sight, and sinus issues; nerves; insomnia; and negative states of mind that include paranoia, hypersensitivity, obsession, and hysteria.

When you need a boost in the areas of intuition and self-reflection, indulge yourself with this color. The frequency of indigo stimulates the brow chakra, also known as the third-eye center. It enhances our sense of knowing and helps us to better understand the big picture, to see clearly.

The vibration of indigo is purifying, integrating, and cooling. What shade are you drawn to?

Pure indigo calls to mind the emotions of the sea, promoting responsibility and trust in personal intuition. Or do you prefer the noble shaded tones that exude deep thought, contemplation, inner calm, and balance?

What we do with our physical environment—our personal space—speaks to our heart and helps us to flourish:

- Accessorize with a piece of indigo clothing or jewelry.
- Throw pillows are a quick way to freshen a room without a lot of expense or effort; indigo is ideal for the bedroom.
- Set the stage for nighttime dreams by painting the ceiling in your bedroom indigo. You can even add glow-in-the-dark stars.
- Take advantage of the healing frequency of indigo crystals, such as lapis lazuli, sodalite, or sapphire.

What we do with our mental and emotional environment is equally important.

Janine shared, "So much of what I struggled with while living in a communal environment were my shadows, my darkness, as well as those of the others I lived and worked with.

"In that environment, I had twelve or so people reflecting back on me on a daily basis. It was both a challenge and a gift at the same time. Finding the balance, creating the space for the shadow and the light to dance, rather than separate, was and is the process of my awakening."

In her intentionally cultivated heart space, Janine was able to offload baggage and increase joy.

3. DIET

Foods that boost our sense of knowing and connectivity include:

- **Dark bluish–colored fruits**—blueberries, red grapes, black berries, and raspberries.
- **Liquids**—red wine and healthful juices, such as açai, goji, and mangosteen.
- **Spices**—lavender and poppy seed.
- **Supplements**—Vitamin D is known as the "sunshine vitamin." It's linked to a cheerful disposition and enhanced longevity. Unique among its vitamin peers, vitamin D is a hormone. It helps the body to utilize calcium. Omega-3 fatty acids can also help to relieve depression naturally.

People who self-medicate for depression with alcohol would do well to eliminate sugar from their diet. Keeping blood-sugar levels steady by eating a diet that's high in complex carbohydrates (such as vegetables) and low in simple carbohydrates (such as white bread and sweets), as well as eating a little protein (a handful of roasted, unsalted nuts) every few hours, will help curb sugar cravings, a frequent problem for people who are giving up alcohol.

The amino acid L-glutamine, which helps regulate blood sugar, has been used effectively to treat alcohol addiction.

4. AROMATHERAPY

The use of rosemary, juniper, hyacinth, lemon, pine, or angelica seed helps eliminate fears associated with intuition and self-reflection (an unwillingness to look within, fear of truth when one's reason is clouded, or fear of sound, realistic judgment). These essential oils encourage clarity, inspiration, focus, concentration, and inner vision.

5. AFFIRMATIONS

When you encounter threats to your mind center—your sense of knowing—effective affirmations to speak out loud are:

I see myself and others clearly.

I am discerning; I exercise sound judgment.

I trust my intuition and insights.

I am conscious and mindful.

I approach life in a purposeful manner.

I utilize positive thinking.

I am courageous and ask, "Why?"

I am open to new ideas.

I am secure with not-knowing.

I function from a place of endless possibilities.

6. THE BUSINESS OF BEING

Intuition and self-reflection in the business world relate to metrics, to measuring success. For a moment, think of your life as a business and write the answers to the following questions:

- How do you define success?
- What are your measuring tools?
- Does your personal success measure up?

My personal definition of success is fulfillment. An added bonus is that people who are fulfilled often sleep better at night and wake up more refreshed.

My friend and colleague Terrill Welch, author of *Leading Raspberry Jam Visions Women's Way: An Inside Track for Women Leaders,* has this to say about success: "My challenge for us is to question all measures attributed to success—not just those that are beyond the quick and easy definition provided by wealth and position.

"I ask that we embrace the multiplicity of success, and carefully explore and articulate what we believe is success in a particular situation and also what consequences result from that success.

"For me, success is not about getting it right and sailing to the finish line of life. Success is about allowing your persistence to sail your vision through every day . . . while the breeze of your passion and potential charts your course."

7. BREATHWORK: FATHER SKY, MOTHER EARTH

Whenever you recognize that you're hosting an unwanted, draining emotion related to issues of intuition, self-reflection, or intellectual wellness, stop what you're doing and focus on your breath. Breathe deeply, slowly, and steadily.

An effective breathing exercise to do is known as *Father Sky, Mother Earth*. Here's how it's done:

- Stand with your feet shoulder-width apart.
- As you inhale through your nose, imagine that you're drawing indigo-colored air down into your expanding belly.
- On the inhalation, raise your right hand, palm up, straight toward the sky while simultaneously pushing your left hand, palm down, toward the earth.
- As you exhale through your mouth, imagine that toxins are leaving your body as your stomach contracts.
- Push your right hand, palm down, straight toward the earth while simultaneously raising your left hand, palm up, toward the sky.
- Repeat this sequence several times.

8. INTELLECTUAL WELLNESS INVENTORY AND VITALITY CHECK

- Are you a self-starter?
- Are you actively engaged in a hobby?
- Do you enjoy the arts—visual, performing, language, culinary, etc.?
- Do you see yourself as a creative person?
- Do you look for ways to use creativity?
- Are you open to new ideas?
- Metaphorically speaking, do you think outside the box and color outside the lines?
- Do you enjoy participating in stimulating conversations?
- Do you enjoy mental challenges like crossword puzzles, chess, Othello, Sudoku, or Rubik's Cube?

If you answered no to any of these questions, it may indicate an area of opportunity for you to improve the quality of your intellectual wellness.

On a scale of one to nine, where do you rate yourself on your current level of mental clarity and intuitive knowing, if one represents sluggishness (confusion, forgetfulness, difficulty concentrating) and nine represents liveliness (sharpness, ability to recall information, capacity for planning and strategizing)?

Is there a difference between where you currently are and where you want to be? If so, write down how you'll close the gap. Be specific.

9. ACTION STEPS

Self-reflection is something we need to intentionally set aside time for. It requires thoughtful planning and mindfulness. To enhance your senses of intuition and endless possibilities, enjoy the following activities:

> **Quick hit:** In your mind's eye, take yourself to your favorite body of water. Pick up a stone, visualize the thing that's holding you back (an emotional hurt, a fear, anything unhealthy), and project that idea into the stone. With all your strength, heave the stone out into the water and let what's holding you back go with it.

> **With a little planning:** Try visual stimulation, such as art therapy (coloring, drawing, or painting) or stargazing. And then do the opposite: using an eye mask, remove viewing and enter the stillness of your mind center. This stimulates connection with our unconscious mind, imagination, memory, inspiration, meditation, intuition, realization, imagery, and dreamwork.

Shift in Perspective

In my experience, shifting one's mental outlook (perspective) even slightly can significantly change the trajectory and reveal the sun coming up beyond the dark horizon.

Don't Miss the Gorillas

Write down whatever you've been so focused on that you've missed seeing the gorillas—the good stuff!

Not-Knowing

For one week, commit to the Soto Zen practice of not-knowing described in the previous chapter.

Self-Portrait

When you make time to reflect, what does your *authentic* self look like? Not the exterior package that you reside in, but your essence. When you study your self-portrait, what does it reveal about you—your impact on the earth and its inhabitants?

- Are you a creator or a destroyer?
- Are you responsible or irresponsible?
- Does your life reveal what inspires you?
- Do you transcend the superficial?
- Does your self-portrait reflect gratitude?

If, upon close examination, you don't care for what you see, acknowledge it, change it, and then move forward. You're the artist; select different colors. You're the author; write a different story. You're the composer; choose different notes. Redefine yourself. No—*amaze* yourself!

Time and Time Again

In many ways, time is more valuable than money. We'll have more opportunities to make money, but once a moment has passed, it's gone forever, and each of us has only so much time.

When we think of time as a commodity and our actions as investments, it can change the way we approach everyday decisions. When deciding how to pass time—spending or investing—we have to rely on experience and intuition.

- Does time seem to move slowly or quickly for you?
- Do you *spend* your time (no return on investment) or invest your time (have something to show for it—body, mind, and/or spirit)?
- If you could go back in time to revisit a single twenty-four-hour window of time, what would it be? During this revisit, you

wouldn't be able to change anything; you can only revisit the scenario. However, you would have your current, full knowledge—your current age perspective.

- When was the last time you were so caught up in *kairos* time (the opportune time, perfect time, supreme moment, or "now") that you transcended *chronos* time (tick-tock, chronological, sequential time, governed by watches, clocks, and calendar pages) and found yourself at soul level?

Self-Reflection as a Practice

Self-reflection is thinking about who we are and the things that are most important to us. But it takes time. Unfortunately, in this fast-paced world it's hard to justify slowing down and stopping for something that on the outside may appear to be nothing.

The good news is self-reflection, though motionless, is an action activity—the activity of quieting the mind and body to allow for reflection to take place. You can establish a reflection practice by following a few basic steps:

- Start a habit by scheduling actual appointments with yourself. These daily appointments need to be interruption-free. I have a little sign on the outside of my home-office door that says THERE BETTER BE BLOOD, FLOOD, OR FIRE!
- Find a place that's right for you. This will be different for every-one, but this geographic location should be quiet, comfortable, and distraction-free.
- Quiet your mind by intentionally putting your shoulders down and taking a few deep, relaxing breaths. A quiet mind doesn't mean an empty mind, a place to run away from what we're feeling. A quiet mind invites self-reflection—being aware of our experiences so we can transform our relationship with problems, fears, and stress so they don't erode the quality of our life.
- Choose a reflection focus for the day. Make a clear mental state-ment of what you want to focus on. If you find that you're drifting away from it, accept what you find. Pay attention to where your thoughts go; let them happen and experience them.

- Somewhat like individual flowers that you pick for a lovely bouquet, gather your random thoughts and reflect on what they mean as a whole. This helps us to discover what issues are most important at the current time.

When self-reflection becomes a daily practice, it yields a dividend—a return value to the heart. It helps us to muffle the daily noise and focus on things that are the most important.

10. PERSONAL ENERGY SIGNATURE

On a sheet of paper, draw a circle that represents your personal energy signature. Considering what you've learned about intuition, self-reflection, and intellectual wellness, on the inside of the circle, list the people, places, and things that are for this self's highest and best good—positive, uplifting, constructive, and healing.

On the outside of the circle, list the people, places, things, and actions you need to avoid to keep this self healthy and balanced. The examples on the following page will help you get started.

SELF-REFLECTION, INTUITION, AND INTELLECTUAL WELLNESS
PERSONAL ENERGY SIGNATURE

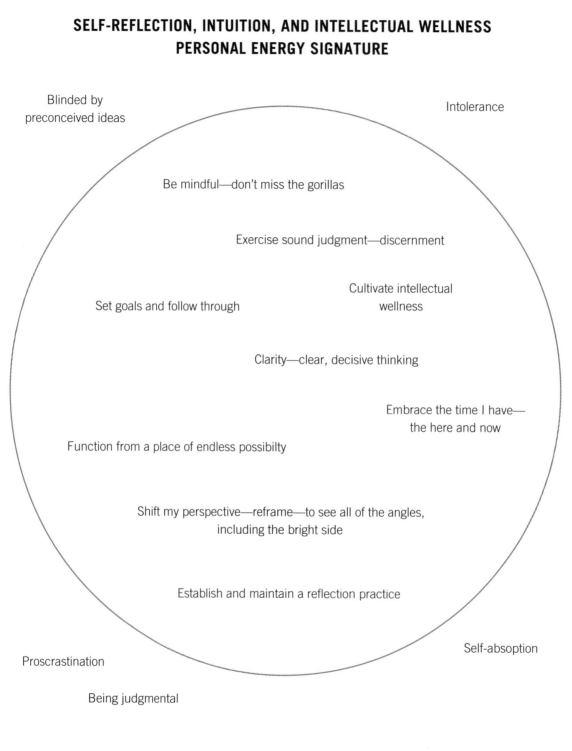

Blinded by
preconceived ideas

Intolerance

Be mindful—don't miss the gorillas

Exercise sound judgment—discernment

Cultivate intellectual
wellness

Set goals and follow through

Clarity—clear, decisive thinking

Embrace the time I have—
the here and now

Function from a place of endless possibilty

Shift my perspective—reframe—to see all of the angles,
including the bright side

Establish and maintain a reflection practice

Self-absoption

Proscrastination

Being judgmental

CHAPTER 15

Self #7: Self-Knowledge

Self-knowledge is responsible for divine connection and spiritual wellness; its purpose is to strengthen the connection with our higher self. When healthy, this self functions from a place of present-moment awareness. Corresponding to the crown chakra, it resonates with the color violet. An inspiring affirmation for this self is: *I am divine*. The shadow side is self-unawareness.

❖ ❖ ❖

Theresa shared, "What's the point? Why was I born? What, exactly, is my purpose in life? I'm forty-three years old and feel like I'm drifting through life aimlessly, like a boat without oars. I have no direction, no idea of destination, and no sense of purpose.

"I go from one experience to the next, one person to the next, seeking to fill the vacuum that I feel inside, yet it never gets filled. When I stop to think about it, it never feels *fulfilled*—momentary satisfaction, yes, but not fulfillment. No connection. I feel disconnected."

Are you aware of being an expression of something much bigger than you are, an extension of source energy?

"The place and time to practice awareness is now. Seize your activity this moment and become aware of what's around and within you. Notice when the mind wants to add a judgment, an explanation, a preference. And then stay with pure awareness a little longer."

—DR. PETER RENNER, practicing Zen lay monk

Do you perpetually feel disconnected from a higher power—be it God, universal consciousness, or simply your higher self?

Do you see everything that happens to you as a lesson for you to learn?

Are you living the legacy that you wish to leave the world?

This self—self-knowledge—nurtures our spiritual nature, the connection with our higher self. The developmental stage begins in early adulthood and continues thereafter.

Self-knowledge is concerned with our essence and integration of the whole. As we continue to grow, this often translates to discovery of the divine, interconnectedness, humanitarianism, and wisdom.

What's important is that each of us discovers for ourselves our individual sense of meaning, our exclusive purpose, and that each of us lives in a way that's consistent with our personal values and beliefs.

In her book *Nothing Special: Living Zen*, Charlotte Joko Beck wrote, "Awareness can take in a multiplicity of things just as an eye can take in many details at once. But awareness itself is one thing only. Awareness is completely simple. We don't have to add anything to it or change it. It is unassuming and unpretentious; it can't help but be that way.

"Awareness is not a thing affected by this or that. When we live from pure awareness, we are not affected by our past, our present, or our future.

"Because awareness has nothing it can pretend to, it's humble. It's lowly. Simple. The practice of awareness is about developing or uncovering a simple mind. It is not easy. It takes endless practice, diligence, and determination."

THE SHADOW SIDE: SELF-UNAWARENESS

When our senses of divine connection and self-knowledge are out of balance, we can experience negative things such as self-unawareness.

....

"The invisible walls of our deepest beliefs can become our greatest prisons or they can become our greatest source of freedom."

—GREGG BRADEN, scientist, visionary, scholar, and author

....

Self-unawareness can manifest itself in a number of harmful ways that become items we tuck into our life's baggage. Depending on their size and impact, we may slip them into a tote that we keep within arm's reach, for handy retrieval, or stuff them into a large suitcase that comes around on the baggage carousel only occasionally. These can include:

Physical: sensitivity to environmental triggers, such as light and sound; chronic exhaustion unrelated to physical illness; issues with the musculoskeletal system; and issues with the integumentary system (skin).

Mental: mystic depression or an inability to see the big picture.

Emotional: an inability to trust life.

Spiritual: fanaticism, living outside the present moment, lack of purpose, and disconnection from divine love.

Carol shared, "In my quest to discover the divine truth of me and my life, I often feel that I'm battling to discover, uncover, and recover."

Divine connection and self-knowledge work hand in hand with spiritual wellness—the foundation of wisdom. It activates the sense that life is meaningful and has purpose; it helps us to implement beliefs that are empowering, nurturing, and encouraging.

Like a tiller made of awareness, spiritual wellness guides us in a direction that is positive, uplifting, constructive, and healing, to a place where we're in harmony with ourselves and the rest of the world.

At the most elementary level, spiritual wellness involves a connection with something that's bigger than we are, a higher power of our choosing. This connection prompts values such as nonjudgment, discipline, conscientiousness, selflessness, and other principles that enhance our inner peace.

Sandi shared, "I've come to believe in the 'God of my own understanding,' the higher power that is constant and immutable, the universe without beginning or end. I'm part of the universe, and so I'm part of God. I can never unravel the holy mysteries of that being, only rejoice that I'm aware of that power and glad to be connected."

Ruth shared, "I spent my entire life doing science and found, in the end, that I was only studying myself. I have now awoken to see that it's my creation and I'm the creator. As I approach the end of time, it's both amazing and painful to reflect on all that I've done, all that I do now, and all that I will do."

The path to spiritual wellness is a personal, unique journey. It may include affirmation, meditation, prayer, or specific spiritual practices that support our convictions, but it may not. It may include aligning ourselves with a religious group or spiritual community of like-minded people, but it may not.

What's important is that each of us discovers for ourselves our individual sense of meaning, our exclusive purpose, and that each of us lives in a way that's consistent with our personal values and beliefs.

Spiritual wellness means that we bring any unhealthy aspects of our religious or spiritual experiences to light—take them out of our baggage—for examination so we can work through them in a healthy and productive way, offloading baggage and increasing joy.

Esther shares, "For me, spirituality is being in harmony and being sensitive to the meaning in my relationship with who I am, the people around me, and the larger universe—those three. That's my trinity. So far, I have experienced the most wonder and mystery not from my own intellectual puzzling but by simply being open to what can be sensed, including the vast information gathering being done by science."

THE VALUE OF BELIEF

Beliefs are something that we embrace, heart and soul. They're something that we accept as truth. Beliefs can revolve around ourselves or others and can include a number of attributes, such as faith and identity.

Limiting beliefs are ideas that hold us back, ideas that keep us from becoming the person we want to be or from doing the things we want to do. They're constraining, restricting, and usually exclusive. Most of the time, they're not even true; they're myths that we allow to control our lives. Many times, we're not even consciously aware that we have these beliefs. They often exist in our subconscious, directing our automatic judgments and influencing our decisions.

If we find ourselves saying things like, "I can't" or "There's nothing I can do," or even if we catch ourselves using words like "never," "always," "all," and "none," then we may have some limiting beliefs.

If we feel as if our life is not how we want it to be and we feel helpless or hopeless about it, then perhaps it's time to examine what we believe.

It's my perspective that any belief worth embracing will stand up to the litmus test of scrutiny.

If we have to qualify, rationalize, make exceptions for, or turn a blind eye to a maintain belief, then it may well be time to release that belief.

The first indication that we have a limiting belief is a feeling. Sometimes we may feel anxious or angry when faced with something that we have limiting beliefs about. Sometimes we may feel overwhelmed, irritated, or depressed, without knowing why.

When we notice that we're experiencing uncomfortable feelings, we need to stop what we're doing and ask, "Why?"

- Why does being around slender people make me feel uncomfortable?
- Why do I get angry when I have to go to work?
- Why do I feel anxious whenever I have to interact with needy people?

Once we begin to recognize the limiting beliefs in our life, we can start to think about how true they are and whether we need to change them so that we can embark on the life path that we want and can experience delight in living.

....

When I first read these thoughts in Osho's work *The Book of Understanding: Creating Your Own Path to Freedom*, I was immediately put off and attracted—both—by what he had to say about belief. With time and careful consideration, I've come to embrace his observation as a call to avoid complacency and maintain a spirit of investigation and questioning.

"I do not believe in believing. My approach is to know, and knowing is a totally different dimension. It starts from doubt; it does not start from believing. The moment you believe in something, you have stopped inquiring. Belief is one of the most poisonous things to destroy human intelligence.

"All the religions are based on belief; only science is based on doubt. And I would like the religious inquiry also to be scientific, based on doubt, so that we need not believe, but we can come to know someday the truth of our being, and the truth of the whole universe."

—OSHO (ALSO KNOWN AS BHAGWAN SHREE RAJNEESH), Indian mystic guru, and spiritual teacher

....

Here are some examples of limiting beliefs:

- I'm not good enough the way I am.
- No one else can do the job as well as I can, so I have to do everything myself.
- When things go well, something always happens to ruin it.
- Anyone who's wealthy is greedy and probably got there by unethical means.
- If I share what I have, then I won't have anything left.
- Thin people are anorexic, and heavy people are lazy.
- To forgive means to condone.
- People outside my religion are going to be punished for eternity.

Empowering beliefs are ideas that launch us forward and help us to become the person we want to be. Empowering beliefs are freeing, encouraging, and inclusive; they nurture and uplift. When we find ourselves harboring a limiting belief, we need to replace it with one that cultivates joy.

....

"Our belief does not change reality or truth. You may sincerely believe something to be true, but you may be sincerely wrong."

—DR. ALAN SIU-LUN WONG, molecular biologist

....

Here are some examples of encouraging beliefs:

- Giving and receiving are the same.
- I embody unlimited, unleashed potential and possibility.
- I have the power to choose.
- I am worthy.
- I already have everything that I need.
- I am capable.
- I accept my body temple the way it is.
- I have enough time for the important things in my life.

Regardless of the religious tradition, spiritual path, or personal perspective we choose to embrace, the potential exists for it to encourage and uplift every aspect of our being and to affect the types of goals we may choose to set for ourselves.

When our senses of divine connection and self-knowledge are in balance, we enjoy qualities from the constructive side of this self. These include mindfulness, inspiration, the ability to trust life, selflessness, courage, and devotion. We feel a connection with source energy, the well from which we draw our faith and values.

ON YOUR MARK, GET SET, GOAL!

My friend Bill shared his thought that self-knowledge may well be equated with peace. He said, "Through self-reflection, self-knowledge could reveal truths that may be appealing—or otherwise. Some of both varieties should be expected."

There are times when self-reflection reveals a need for change. Goal setting and making resolutions can be a reaction to the knowledge that we're not living for the highest and best good. It can be a means that moves us toward living to our highest potential.

According to the Statistic Brain Research Institute, the top ten New Year's resolutions for 2016 are:

1. Lose weight.
2. Get organized.
3. Get out of debt.
4. Exercise more.
5. Enjoy life more.
6. Quit drinking.
7. Quit smoking.
8. Learn something new.
9. Help others.
10. Spend more time with family and friends.

Unfortunately, the disconnect between the achievement of goals and resolutions and their reality is quite common.

Why does this disconnect exist, and why does it seem to be so prevalent? Maybe it's because our goals and resolutions aren't "smart."

In many corporate environments, there's a lot of buzz about setting goals—but not just any goals. SMART goals are used to measure performance during the annual review process.

My friend Ben works in the corporate world and shared the following formula for completing goals: *focus + attention x commitment = the highest probability of goal attainment.* When coupled with the affirmation "I attract everything that I desire," it creates a winning combination.

SMART is an acronym for the five characteristics of well-designed goals. The letters stand for "specific, measurable, attainable, realistic, and time-bound."

> *Specific:* Goals must be clear, concise, and articulate. They must state expectations such as what, when, and how.

> *Measurable:* If our goals aren't measurable, we won't know whether we're making progress toward successful completion. Measurable goals have milestones to indicate progress.

> *Attainable:* Goals must be within reach. If they're set too high or too low, they're meaningless.

Realistic: A goal must represent an objective toward which we're *willing* and *able* to work.

Time-bound: Goals must have a starting point, an ending point, and a fixed duration. Goals without completion deadlines tend to get consumed by the day-to-day interruptions that invariably come up.

After a presentation I gave at a women's retreat, I received an e-mail asking me what *my* personal goals are. I replied with the following list of desires to which I aspire. You'll notice that they're daily aspirations. They're specific, measurable (*either I am or I'm not*), attainable, realistic, and time-bound to each day of my life. Some lifelong desires can be achieved daily.

If you haven't formulated personal goals yet—desires, aspirations—perhaps you could use some of the following as seed thoughts to help you get started:

- Keep the energy of each "self" healthy and balanced.
- Accept and respect myself and others "as is."
- Be authentic—always.
- Be a positive, uplifting, constructive, and healing influence. My mother used to say, "Laurie, be a pleasure wherever you go, not whenever you go."
- Live in the present moment.
- Live my purpose: be a conduit for divine grace, a mindful agent of heart-based change.
- Listen "between the lines" and be sensitive to what people aren't saying.
- Integrate the wisdom that I have with the life that I live.

KARMA

Self-knowledge is closely related to spirituality; they work hand in hand. As a holistic health practitioner, I see a direct connection between health and spirituality. We're not just biological in nature; we're body, mind, and spirit. All of these aspects are interconnected. We function as a whole. We heal as a whole. As such, part of my job is to help others become more intimate with their spirituality—with source energy.

As I stated at the beginning of this book, we're spiritual beings on a human journey, here on a temporary layover in the classroom called life for the specific purpose of learning lessons before continuing on. Some people refer to these lessons as *karma*.

....

"My actions are my only true belongings. I cannot escape the consequences of my actions. My actions are the ground upon which I stand."

—THICH NHAT HANH, Buddhist monk, teacher, author, poet, and peace activist

....

Enzo, the old soul and canine narrator of Garth Stein's book *The Art of Racing in the Rain*, said, "I know that karma is a force in this universe and that people will receive karmic justice for their actions. I know that this justice will come when the universe deems it appropriate and it may not be in this lifetime but in the next, or the one after that. Their current consciousness may never feel the brunt of the karma they have incurred, though their souls absolutely will. I understand this concept."

Karma is a Sanskrit word that means "action." In many people's eyes, karma functions like fate, and bad fate, at that. It's an inexplicable, unchangeable force reaching out of our past, for which we're somehow vaguely responsible and against which we're powerless to fight. "I guess it's just my karma," I've heard clients say when something bad happens and they don't see any alternative to resigned acceptance.

....

"How people treat you is their karma; how you react is yours."

—WAYNE DYER, American self-help advocate, lecturer, and author

....

The fatalism implicit in this statement is one reason why the concept of karma repels so many people. It sounds like a callous justification for suffering and unfairness.

"If he's poor, it's because of his karma."

"If she's been mistreated, it's because of her karma."

From this, it's but a short step to saying that he or she *deserves* to suffer and so doesn't merit our help.

The philosophical explanation of karma differs somewhat between traditions, but the general idea is basically the same:

Through the law of karma—cause and effect—the result of every action creates present and future experiences, making each of us responsible for our own life and the pain and joy it brings to those in our sphere of influence.

The early Buddhists used flowing water to symbolize free will within karma. It illustrated that sometimes the flow from the past is so strong that little can be done except to stand fast, but there are also times when the flow is gentle enough to be diverted in almost any direction.

Instead of promoting resigned powerlessness, flowing water focuses on the liberating potential of what our mind can do with every moment.

Regardless of the school of thought, the karmic litmus test is to examine the *motive* that underlies our present actions.

Despite the ways in which the past may account for many of the inequalities we see in life, the measure of human beings is not the hand they're dealt. Rather, it's how they play that hand. Because we're all interconnected, that decision affects everyone.

In thinking about karma, I often consider how our current action—or inaction—affects the global community, not only the human race but the other lives we share this planet with, animals and plants alike.

Seven-generation sustainability is a sound ecological concept that admonishes the current generation of humans to work for the benefit of the seventh generation into the future and to replenish what we use, leaving enough for the next seven generations in line. Clearly, most people do not make decisions with their descendants in mind.

....

The belief in seven-generation sustainability was lived by the people of the Six Nations, also known as the Iroquois Confederacy. The Six Nations is composed of the Mohawk, Oneida, Onondaga, Cayuga, Seneca, and Tuscarora tribes.

"In every deliberation we must consider the impact on the seventh generation . . . even if it requires having skin as thick as the bark of a pine."

—THE GREAT LAW OF THE IROQUOIS

....

Every act contributes in some way to an outcome. What we do has significance. Just imagine if humankind recognized nature as a critical partner—the positive global change would be staggering!

Earth is the third planet from the sun. The Greek word "Gaia" translates as "Mother Earth," and that's how we've come to know her. We know the universe is a living thing and that everything in it is connected. When we embrace this knowledge and live it, there'll be a tremendous shift in global behavior. We'll cease dumping, strip-mining, and polluting. We'll be mindful of the earth and treat her with respect.

As I mentioned in the chapter on self-preservation, the word "spirit" comes from the Latin *spirare*, which means "to breathe." Spirit is quite literally our life force.

The characteristics of spirit—source energy, divine love—include being unconditional, as opposed to conditional; accepting, not rejecting; being constructive, not destructive; being inclusive, not exclusive; uniting, not dividing; building up, not tearing down; and being positive, not negative.

You may have noticed that I don't use a gender designation when referring to divinity. It's my personal belief that spirit is either gender free (neither male nor female) or fully both, but not singularly one or the other.

PATHS TO SERENITY: PRAYER, MEDITATION, AND STILLNESS

Regardless of the religious tradition or spiritual path, at least one basic ingredient is shared: prayer and/or meditation.

....

"Why is it that when we talk to God we're said to be praying, but when God talks to us we're schizophrenic?"

—LILY TOMLIN, American actress, comedian, writer, and producer

....

I'm often asked if prayer and meditation are the same thing. In my experience, they're similar yet different:

Prayer is *talking with* divine love.
Meditation is *listening to* divine love.

Most of us have the talking part down pat. Many of us struggle with the listening part.

Monica shared, "Even though it's simple, it's not always easy." Simple and easy aren't the same. Simplicity is efficiency, a clearing of clutter, mental or otherwise, while easy is uncomplicated and trouble-free.

Prayer

Kathy shared, "I believe that one of the best prayers one can say involves no words. It involves an exquisite presence to what is unfolding in the moment. The heart opens in gratitude. It prays by itself in those moments. The world reveals itself as sacred, holy, and divine."

Whether we pray out loud or speak from the quietness of our mind, our words and thoughts are things—they have a vibration—which means they're powerful.

In her book *The Dynamic Laws of Prayer*, Catherine Ponder wrote, "When you pray, you stir into action an atomic force. You release a potent spiritual vibration that can be released in no other way. Through prayer you unleash a God energy within and around you that gets busy working for you and through you, producing right attitudes, reactions, and results."

In his book *The Art of Spiritual Healing*, spiritual healer and mystic Joel Goldsmith wrote, "You begin to see that God cannot give and God cannot withhold. You can shut yourself off from the grace of God, but through prayer, you can be reunited with your Source. Your prayer will not be a seeking of any thing; it will be an asking and a knocking for more light, greater spiritual wisdom, greater discernment."

People generally operate from one of three places: thought, feeling, or emotion. We can have emotion and be emotional about something, or we can think and be thoughtful about something. But when we marry thought with emotion, we produce feeling. As Gregg Braden said in his book *Secrets of the Lost Mode of Prayer*, "The feeling *is* the prayer."

Meditation

Think of meditation as mental floss, an opportunity to get the junk out.

....

"Meditation is observing that thoughts, emotions, feelings, and sensations arise and fall away, bringing attention to the neutral breath, and watching all that stuff float by—like an angler sitting at the riverbank—observing and letting flotsam be flotsam."

—DR. PETER RENNER, practicing Zen lay monk

....

Meditation is a willingness to be quiet and listen to that "still, small voice within" without reacting. It's an invitation to get to know yourself honestly and sincerely.

Success and failure aren't part of meditation; it's a matter of fullness. I've come to think of it as a way of life. In my experience, people whose existence is a living meditation teach more by who they are than by what they say.

Not a skill to be mastered, meditation is an awareness that already exists inside you, one that you find with your heart, not your head.

Meditation may not be easy, but it's simple.

What do you long for?

What do you bring into your life that makes you feel ill?

What do you bring into your life that makes you feel healthy, vibrant, and alive?

What makes your heart hurt?

What makes your heart feel light and free?

The answers to these questions and more can be found in stillness.

Stillness is dynamic; it's unconflicted movement (no friction). It can be experienced whenever there is total, unrestricted participation in the moment we're in, when we're unreservedly present with whatever we're doing.

Stillness is a natural rhythm in the cycle of life. In the space that stillness creates—sacred space—we have the opportunity to quiet the mind and body, regroup, recharge, reconnect, and find a point of reference, something to measure against. To find the wisdom, we need to move forward; it's there that the strength of serenity embraces us.

Stillness in Motion: Movement Meditation

I like to think of movement meditation as stillness in motion. The outside body is moving, but inside the thoughts are calm and still, and the energy is smooth and refined.

Movement meditation is the circulation of energy through movement of the body. The graceful images of people gliding through dance-like poses as they practice movement meditation are compelling. Simply watching them is relaxing. Through gentle movements that connect the mind and body, movement meditation reduces stress and promotes serenity.

Different forms of movement meditation, such as tai chi, yoga, and qigong, are noncompetitive, self-paced systems of gentle physical exercise and stretching that involve a series of postures or movements done in a slow and graceful manner; each posture coordinates with breathing and flowing into the next without pause.

Movement meditation doesn't require physical prowess. Rather, it emphasizes technique over strength. It's generally safe for people of all ages and fitness levels. Many people find it appealing because the movements are low impact and put minimal stress on muscles and joints.

Despite its ancient history, movement meditation has been studied scientifically only since the 1960s. The results of that research suggest that it offers numerous benefits, including:

Energy, stamina, and agility: increased feelings of well-being and overall health.

Sleep quality: staying asleep longer at night and feeling more alert during the day.

Cardiovascular fitness: lower resting heart rate; normalized EKG, blood pressure, and cholesterol levels.

Chronic pain: significant pain reduction from all causes, including injury, surgery, arthritis, and fibromyalgia.

Respiratory health: slower respiratory rate, improved gaseous exchange, significant benefits for asthma and bronchitis.

Immune system: better targeting of antigens, significant anticancer effect.

Circulation: improves microcirculation; prevents vascular spasms; extremely helpful for angina, migraine, and Raynaud's disease (cold hands and feet).

Brain: improves cerebral blood flow; lowers incidence of stroke; reduces frequency and intensity of seizure disorders; slow, high-amplitude brain waves suggest relaxed and integrated state of consciousness.

···

"Inhalation through the right nostril stimulates the left side of the brain, and inhalation through the left nostril stimulates the right side of the brain. Research has proven that the brain swaps the dominant nostril we breathe through every ninety minutes."

—EDWARD STEINER, MD, biochemist, nutritionist, and longevity researcher

···

Musculoskeletal: improves muscle strength and definition, posture, balance, strength, stamina, flexibility, and coordination; slows bone loss in women after menopause.

Mental health: decreases stress, anxiety, obsessive-compulsiveness, and depression; improves mental acuity, memory, and interpersonal sensitivity.

Longevity: improves vital capacity, cholesterol and hormone levels, kidney function, vision and hearing, skin elasticity, bone density, digestion, strength, and libido.

In a *Psychology Today* article titled "The Benefits of Meditation," Colin Allen said, "Maybe meditation isn't so mysterious after all. Neuroscientists have found that meditators shift their brain activity to different areas of the cortex—brain waves in the stress-prone right frontal cortex move to the calmer left frontal cortex.

"This mental shift decreases the negative effects of stress, mild depression, and anxiety. There is also less activity in the amygdala, where the brain processes fear."

My friend Bob Bloom, author of *Taming the Tiger of Emotion: A Radical Change of Mind*, shared, "One of the practices I've been guided to incorporate into my daily routine is to take some time each day to just sit and 'be well.' This is an intuitive practice that asks me to connect with the energy or value of 'wellness' and breathe it into my being.

"To accomplish this task, I sit for a moment and quiet my mind. Then I invite my heart to bring the energy of 'be well' forward so I can know it, feel it, and experience it. As I feel the energy rise within me, I invite every cell within my mind and body to open up to receive this vital energy. I just sit and breathe it in."

In an article entitled "Alterations in Brain and Immune Function Produced by Mindfulness Meditation," which appeared in *Psychosomatic Medicine*, Jon Kabat-Zinn, PhD, of the University of Massachusetts Medical School, published the results of a study that recorded the brain waves of stressed-out employees of a high-tech firm in Madison, Wisconsin, then split the subjects randomly into two groups. Twenty-five people were asked to learn meditation over eight weeks, and the remaining sixteen were left alone as a control group.

All participants' brain waves were scanned three times during the study:

- At the beginning of the experiment
- Eight weeks later, when the meditation lessons were complete
- Four months after that

The researchers found that the meditators showed a pronounced shift in activity to the left frontal lobe at the eight-week point, as well as four months after that. In other words, they were calmer and happier than they were before they learned meditation.

THE CONNECTION TO MYSTICISM

A mystic is a person who lives to discover the deepest truth of our being as incarnate souls and to understand humanity's greatest potential as a reflection of source energy—divine love. Their primary interest is discovering the reason for humankind. The mystic views life as an abundant opportunity to discover, realize, and express divinity.

How does a person determine if they're a mystic? According to Evelyn Underhill, an English Anglo-Catholic writer and pacifist known for her numerous works on religion and spiritual practice, "if you have opened your soul to the divine in complete surrender, knowing that God is ultimately in control, and your mission is to listen, with a singularity of purpose, to the voice of God wherever that may be found," then you are a mystic.

Where does one find the divine speaking? Ms. Underhill answers, "in the plight of the oppressed, in the dark days of the soul, and in the kitchen scrubbing pots."

....

"What does mysticism really mean? It means the way to attain knowledge. It's close to philosophy, except in philosophy you go horizontally, while in mysticism you go vertically."

—ELIE WIESEL, Romanian-born, Jewish American writer, professor, political activist, Nobel Laureate, and Holocaust survivor

....

In her article "The Dark Side of Mysticism: Depression and 'The Dark Night,'" Dr. Mary Jo Meadow, professor of psychology and religious studies at Mankato State University, said, "Most people writing about mysticism emphasize mystical exaltation, ecstasy, and union with God, divinity, value.

"Such experiences—the crown of mystical endeavor—are surely important aspects of mysticism. However, mystics also acknowledge periods of dryness, darkness, and religious despair—the keenly felt absence of God. These features seldom receive scholarly consideration in spite of their importance in virtually all mystics' experience."

Religious despair, often equated with meaningless suffering, occurs when a person feels cut off from divine love and tries to live in disconnected emptiness. Some of the signs that a person might be experiencing religious despair may include depression, hopelessness, suicidality, anxiety, indifference, the inability to experience pleasure from activities usually found enjoyable, insomnia or hypersomnia, irritability, and involuntary crying or uncontrollable episodes of crying and/or laughing.

Another common trait of mystics is their connection with spiritual entities. Many spiritual traditions include the belief in the existence of angels. In my personal experience I use a twofold approach when working with spiritual entities of light. Because we live in a free-will world, not only do we need to *ask for help*, we also need to *give permission* for them to intervene on our behalf.

If you think in terms of a football game, most of the action is taking place on the field (life), but not everyone is in the game. There are people on the sidelines anxiously waiting to help (angels). However, they can't join the action until they receive permission from the coach.

For the longest time, I worked with angels from a single approach—*help!* Did it work? Yes, but I was always part of the solution. The difference with the twofold approach is that I'm the recipient of the solution. When we give angels permission to intervene on our behalf, they join the game, take the ball, and run for a touchdown.

It's important to note that "our behalf" means for our highest and best good. Angels bring about outcomes that are positive, uplifting, constructive, and healing.

There are times in our limited human vision when what we think would be amazing for us, would actually be detrimental. We can only see down the road of life until there is a bend or a curve on the distant horizon.

Angels, however, have a perfect aerial view. They can see what's going to happen around the bend. Subsequently, they may well answer with a no.

We need to accept yes and no answers with equal grace.

IT'S NOT WHAT YOU THINK

Dena Eakles is the founder of Echo Valley Farm in Ontario, Wisconsin. The farm community is governed by consensus and by the desire to live in harmony with one another and the land. Dena came to our healing studio to speak with our clients about the Medicine Path. She shared, "The Medicine Path is a culmination of my continued study with traditional healers. To these people, the root of medicine is spirit. And to treat the body or the mind without this acknowledgment is just not done."

Many people in the audience raised their hands and asked questions. Some of them included phrases such as, "Dena, what's your opinion on . . ." and "Dena, what do you think about . . . "

Dena smiled and graciously responded to the many questions. After awhile she said, "Don't ask me what I think; ask me what I know. It's not what 'I think' that you want to hear. Rather, it's what 'I know.'"

She went on to say, "Doubt is our enemy," and suggested, "When you speak, it should be from a place of certainty or you should be still until you arrive at that place."

In essence, what Dena was saying was, "Ask me for the facts and then draw your own conclusions." During her presentation, Dena shared *Plato's Theory of Knowledge*. She said there are four levels of knowledge, which I've paraphrased below:

> **Opinion:** This is the lowest rung on the ladder of knowledge. A person who's driven by the opinion of others is working from the lowest level of intellect.

> **Belief:** This is the next rung up on the ladder of knowledge. We're all aware of how beliefs have the ability to spur people to action (e.g., September 11, 2001).

> **Fact:** This is the third rung up on the ladder of knowledge. If you're at least fifty years old, you've lived through at least three different food pyramids, each of which the US government has released as fact. If you're more than sixty years old, you'll remember that in the 1940s and '50s, the surgeon general of the United States enlisted the help of Hollywood movie stars and famous athletes to promote smoking on television and at movie theaters because it was thought to be healthy!

> **Knowing:** "Know thyself" is the highest rung on the ladder of knowledge. There's a difference between knowledge and knowing:

Knowledge is an intellectual process; it's something we're aware of or familiar with because we learned it. A common misnomer about knowledge is that "knowledge is power." Knowledge is organized information.

....

"The real power behind whatever success I have now was something I found within myself—something that's in all of us, I think: a little piece of God just waiting to be discovered."

—TINA TURNER, American singer and actress

....

Knowing, on the other hand, is powerful. It's a result of personal experience, reflection, and independent thinking. Knowing is unique; it comes from ownership. Ultimately, to understand oneself is to understand other human beings as well.

The following excerpt was penned by Theresa of Avila in her work, *Interior Castle*. "Wouldn't it show great ignorance, my daughters, if someone when asked who he was didn't know and didn't know his father or mother or from what country he came?

"Well now, if this would be so extremely stupid, we are incomparably more so when we do not strive to know who we are, but limit ourselves to considering roughly these bodies.

"Because we have heard and because faith tells us so, we know we have souls. But we seldom consider the precious things that can be found in this soul, or who dwells within it, or its high value."

HOW WELL DO YOU KNOW YOURSELF?

What has your *intention*, and what has your *attention*? It's really important to know the answer to these questions, but first, let's clarify the difference:

Intention comes from the emotional/feeling part of the brain.

....

"It is not good enough for things to be planned—they still have to be done; for the intention to become a reality, energy has to be launched into operation."

—WALT KELLY, American cartoonist, notable for his comic strip *Pogo*

....

It's a desire and a goal. It's something we're focused on, something we want to make happen, something that we aspire to do. It remains invisible until it comes into being.

In her book *Pocketful of Miracles: Prayers, Meditations, and Affirmations to Nurture Your Spirit Every Day of the Year*, Joan Borysenko said, "Intention provides the energy that motivates our continuing efforts."

Attention comes from the mental/thinking part of the brain. It's the visible tasks, processes, and individual action steps we must take in order to achieve our intention. These visible action steps have the power to inspire others. Let's use the following scenario as an example:

Your intention (invisible dream) is to take an extended vacation to Provence, France. Your attention (visible action steps) then must be focused on saving money for the trip;

getting a passport; gathering weather-appropriate clothing; obtaining suitcases; reserving lodging, meals, and ground transportation; establishing an agenda; and making arrangements to take time off from work.

There are some people who never realize their intention. Why? Because their attention was not in line with their intention, it was elsewhere. It could be that they allowed external factors to interfere with their attention. Some of those factors are in their control, while others are outside their control.

Let's use the Provence, France, example. Events that are *inside your control* but derail you from the necessary action steps to achieve your intention could include:

- Making poor financial decisions.
- Agreeing to the influence of someone else who has a "better" plan for you (e.g., parents who want you to go back to school; a love interest who doesn't want you to go).
- Procrastination—you simply put it off.

Events that are *out of your control* and derail you include:

- Not saving enough money because you had to unexpectedly replace your vehicle after it was totaled in an accident and had to pay subsequent medical bills.
- Getting laid off from work.
- Suddenly finding yourself in a long-term-caregiving position for a loved one.

Have you always wanted to write a book?
Have you intended to take voice, dance, or piano lessons?
Have you had a burning desire to learn to fly or scuba dive?
Have you always yearned to take a hot-air-balloon ride or intended to travel?
Have you meant to learn another language or take a pottery class?

If your *intention* and your *attention* are in sync with each other, you'll meet with success.

Self-knowledge is the culmination of who we are—our core, our very essence, our sense of divine connection. When we're confident in our self-knowledge, our sacred awareness is amplified and our spiritual nature moves forward; it evolves.

When this self is healthy and in balance, there's an abundant return value to the heart. In this case, the dividends include tangibles such as living at the source and understanding that we're a reflection of source energy—divine love—that we're all connected, that we are one.

In the following chapter, you'll find several keys—practical tips, tools, and exercises—to strengthen the connection with your higher self and offload baggage associated with self-knowledge.

CHAPTER 16

Keys to Self-Knowledge: Strengthen the Connection with Your Higher Self

> "We have all a better guide in ourselves, if we would attend to it,
> than any other person can be."
>
> —JANE AUSTEN, British novelist

1. MIND-BODY CONNECTION

Self-knowledge is associated with the musculoskeletal system and the integumentary system (skin). If you're experiencing issues in any of these areas, it's time to make an appointment with your health care provider.

2. COLOR THERAPY

Violet is associated with self-knowledge, connection, spiritual wellness, and the divine.

It enhances creativity, wisdom, and inspiration. It's the color of royalty. Think of juicy plums, purple grapes, the velvet petals of an African violet, or the rich color of eggplant. When was the last time you picked turnips fresh from the earth? Have you ever seen a spiny purple sea urchin on the ocean floor while snorkeling, or been waved at by an iris dancing in the breeze?

The *positive* properties of violet are expressed as inspiration, dignity, creativity, nobility, spiritual awareness, altruism, independence, and personableness.

The *negative* properties of violet are described as fanatical, perfectionist, self-doubting, self-destructive, and alienated.

The *healing* properties of violet are cleansing and antiseptic and can address physical symptoms, such as epilepsy, neuralgia, and multiple sclerosis, and negative states of mind that include neurosis, despair, loss of faith, and lack of self-respect. Violet can also be used to suppress the appetite.

When you need a boost in the areas of divine connection and self-knowledge, indulge yourself with this color. The frequency of violet refreshes the crown chakra, the gateway to our spiritual nature. This energetic center is where we consent to higher guidance for personal transformation.

....

"Enlightenment is recognizing that we're all connected, then consciously living that realization—our thoughts, words, and actions an unshakable reflection of that understanding."

—LAURIE BUCHANAN, holistic health practitioner and transformational life coach

....

The energy of violet helps to assimilate our day-to-day experiences into wisdom, waiting at the ready for translation into enlightenment. It encourages a peaceful environment, relieves tension, and promotes inner strength, wisdom, and kindness. Violet helps us to change negatives into positives and brings about increased feelings of spiritual connection.

The vibration of violet is strengthening, cleansing, and purifying. What shade are you drawn to?

Pure violet emits the clarity of blue and the warmth of red. It speaks of grandeur and reverence. Or maybe you enjoy the lighter, airy shades that are elusive and intriguing, while the deeper purple tones are shadowy and peaceful, inviting deep relaxation and meditation.

What we do with our physical environment—our personal space—speaks to our heart and helps us to flourish:

- Accessorize with a piece of violet clothing or jewelry.
- Mix and match vases of violet and purple flowers in any room in your home: lavender, lilacs, impatiens, verbena, iris, alyssum, bachelor buttons, asters, crocus, lilac, pansies, gladiolas, snapdragons, wisteria, tamarisk, lupine, and clematis.
- Because of its calming properties, violet is an excellent choice to

use during meditation. Enhance your sacred space with a violet or purple *zafu* cushion to augment your meditation practice.
- Take advantage of the healing frequency of violet or purple crystals, such as amethyst, sugilite, or lepidolite.

3. DIET

Foods that boost our sense of mental illumination and divine connection include:

- **Air**—fasting.
- **Liquids**—water for detoxing.
- **Incense and smudging herbs**—sage, copal, myrrh, frankincense, and juniper.
- **Supplements**—Vitamin B complex supports mental health, including improved memory, concentration, and mental clarity.

4. AROMATHERAPY

The use of neroli, rose, sandalwood, and frankincense helps to eliminate fears associated with spirituality and self-knowledge and to establish a clear connection with your higher self. These essential oils encourage inspiration, introspection, resolution, wisdom, and enlightenment.

5. AFFIRMATION

When you encounter threats to your sense of sacred awareness, effective affirmations to speak out loud are:

I am open to seeing my higher good.
I have the courage to live consciously.
I aspire to *be*.
I see the oneness of all things.
I pay inner attention.
I have a deep sense of spiritual connection.
I know who I am; I live who I am.

I embrace the mysteries that I encounter.
I have the courage to question my beliefs.
I function from a place of present-moment awareness.
I create a doorway of miracles for others to walk through.

6. THE BUSINESS OF BEING

Divine connection and self-knowledge in the business world relate to goodwill. For a moment, think of your life as a business and write the answers to the following questions:

- What are you giving back to the community?
- If your personal goodwill were a pebble tossed into a still lake, how far would the ripple effect travel?

7. BREATHWORK: INNER SANCTUARY

When we enter stillness, we drink deeply from the well of source energy. From this place, we can move back into the busy world refreshed. One of the easiest ways to enter sacred space—your inner sanctuary—is through this breathing exercise. Here's how it's done:

- Close your left nostril with the index finger on your left hand.
- Inhale slowly and fully through your right nostril. In your mind's eye, imagine that you're drawing violet-colored air down into your expanding belly.
- Hold the breath after this inhalation for a mental count of six; simply note whatever comes into your awareness.
- Close your right nostril with the index finger on your right hand.
- Exhale slowly and completely through your left nostril; imagine that toxins are leaving your body as your stomach contracts.
- Don't hold your breath after exhalations, only after each inhalation.
- Do this for three minutes; then reverse the nostril through which you inhale and exhale for another three minutes.

Once you feel calm and still, ask your higher self for guidance and then wait patiently until a sense of knowing enters your conscious awareness. It may be a profound sense of peace.

The author of this definition of peace is unknown, but it speaks volumes: "Peace. It does not mean to be in a place where there is no noise, trouble, or hard work. It means to be in the midst of those things and still be calm in your heart."

8. SPIRITUAL WELLNESS INVENTORY AND VITALITY CHECK

- Do you enjoy a sense of inner peace?
- Do you feel a connection with a higher power?
- Do you have a sense of meaning and purpose in your life?
- Do you enjoy inner wealth?
- Do you view everyday life as sacred?
- Do you feel compassion for other people?
- Are you tolerant of beliefs other than your own?
- Do you live a life that's consistent with what you believe?
- Do you carve out time for relaxation, meditation, or prayer?
- Do you feel a sense of awe about life?
- Do you have rituals that help you integrate the spiritual into your life?
- Do you feel it's safe to examine and question what you believe?
- Is there harmony between your inner landscape and outside physical forces?

If you answered no to any of these questions, it may indicate an area of opportunity for you to improve the quality of your spiritual wellness.

On a scale of one to nine, where do you rate yourself on your current connection to something larger than you that gives you purpose and meaning, if one represents disconnection (feeling hopeless, lost, stuck, adrift, purposeless), and nine represents connection (feeling inspired, guided, purposeful, clear, peaceful)?

Is there a difference between where you currently are and where you want to be? If so, write down how you'll close the gap. Be specific.

9. ACTION STEPS

To strengthen the connection with your higher self and heighten present-moment awareness, try these activities:

Quick hits: Establish a relationship with source energy, be it through prayer, meditation, or both. Develop the daily practice of gratitude. Quick—name five things that you're grateful for.

With a little planning: Expand your awareness and appreciation of the rich palette of different religions and spiritual traditions by reading about them. You'll find a wide spectrum of books on this topic at your local library. Hold heart-based intent (light, divine love) for yourself and other people. This practice promotes health and well-being for both the sender and the receiver. It activates heartlight—illumination of the sacred space within.

Internal Inventory

Ask yourself the following questions. To be complacent or indifferent is to be unaware—oblivious.

- What is my relationship and responsibility to myself?
- What is my relationship and responsibility to others?
- If there is a God, what is my relationship and responsibility to that entity?
- If she or he cares, why is there so much pain and suffering in the world?
- Why me? Why am I here?
- What's the purpose in all this, and how, exactly, do I fit in?

Movement Meditation

Movement meditation destroys free radicals (a major cause of tissue degeneration) by stimulating activity of the enzyme superoxide dismutase. To reap the greatest stress-reduction benefits from movement meditation, practice it regularly. Many people find it helpful to practice in the same place and at the same time every day to maintain a routine.

To do this comfortably, you'll need loose-fitting clothes that don't bind, bare feet so you feel connected to the earth's energy, space to move freely, and tranquil, uplifting music that engages your heart.

While standing still, take several deep inhalations through your nose, exhaling through your mouth. Mentally count to six as you inhale the breath all the way down into your lower belly. Mentally count to eight as you exhale the breath, making your exhalations deeper than your inhalations. Once you feel comfortable with circular breathing, you'll be ready to add in movement.

With feet apart and knees slightly bent, relax your head, shoulders, and arms. Keep your hips and pelvis loose. Visualize your feet standing on soil. In your mind's eye, picture roots growing from the soles of your feet, extending deeply into the earth, from which they draw *chi*—essential life-force energy.

You can stay in this position and sway to the music, or, once you have connected with the energy you need, you can picture yourself as a blossom, slowly opening, and sway with the music. Pick up your feet and dance, if you prefer. Allow yourself to get lost in the sensation of movement and the beauty of your body as it moves. Feel the areas of your body that are tight, and let the movement loosen them.

Oftentimes people start the practice of movement meditation to relieve the increasing amount of stress and anxiety they face in their lives. Over time they find that their practice has gone beyond mere stress relief. For many, it's a great way to connect to spiritual wellness. They find that movement meditation gives them a deeper sense of themselves and expands their awareness of who they are, especially when they meditate in the *heart*, instead of the mind. It's a good place to begin any journey of self-discovery—a journey that leads to inner wealth.

Metta Meditation

Metta is unconditional love and kindness, a powerful feeling of wishing yourself and others well.

- Sit comfortably upright—but not rigidly—in a chair, away from the backrest if you can.
- Focus on your breathing. Follow the air flowing through your nostrils, right into your belly. Do this for a few breaths.
- Place your attention in the center of your chest, around your heart. Rest here for a few minutes.
- Recall a time when you felt loved unconditionally. Remember how it felt, and sit with this feeling. If you can't remember such an experience, then just imagine receiving unconditional love. It works just as well. Sit with this feeling for a few minutes.

- Say these words in your mind: *May I be happy. May I be well. May I be at peace.*
- Think of someone you love—someone very close to you. Then say to yourself, *May he/she be happy. May he/she be well. May he/she be at peace.*
- In your mind's eye, picture someone you feel neutral about. Then say to yourself, *May he/she be happy. May he/she be well. May he/she be at peace.*
- In your mind's eye, picture someone you don't care for. Then say to yourself, *May he/she be happy. May he/she be well. May he/she be at peace.*
- Allow this feeling to radiate out further—to everyone in your building, suburb, state, or country. Say to yourself, *May they be happy. May they be well. May they be at peace.*
- Finally, let it radiate to everyone and everything in the world. Say to yourself, *May they be happy. May they be well. May they be at peace.*
- Just sit and be still for a few minutes. Rest in any feelings of loving-kindness that you experience.

Intention and Attention

Closely observe what has your intention and what has your attention; then write it down. Which of your intentions have you followed through on? Which of your intentions have been derailed? Why? For the intentions you followed through on, what had your attention and enabled you to realize your goal? In other words, what was your formula for success/fulfillment?

10. PERSONAL ENERGY SIGNATURE

On a sheet of paper, draw a circle that represents your personal energy signature. Considering what you've learned about divine connection, self-knowledge, and spiritual wellness, on the inside of the circle, list the people, places, and things that are for this self's highest and best good—positive, uplifting, constructive, and healing.

On the outside of the circle, list the people, places, things, and actions you need to avoid to keep this self healthy and balanced. The examples on the following page will help you get started.

SELF-KNOWLEDGE, DIVINE CONNECTION, AND SPIRITUAL WELLNESS
PERSONAL ENERGY SIGNATURE

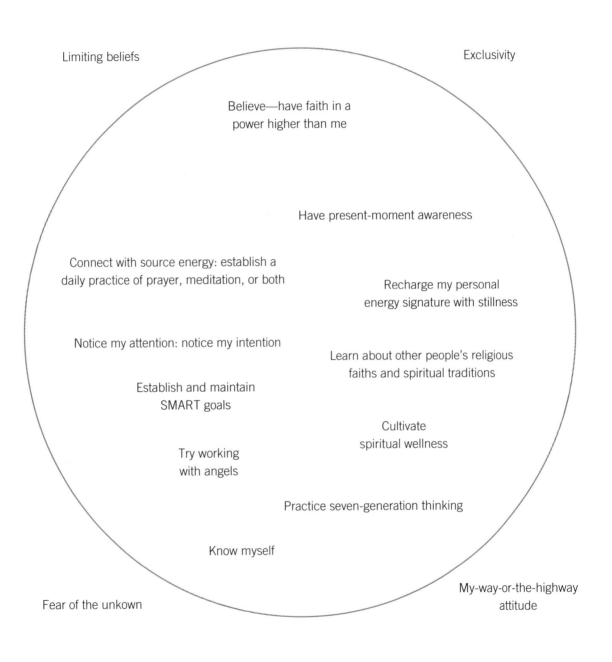

Limiting beliefs

Exclusivity

Believe—have faith in a
power higher than me

Have present-moment awareness

Connect with source energy: establish a
daily practice of prayer, meditation, or both

Recharge my personal
energy signature with stillness

Notice my attention: notice my intention

Learn about other people's religious
faiths and spiritual traditions

Establish and maintain
SMART goals

Cultivate
spiritual wellness

Try working
with angels

Practice seven-generation thinking

Know myself

My-way-or-the-highway
attitude

Fear of the unkown

CHAPTER 17

Integrating the Seven Selves: A Rainbow of Color

"I've always taken *The Wizard of Oz* very seriously, you know. I believe in the idea of the rainbow. And I've spent my entire life trying to get over it."

—JUDY GARLAND, American actress and singer

Color is energy made visible. Each of the seven selves is associated with and influenced by a specific color. Just as a dazzling rainbow isn't perfect and beautiful without all of its colors, the same holds true for us—it takes all seven selves working hand in hand for us to be at our personal best.

Represented by different colors, each self carries out a unique set of responsibilities:

> *Red* supports self-preservation, survival, and physical wellness. It enhances our sense of groundedness and helps us to function from a place of courage.

> *Orange* encourages self-gratification, pleasure, and occupational wellness. It increases our sense of delight and helps us to function from a place of personal respect.

> *Yellow* uplifts self-definition, personal power, and social wellness. It cultivates our inner landscape and helps us to function from a place of humble dignity.

Green nurtures self-acceptance, love, and emotional wellness. It develops our emotional empowerment and helps us to function from a place of compassion and forgiveness.

Blue promotes self-expression, creativity, and environmental wellness. It unleashes our creative flair and helps us to function from a place of original thought.

Indigo furthers self-reflection, intuition, and intellectual wellness. It boosts our insight and helps us to function from a place of endless possibility.

Violet strengthens self-knowledge, divine connection, and spiritual wellness. It increases our connection with our higher self and helps us to function from a place of present-moment awareness.

Just as a colorful rainbow reflects visible vapors of the earth's life, our seven selves reflect the vibrancy of our individual lives.

Throughout life, we'll continually evaluate each self and determine which one to polish next. Initially, the effort may seem monumental. But it gets easier over time. With regular attention, it becomes a matter of fine-tuning this one, and then that one, to keep them balanced and working in harmony. Periodically, it's helpful to sit with all seven selves at once. This concept is accomplished easily by doing the following meditation.

RAINBOW MEDITATION

From buttons, beads, and snippets of soft yarn to bits of smooth sea glass, fabric swatches, and everything in between—including small pieces of ceramic tile, crystals, crayons, and an assortment of glassy marbles—start collecting colors.

Barbara shared, "I'm beginning my color collection so that when I sit down to this meditation, depending on what I need, I'll have my colors right here to select from for support. Sometimes they might even be the object of my meditation. There's something very mindful about color selection and matching it to my feelings and where I might need extra strength or a closer connection."

You may want to light a candle, dim the lights, and play music softly in the background. Each exhalation is designed to offload emotional baggage from a particular self, creating space for unleashed, unlimited potential and possibility—*for joy!*

Sit with your feet flat on the floor, back upright and supported against a chair, hands resting comfortably on your thighs, eyes gently closed. Take a few deep, letting-go breaths, directing attention to your body's still point where in-breath becomes out-breath. In your mind's eye, picture roots growing from the soles of your feet down through the floor, deep into the earth, grounding and centering you like an ancient, wise tree.

Self-Preservation

Bring your attention to the tip of your tailbone, your foundation, where self-preservation resides. In your mind's eye, inhale the color *red*—slowly, deeply, and steadily—through your nostrils, drawing the breath past your chest and all the way down into your belly.

Now exhale the "waste"—any toxic thoughts or emotional baggage—through your mouth. Using the power of intent, say, "The energy of divine love fills my self-preservation. I invite the healing energy of divine love to flow."

Self-Gratification

Shift your attention to the area just below your belly button, where self-gratification resides. In your mind's eye, inhale the color *orange*—slowly, deeply, and steadily—through your nostrils, drawing the breath past your chest and all the way down into your belly.

Now exhale the "waste"—any toxic thoughts or emotional baggage—through your mouth. Using the power of intent, say, "The energy of divine love fills my self-gratification. I make choices that are for my highest good."

Self-Definition

Direct your attention to your solar plexus, the area just below the point on your chest where your rib cage meets, where self-definition resides. In your mind's eye, inhale the color *yellow*—slowly, deeply, and steadily—through your nostrils, drawing the breath past your chest and all the way down into your belly.

Now exhale the "waste"—any toxic thoughts or emotional baggage—through your mouth. Using the power of intent, say, "The energy of divine love fills my self-definition. I choose to fill my world with joy."

Self-Acceptance

Bring your attention to the center of your chest, your heart, where self-acceptance resides. In your mind's eye, inhale the color *green*—slowly, deeply, and steadily—through your nostrils, drawing the breath past your chest and all the way down into your belly.

....

"Beyond the scientifically proven results of meditation, such as reducing stress, relieving anxiety, and strengthening the immune system, meditation also offers many spiritual benefits.

Now exhale the "waste"—any toxic thoughts or emotional baggage—through your mouth. Using the power of intent, say, "The energy of divine love fills my self-acceptance. I lovingly forgive and release the past."

Self-Expression

Move your attention to the divot in your throat, where self-expression resides. In your mind's eye, inhale the color *blue*—slowly, deeply, and steadily—through your nostrils, drawing the breath past your chest and all the way down into your belly.

Now exhale the "waste"—any toxic thoughts or emotional baggage—through your mouth. Using the power of intent, say, "The energy of divine love fills my self-expression. I speak my truth with ease and grace."

Self-Reflection

Direct your attention to the point between and slightly above your eyebrows, where self-reflection resides. In your mind's eye, inhale the color *indigo*—slowly, deeply, and steadily—through your nostrils, drawing the breath past your chest and all the way down into your belly.

Now exhale the "waste"—any toxic thoughts or emotional baggage—through your mouth. Using the power of intent, say, "The energy of divine love fills my self-reflection. I see all things with insight and inspiration."

Self-Knowledge

Bring your attention to the top of your head, where self-knowledge resides. In your mind's eye, inhale the color *violet*—slowly, deeply, and steadily—through your nostrils, drawing the breath past your chest and all the way down into your belly.

Now exhale the "waste"—any toxic thoughts or emotional baggage—through your mouth. Using the power of intent, say, "The energy of divine love fills my self-knowledge. I am divinely inspired to live as I am meant to live. Thank you. And so it is."

❖ ❖ ❖

Having reached this point in the book, you've completed the tips, techniques, and self-health exercises located in the "key" chapters. In having done so, you have few, if any, bags left. You've worked hard to examine and offload baggage that contained physical, mental, emotional, and spiritual issues associated with the seven selves: preservation, gratification, definition, acceptance, expression, reflection, and knowledge.

The only luggage you should have left is for fun—just big enough for a swimsuit, snorkel, mask, and camera. So come on—you don't need an invitation to your own life!

WHAT COLOR IS YOUR PALETTE?

From soft pastels to bold hues, women are particularly attuned to color.

For decades, many of us have purchased makeup, clothing, and accessories based on our color palette. A qualified makeup artist or style consultant can do a color analysis on you, based on your original hair color, eye color, and facial skin tone, and, depending on their training, might tell you that you're light, dark, neutral, bright, cool, or warm.

....

"Without black, no color has any depth. But if you mix black with everything, suddenly there's shadow—no, not just shadow, but fullness. You've got to be willing to mix black into your palette if you want to create something that's real."

—AMY GRANT, American singer-songwriter, musician, author, and actress

....

Or you might be informed that you're a winter, spring, summer, or autumn. Winters and summers have cool coloring (pinkish skin undertones), while springs and autumns have warm coloring (golden skin undertones).

Yet again, you may discover that you have a morning, noon, or sunset palette—depending on how you look at those times of day.

Selecting makeup and clothing from our color palette helps to ensure that we won't end up with a drawer full of makeup or a closet full of clothes that we'll never use. An added benefit of limiting color choices in our wardrobe is that it's easier to coordinate clothing and we save time, space, and money.

And while this is true for the outside of the package we reside in—our physical body—we also have a color palette for the inside, the part that reflects our life's choice points. In my purse, I carry a little mirror. The back is inscribed with a quote by French writer and aviator Antoine de Saint-Exupéry. It says, "What is essential is invisible to the eye."

....

"You know when you take the paint off an old canvas and you discover that something's been painted underneath it? That's what I feel like—that part of the old is coming through the new."

—CARLY SIMON, American singer-songwriter, musician, and
author of *Smile and Say "Cheese"*

....

If a photograph were taken of your life right now, would it accurately capture how you want the final product to look?

Donna took a weeklong *National Geographic* class in France to learn how to use her camera more effectively. Her art medium is painting on canvas, not photography, so I didn't understand why she was taking the class, until she explained that she often photographs what she's going to paint and works from her photographs. And even though the photograph isn't the end result, it has a tremendous impact on the final product. In other words, the more accurately Donna captures what she sees with her eyes, the better her painting will be.

I share this story with you for several reasons. If we think of our life as a canvas, the way we live—how we respond to life's choice points—is how we add color, dimension, character, and depth.

Our daily living—what we say, what we do, how we do it, our interests, the relationships we cultivate—are all brushstrokes on our life canvas, the masterpiece that we call *My Life*.

No work of art that truly captures our attention is created exclusively from one color. It's a combination of colors, shades, and tones. It's not composed of all light hues, nor is it all dark. It's the use of both—the contrast—that gives it rich texture. It's the slight nuance that draws our attention to detail. It's the uniting of these elements that brings it to life and causes it to capture our attention with its beauty.

....

"There is only one thing more painful than learning from experience, and that is not learning from experience."

—LAURENCE J. PETER, past associate professor at the
University of Southern California

....

The same is true of our life's canvas.

If we focus on only one aspect of self, we'll be desperately out of balance. To experience stability and harmony, each aspect of our self must come into play.

During life's journey, the intensity of focus will shift from one aspect to another. We may even find that we're working on multiple aspects simultaneously. This depends, in great part, on our age and current circumstances. For instance, when we're in our teens, we have a strong self-focus. However, as we gain insights from life experience, our focus turns outward.

The wider the brushstroke of our experience, the more fully each aspect of self is fed. The more we cultivate ourselves—read, travel, experience different cultures and their traditions, are inclusive in our relationships, experience the arts, take advantage of learning opportunities, and have a variety of interests—the more each aspect of self is strengthened. This, in turn, provides us a strong platform to stand on when we're plagued by life's storms. And we will be.

My friend and colleague Linda is a psychotherapist. In 2005, her husband, Bill, suffered an accident that left him unable to walk without the use of two canes, unemployed, unable to drive, and almost homebound. Since then, he's had two significant memory losses, although he does remember that they're married.

Linda has a buoyant attitude about their circumstances. She told me, "The best university is adversity."

"I'm not afraid of a storm, for I'm learning to sail my ship."

—LOUISA MAY ALCOTT, American novelist

We learn the most from the hard things in life.

Each of us will encounter times when we must endure experiences that boil us down to our very essence. There are few exceptions.

My friend Sandi said, "While it's true that storms clear the air and leave the world a brighter place, you must first weather that storm—not always easy. There are times when we face unsettled weather on many fronts at the same time, and that can cause an internal battleground that's hard to escape."

It's important to feel our way through that weather.

These rich ingredients are what we—the artist—draw from to paint our life's canvas. They're the colors we choose.

DON'T OUTSOURCE YOUR LIFE—WRITE IT YOURSELF

In her book *There Is a Flower at the Tip of My Nose Smelling Me*, Alice Walker has a line that I love: "There is a pen nestled in my hand writing me."

Oh, to enjoy this life as our own novel unfolding.

When I asked Brenda to tell me what the title of a book about her life would be, she responded with a smile, "*It Takes a While, but She Figures It Out.*"

Then I asked her to tell me about the most important chapter.

Leaning back comfortably, eyes closed, she folded her hands across her stomach and replied, in storyteller fashion, "She felt so blessed with a wonderful family. She smiled a lot and was happy. She had a husband who loved her, four fabulous children, and the comforts of a beautiful home.

"Through life she worked hard and tried hard to do the right thing: first for her boss, then her husband, and then her children. But as her children were growing, she realized that she had stopped growing.

"She realized that what she wanted for her children were not things you could teach with words. You couldn't read instructions to them for how to feel joy and live a life full of love. You couldn't teach them how to feel confident and full of passion and purpose.

"She realized she had to live it—be it—in order to teach it.

"She knew she needed to change. And she knew to look inside for the answer, instead of always looking outside.

"With a very busy household and old habits keeping her prisoner, the steps were tiny, but little by little she started listening with her heart and began to understand."

I asked Brenda, "If I were to sneak ahead and read the final chapter of your life, what would I find? Since it hasn't been written yet, tell me how you'd like it to end."

Eyes still closed, Brenda said, "Life was good. With a lot of love and many mistakes, she found her way and spent most of her life filled with gratitude, joy, peace, and passion.

"As good energy always seems to spread, her husband and children found their way, too."

ARE YOU LIVING YOUR EPITAPH?

When asked what she would like engraved on her headstone, Erma Bombeck replied, "I *told* you I was sick!"

Her response has always made me laugh. It's a great question, one I often ask my clients. Once I receive the answer, I typically ask, "Is that a statement that you currently live up to?"

The completed work of art—your life's canvas—can be likened to a living version of a written epitaph.

Swedish chemist Alfred Nobel heard a premature version of his epitaph when his brother died and a French newspaper mistakenly ran an obituary for Alfred, calling him "the merchant of death" for having created dynamite.

Upon hearing this, he determined that wasn't the way he wanted to be remembered, and he made plans to set up and create the Nobel Prize organization for people who conferred the greatest benefit to mankind in physics, chemistry, physiology or medicine, literature, and peace.

Imagine what would have happened if he hadn't heard that epitaph or thought about how he would be remembered once he'd died?

The famous Latin saying "Bidden or unbidden, God is present," was so important to Carl Jung that he had the phrase carved, bronzed, and hung over his home entrance as a physical reminder of God's tangible availability. This plaque served as a lifetime memorial about his conviction—his heartfelt passion—that there's nowhere a person can run that's away from God. That saying is also on his tombstone as an epitaph.

April, a fiery redhead, answered my epitaph question with, "Just one word, 'debauchery,' and all of the letters will be crooked. I like how the word sounds and the meaning—'excessive indulgence in sensual pleasures; seduction from morality, allegiance, or duty.' I still want to shock people after I die."

Phoebe, a woman of great humor, smiled with delight and answered, "Oh, I've got it all planned out. It'll be one of those flat stones you can mow right over, and it's going to say, 'Tap-dance here.'" Then she threw her head back laughing!

More and more people are moving toward cremation, including me. But if I did have a headstone, I would want it to say JOIE DE VIVRE—enjoyment of life; exultation of spirit.

THE BUSINESS OF BEING: WHAT'S YOUR LEGACY?

Profit in the business world is the bottom line on top. If a company has clearly defined and is incorporating—living—all of the business principles that we've covered in this book, it's much more likely to operate in the black. And while this book isn't about being in business, it is about the business of being.

For a moment, think of your life as a business. How are you doing overall? How are you *really* doing?

If you've woven the many tips, techniques, and exercises you've learned in this book into your lifestyle, you'll see a "profit" in this lifetime—*joy!* It's revenue that you're currently investing in two directions simultaneously:

> **Forward:** When we draw our last breath, our "profit" is what we reap, karmically speaking. It's what comes back to us based on our motivation, words, thoughts, and deeds.

> **Backward:** When we draw our last breath, our "profit" is known as the legacy that we leave, especially to those in our sphere of influence.

As human beings, we're energy. Each of us has a personal energy signature. One of the fundamental laws of physics states, "Energy can be transferred from one form to another but neither created nor destroyed."

As such, birth is not a beginning; it's a continuation. That lends tremendous comfort because we then understand that, equally true, death is not an end; it's merely a continuation. In either case, it's a change from one form to another.

Rabindranath Tagore became Asia's first Nobel laureate when he won the 1913 Nobel Prize in Literature. One of the writings that he's best known for is "Death is not extinguishing the light; it is putting out the lamp because dawn has come."

When recognized as a continuation, death is no longer a threat or a tragedy; it's not a defeat or necessary evil that we have to brace ourselves against. Rather, it's a joyful fruition we can enter without fear.

....

"At the evening of life, you will be examined in love."

—ST. JOHN OF THE CROSS, Spanish mystic, Carmelite friar and priest

....

If you ever find yourself in a circumstance where you have to explain death to a child, one of the best books I've ever read is *The Fall of Freddie the Leaf: A Story of Life for All Ages*, beautifully written by Leo Buscaglia. This strikingly simple tale illustrates life and death with a leaf named Freddie, his leaf friends, and the changing seasons.

Intended or not, the canvas of our life is being painted. With intention, then, we can create something that's awesome and inspiring, as did Harriet Tubman, who was born into slavery in 1820. As a child, she was beaten and whipped by various owners. Early in her life, an angry owner threw a heavy metal weight with the intent to hit another slave. It struck her instead. The resulting head injury caused disabling seizures and headaches, but she didn't let these difficulties stop her.

When she was twenty-nine, Harriet escaped to Philadelphia but then immediately returned to Maryland to rescue her family. One group at a time, she slowly snuck relatives and other slaves out of the state to freedom. Traveling by night in extreme secrecy, Harriet—or Moses, as she was called—never lost anyone. Large rewards were offered for many of the slaves, but no one ever gave her away.

....

"Every great dream begins with a dreamer. Always remember, you have within you the strength, the patience, and the passion to reach for the stars—to change the world."

—HARRIET TUBMAN, African American abolitionist and humanitarian

....

In 1850, the US Fugitive Slave Law was passed. The only thing this meant to Harriet was that she needed to guide fugitives farther north, into Canada, where she also helped them find work.

When the American Civil War began in 1861, Harriet worked for the Union Army, first as a cook and nurse and then as an armed scout and spy. She was the first woman in US history to lead an armed expedition in the war. Part of her work included guiding the raid on the Combahee River that liberated more than seven hundred slaves.

After the war, Harriet returned to her family's home in Auburn, New York, where she was active in the women's suffrage movement and took care of her aging parents. Near the end of her life, she was admitted to a home for elderly African Americans that she'd help to open years earlier.

After her death in 1913, Harriet Tubman became an icon of American courage and freedom. Not constrained by time or distance, her ripple effect is far-reaching. Generations later, her legacy continues to have awe-inspiring global impact.

We all live different lives. We have individual interests, lifestyles, and needs. The common denominator is death. Each of us is going to die, no matter whether we're multimillionaires who live in mansions or homeless people who live on the street. We don't have a choice about this inescapable fact.

However, how we face death, and what we do with the time we're given here, is totally up to us; it's a choice. The culmination of our life experience is our life story, our legacy—something we leave behind after we've drawn our last breath.

....

"All of our life stories and the history of the world were written by the same hand."

—PAULO COELHO, Brazilian poet and writer

....

Have you ever thought about what your legacy will be, what *you'll* be remembered for?

Legacy isn't necessarily about prosperity or about leaving a sum of money to our children or grandchildren. Rather, it's about making a positive contribution.

I keep a little handwritten note on my desk that says, "Never underestimate the influence you have on others." This serves as an important reminder that people are affected by me. They're affected by you, too. Each person is affected in some way (positively or negatively) by what we think, say, and do—or fail to do; each person is affected by our personal energy signature.

As a child, sibling, parent, neighbor, coworker, partner, spouse, etc., you know what it's like to be on the receiving end of other people. What's it like to be on the receiving end of you?

We each hold our own paintbrush; each of us has our own life canvas. But the same spirit exists between paintbrush and canvas for everyone.

Likewise, legacy is about abundance, not prosperity. If we're *authentically* living our purpose and our higher self—not our ego—is driving the car, then we'll naturally be a magnet for abundance: health, peace of mind, joy, gratitude, contentment, quality relationships, a love of what we do, emotional fulfillment, integrity . . . the list goes on.

We may not be *wealthy*, but our life will indeed be *rich*. And our legacy—the culmination of our life experience—will be one of true and lasting value.

THE PRACTICE OF LETTING GO

Most of us hold on to things—relationships, places, habits, and emotions—that no longer serve us well, yet we embrace them. Sometimes it's because of fear that we allow these attachments to stand in our way and block joy. Yet letting go is something we do repeatedly throughout our lives.

In parenting, it happens when our child gets on a school bus that first time, again when they move away from home, and yet again if they get married—all tearful, emotional events. Repetition doesn't make it easy. Letting go is hard. Really hard.

Letting go is also multilayered—it includes grief and grieving, letting go of mistakes, finding and embracing new love, forgiving and being forgiven. The ability to forgive and let go of past hurts is one of the most critical challenges many of us face on the road to personal peace and joy.

Forgiveness can be defined as the decision—a conscious choice—to let go of resentment, anger, and thoughts of revenge as a result of real or perceived offense, hurt, or wrongdoing. The reason many people hang on to these is the belief that to forgive means to condone.

. . . .

"Forgiveness is a choice. It is the process of uncovering and letting go of anger while restoring hope and moving on with life."

—DR. ROBERT ENRIGHT, professor of educational psychology, University of Wisconsin, and pioneer in the scientific study of forgiveness

. . . .

But forgiving someone doesn't mean denying a person's responsibility, nor does it mean minimizing or justifying whatever it was that took place. It does mean to let go of it.

Not forgiving is like embracing an anchor: it pulls us down. When we release it—let go of it—we refuse to play the victim role and we resurface. We're not denying the existence of the anchor. Rather, we're choosing to let go of the control and power that it has over us, choosing to live unencumbered by it, to move on with life, and not to let it define who we are.

A Glance at the Future

I've chosen to end this book with an amazing true story of how Susan Wisehart, author of *Soul Visioning: Clear the Past, Create Your Future*, used holographic time to take me forward in time to see my future self. I was somewhere in my very late eighties or early nineties, and I was referred to as Granny B.

"Once confined to fantasy and science fiction, time travel is now simply an engineering problem."

—MICHIO KAKU, American physicist, professor of theoretical physics, City University of New York, cofounder of the String Field Theory, and author

One of the things that clinical hypnotherapists learn in our training is past-life regression. When that's done accurately and well, it's very interesting. But just like anything that you get a lot of (chocolate cake, pizza, ice cream), it can become monotonous or boring after a while. So when Susan Wisehart invited me to move *forward* in time that really piqued my curiosity.

My husband, son, and I went to the Infinity Foundation in Highland Park, Illinois, where we were part of a group of about sixteen people. After the first part of the day, we returned from lunch to find that our chairs had been replaced with yoga-style mats, which we each lay on.

Susan started talking in a voice, tone, and rhythm that are common in hypnotherapy and guided imagery. I was thinking, *Oh, brother, what's new about this?*

I can't tell you the who, what, when, where, why, or how of it—I don't have those answers—but I found my current self in a tropical location. It was as if all of my molecules and atoms came together—reassembled themselves—in that geographic location.

Looking around, I saw, in the near distance, my future self. She turned around and looked my current self square in the eyes.

I felt compelled to walk forward, hands extended. She took them in hers. And for some reason, I had the feeling that the clock was ticking very fast, that I was about to run out of time with her.

I looked into her eyes and said, "Please tell me what I need to do to get here."

With a smile and a twinkle in her eye, she said, "Let go."

It was at that point that I started wondering about my husband. And though I didn't voice any questions, she answered me with her mind. Turning to my left, in the distance I saw Len sitting on the end of a dock wearing a baseball cap, fishing pole in hands, feet dangling over the water. He was obviously content. Somehow I "knew" that his back being to us meant he was dead. But I also "knew" that everything was okay. He was quite well on the other side.

Just then, a tall, slender young woman with shoulder-length brown hair came up to me with a tray of sweating glasses of water and said, "Granny B., would you like something to drink?"

Just like I "knew" about Len, I "knew" that she was my granddaughter. I would guess that she was somewhere in her late twenties or early thirties. In current time, my son was not even married.

I looked back into the smiling eyes of my future self, who was still holding my hands. She conveyed the message "let go" one more time (nonverbally), and I dissolved (for lack of a better description), and then everything came back together again. I was physically reassembled back at the Infinity Foundation in Highland Park.

....

"We must be willing to let go of the life we have planned, so as to accept the life that is waiting for us."

—JOSEPH CAMPBELL, American mythologist, lecturer, and writer

....

To this day, I'm not exactly sure what it is that I'm supposed to let go of. I'm confident my future self wasn't specific on purpose, because now every time I hit a bump in the road, my current self simply remembers her words.

In not being specific, she made letting go a current, regular practice.

Letting go is another example of something that is simple but not easy. It involves allowing things to change. It requires an ongoing examination and revision of closely held thoughts and ideas, and an ongoing willingness to release them.

Lindsay shared, "The wisdom of my life's lessons is to step out of my own way and let go of the attachment to how I imagine I should be."

T. S. Eliot wrote, "Teach us to care and not to care." Letting go is that practice.

The following tale, "Two Monks and a Woman," is an old Zen story you may have heard before. There are many versions, but the origin is unclear. It reminds me of how easy it is to hold on to unpleasant memories. By reliving previous events in our mind, we kindle that energy. This, in turn, can trigger anger, blame, and so on, and fuel our own misery. It can also hinder us from cultivating love and compassion toward others.

Two monks were making a pilgrimage. During their journey, they came to a river with a strong current. As the monks were preparing to cross, they saw a young, beautiful woman standing in tears, unable to cross. She was afraid of the current and asked if they would help her.

....

"The path to health and happiness is often not a path of adding to or gaining something, but of removal or letting go. This is a critical principle of healing that is rarely discussed.

"The media, books, and even parents often encourage us to obtain more, to attain great heights, to grow and accumulate degrees, things, friends, children, money, and so on. All of this has its place. However, its opposite—learning to let go of the past, in particular, and of all attitudes, emotions, things, friends, and other 'baggage' that are holding one back—is often a hidden key to happiness and healing. It is a must to make room for more wonderful things to come."

—LAWRENCE WILSON, MD, nutrition consultant, and author

....

The younger and more exacting monk was offended at the very idea and turned away with an attitude of disgust. The older one didn't hesitate. Picking her up on his shoulders, he carried her across the river and set her down on the other side. She thanked him and went on her way.

When the younger monk reached the other side, they resumed their walk, the older one in perfect equanimity, enjoying the beautiful countryside, the younger withdrawn and brooding. At last, he could contain his silence no longer and spoke with some agitation. "Brother, we are taught to avoid contact with women, and there you were, not just touching a woman but carrying her on your shoulders!"

The older monk looked at the younger one with a loving smile and said, "Brother, I set her down hours ago; you are still carrying her."

How does one let go?

For me, it means being open to receiving change and inviting the energy of my higher self—divine love—to fill my heart and direct my thoughts with things that are positive, uplifting, constructive, and healing.

The investment in the everyday act of letting go has a large dividend: it leads to a deep, enriched life.

LA PIÈCE DE RÉSISTANCE

In his work *The Little Book of Atheist Spirituality*, author André Comte-Sponville writes about people "turning their lives into works of art."

If we knew for certain that our daily lives were actually artistic expressions—a perfectly executed pirouette in an intricate ballet, a delicately applied brushstroke in a magnificent painting, an exquisite piece born on a potter's wheel, or a thoughtfully constructed line in a poetic phrase—would we do things differently?

....

"Only put off until tomorrow what you are willing to die having left undone."

—PABLO PICASSO, Spanish painter, draftsman, and sculptor

....

This deliberate way of thinking adds to mindful productivity and enhances the desire to taste and enjoy each moment.

It also helps us determine what to put on our to-do list and what to leave off. Part of the decision-making process includes asking ourselves:

- Is this going to add to or detract from the end result of the creative piece?
- Is the ripple effect going to be positive, uplifting, constructive, and healing?

To do anything less compromises our inner alchemy—our personal transformation.

....

"Life is a great big canvas; throw all the paint on it you can."

—DANNY KAYE, American actor, singer, dancer, and comedian

....

At the beginning of this book, I shared with you that just before my fiftieth birthday I went on a brief hermitage—took time away by myself—to think through the colors on the palette of my life. The single truth that kept surfacing over and over again was: *whatever you are not changing, you are choosing*. That discovery gave birth to this poem:

I am what I decide to be
The blending of color
The integration of selves
I am a bright shade used to stand out
I am a soft shade used to merge in
There is no other design like mine
I am a combination of textures
I am shadow and I am light
The fusion of your every aspect
I am a reflection of your essence
I am what sets you apart
I am your life's canvas
The expression of your soul
Extraordinary
A masterwork
I am
La pièce de résistance

Best enjoyed without baggage, the journey, not the destination, is what matters. Travel light, travel fast, Godspeed.

CHAPTER 18

It's An Inside Job: Internal Inventory Questions

"There came a time when the risk to remain tight in the bud was
more painful than the risk it took to blossom."

—ANAÏS NIN, French-Cuban author

Designed to provide you with a question a day for a year's worth of journaling, the following 365 thought-provoking questions aren't meant for quick yes or no answers. Rather, they're ideal for contemplation as you go about your day—commuting to work, completing your *ta-dah* list, enjoying a cup of tea—or for group consideration and discussion at conferences, in retreat settings, or anywhere women gather.

Intended for you to interpret your own way, the questions have no right or wrong answers. Their sole purpose is to nudge you inward for an internal inventory—an examination—of your beliefs, to discover the colors on your life's palette, and to help you see what you should continue to embrace and what, perhaps, you should release.

Where appropriate, mentally add "and why?" to the end of the question. This will help you to more closely examine the motivation, inspiration, belief, and driver behind your answer.

If what you discover is positive, uplifting, constructive, and healing, it's a welcome friend as you continue life's journey. However, if what you discover is otherwise, it's time to offload that weight in your baggage, creating space for increased joy—*now!*

1. What are you still learning about yourself?
2. Are you open or closed to the input of others?
3. How old do you feel?
4. If, for some reason, you had to leave your home in a hurry and could take only three nonliving items with you, what would those three items be?
5. What is your definition of trust?
6. Why is trust easy or difficult for you?
7. In retrospect, what do you wish you'd paid more attention to?
8. What do you know for sure?
9. What do you think about "ownership?" What do you truly own?
10. How would your next-door neighbors describe you?
11. What's the bravest thing you've ever done?
12. What can you do right now to make a positive difference?
13. What places of the world are sacred to you?
14. How do you get past what keeps you up at night?
15. Whom do you admire?
16. What have you not been successful at changing about yourself?
17. When you feel stressed, what do you do to relax?
18. In life, what is your favorite role to play?
19. Who or what has the ability to cause you to ignore your personal values?
20. Where do you find beauty in your world?
21. What topics do you tend to avoid?
22. How far off course are you from your ideal life?
23. If you could talk with anyone right now, alive or dead, who would it be?
24. What single practice has made the biggest difference in your life?
25. Do you voice your choice?
26. What is your all-time favorite photograph?
27. When is it better to be sorry than safe?
28. What troubles you about the future of our world?
29. When do you feel exposed and vulnerable?
30. What do you feel passionate about?
31. Did you choose your work, or did your work choose you?
32. What's the biggest secret you failed to keep?
33. How often do you pay conscious attention to your breathing?

34. Do you believe—really believe—that everything happens for a reason?
35. Who or what has had the greatest influence on how quickly you achieve your goals?
36. What was the last thing you asked for?
37. What's on your "bucket list"—the things you want to do before you die? What's holding you back?
38. Whom would you like to get to know?
39. What are you here for? What's your purpose in life?
40. Whom do you miss the most?
41. What's your definition of art? What form of art moves you the most?
42. Have you ever lied about your age?
43. What purpose do relationships serve?
44. What makes you need to vent? How do you vent?
45. Do you follow your intuition?
46. How do you respond to uncertainty?
47. What is your relationship to money?
48. What purpose does guilt serve?
49. What is your preferred method of communication?
50. What's the most useful piece of advice you've ever received?
51. What was the last game you played?
52. What have you found to be the most beneficial attitude?
53. What was the best thing you learned from the worst job you've had?
54. What was the last intention you set?
55. When was the last time you cried?
56. Given how short life is, why is it that you do so many things you don't like, and like so many things you don't do?
57. When you listen with your heart, what do you hear?
58. What feeds your optimism? Likewise, what feeds your pessimism?
59. What's the best decision you've made in your life so far?
60. How do you smooth your rough edges?
61. What separates you from the crowd?
62. Who was the best teacher you ever had? What set him or her apart?
63. Describe "the one who got away."
64. When do you and don't you like spending time with others?
65. Where did you last find inspiration?
66. Who are your people?

67. How would you describe a life well lived?

68. What does your heart want most right now?

69. Do you go out of your way to appear happy and positive?

70. Describe the terrain of your life's path.

71. If you could go back in time and have a five-minute conversation with yourself ten years ago, what would you say?

72. When was the last time you were amazed?

73. What's your idea of the perfect day off?

74. Is it always better to know the truth, even when it hurts?

75. Describe the sound of your laugh.

76. What was the last story you told?

77. What's the most important thing you're putting off?

78. What is something you never believed in until you experienced it?

79. What is something you believed in until an experience changed your mind?

80. In five words or fewer, describe how you feel when you're in sync with your heart.

81. To whom or what do you give authority?

82. When did you do the most growing up?

83. What three films have most inspired you?

84. What three books have most inspired you?

85. What constitutes a miracle?

86. What work are you meant to accomplish?

87. Why is there suffering?

88. What are the top five things you're most grateful for?

89. What is your responsibility?

90. What's the most trouble you've ever been in? How did you resolve it?

91. What's your relationship to perseverance?

92. Who do you want to be, and what do you want to do when you grow up?

93. How do you define luck?

94. If you had a time machine that would let you spend one hour in a different time, what date would you go to?

95. Who or what makes you laugh out loud?

96. When do you feel exposed?

97. What is people's first impression of you?

98. If you were to go back to school, what would you study?

99. What captures your attention?
100. What's the biggest risk you considered taking but didn't?
101. When all is said and done, will you have said more than you've done?
102. What's in a name? Does yours suit you?
103. To what extent does simplicity play a role in your life?
104. What was the last risk you took?
105. In what areas of your life do you want to learn more?
106. Where do you feel freest?
107. What do you expect from life? What does life expect from you?
108. If you could have any job in the world, what would it be?
109. When do you feel most afraid?
110. Who is the most important person in your life?
111. What are the ingredients of a good conversation?
112. If you could have any superpower, what would it be and what would you do with it?
113. What would you most like to teach?
114. What brings you solace?
115. What's your favorite thing about yourself?
116. Who lets you know that you matter? Whom do you let know that they matter?
117. What makes you punctual, or not?
118. What culture outside your own most intrigues you?
119. What life experience contributes most to your capacity for empathy?
120. What brings balance to your life?
121. What would surprise some people to know about you?
122. Where do you go when you daydream?
123. What do you do when you don't know what to do?
124. What's the most irrational thing you've ever done?
125. Are you the kind of person whom you would want to have as a friend? What would make you a better friend?
126. Where is the most magical geographic location you've ever been?
127. If happiness were the global currency, what type of work would make you rich?
128. How has *giving* forgiveness, or the lack thereof, played a role in your personal health and wellness?

129. How has *receiving* forgiveness, or the lack thereof, played a role in your personal health and wellness?
130. To date, what has been your most significant contribution?
131. If life were a scavenger hunt, what would be on the list of things that you're looking for?
132. Do you play as hard as you work? Do you work as hard as you play?
133. If not now, then when?
134. If you were a judge, what one word would best describe you?
135. Who is the wisest person you know?
136. How do you say no?
137. If you were stranded on a desert island and you could take only one book with you, which one would it be?
138. What comes easily for you?
139. How did you get into the work you do now?
140. When was the last time you whispered?
141. If you had only one hour to live, what would you do with those sixty minutes?
142. In your perspective, is there a difference between spirit and soul? If so, describe it.
143. Who is the funniest person in your life?
144. Are you kind to yourself?
145. If children are the future, what do you feel is the most important value to teach them?
146. To what degree have you controlled the course your life has taken?
147. What is your relationship to conflict?
148. What are you lacking in your life?
149. Do you *spend* your time or *invest* your time?
150. What can't you say no to?
151. Is there anything you need to confess?
152. How do you determine if something is true? What are your criteria?
153. Do you see yourself as a creative person?
154. Where do you turn for help?
155. Do you feel lonely when you're alone, or do you enjoy your own company?
156. What would you like to commit to?
157. What did you damage last?
158. How do you deal with the unknown?

159. Who looks up to you?

160. Do you stay focused on the task at hand?

161. What would you like to let go of? When are you going to let go of it?

162. If you had to describe yourself in terms of climate, what weather are you today?

163. If tapping your heels together three times would instantly transport you anywhere in the world, where would you go?

164. What has the power to make you smile without fail?

165. Who are your unsung heroes?

166. What is your relationship to indifference?

167. What seemingly foolish choice turned out to be wise?

168. What is changing within you?

169. What's the atmosphere in your home?

170. Do you apologize when you should? Do you apologize when you shouldn't?

171. If you could give one gift to the elderly, what would it be?

172. What makes you feel accomplished?

173. What's the best surprise you've ever received?

174. Have you ever lied about your heritage?

175. Are you more concerned about doing things right or about doing the right things?

176. If you could ask any leader a *single* question, what leader would it be and what question would you pose?

177. What does your highest-self want?

178. What three words best describe your mother?

179. Where are you on your journey?

180. Would you prefer to have less work to do, or more work that you actually enjoy doing?

181. Would you like to be famous?

182. Who in your life is beautiful inside and out?

183. How do you define power?

184. If you could experience a different lifestyle for one week—a Buddhist monk, chocolatier, movie star, pianist, political leader, deep-sea fisherman, brain surgeon, stand-up comedian, tribal member, sculptor, or farmer—what would it be, and why?

185. What do you remember being especially proud of as a child?

186. If you could develop one new habit, what would it be?

187. How would you describe your sense of humor?
188. If you could change history and remove one scientific break-through, what would it be?
189. What's something that you experience differently than most people?
190. When was the last time you felt depressed? What was the cause?
191. If you knew that the world was going to end tomorrow, what would you do today?
192. What is your pet peeve?
193. Is there a part of your work that doesn't seem like work?
194. Do you use relationships as a mirror?
195. What does your family want most?
196. What in life are you most sure of? What in life are you least sure of?
197. What do you regret?
198. Would you rather be extremely intelligent or extremely good-looking?
199. What single material possession do you treasure the most?
200. Have you ever coveted things that belong to others?
201. Sum up in a single word: What kind of person are you?
202. What is your personal definition of success? Are you successful?
203. What was your most recent aha moment?
204. Why is it that the things that make you happy don't make every-one happy?
205. If you had the opportunity to make a single-sentence statement on television to millions of viewers—for instance, on Super Bowl Sunday—what exactly would you say?
206. What makes you content/gives you the most satisfaction?
207. What single quality stands head and shoulders above the rest in the most influential person who raised you?
208. What's your most vivid childhood memory?
209. Karmically speaking, if what we think, say, and do comes back to us, what's in store for you?
210. What do you see that others don't?
211. With whom do you compete?
212. Describe your wealth.
213. How do you overcome what stops you from taking risks?
214. What role does color play in your life?
215. What's the most magical thing that's ever happened in your life?

216. What's your all-time favorite type of music?
217. What is your strongest skill?
218. If you could live forever, would you?
219. Where are you most comfortable?
220. If you haven't achieved "it" yet, what do you have to lose?
221. What value is the most important for you right now?
222. What is your favorite taste: sweet, bitter, sour, or salty?
223. What is at the root of your need to be heard?
224. Do you act your age?
225. If you could be any animal, insect, fish, or bird for a day, what would you choose?
226. When was the last time you lied, to whom, and why? How did it work out for you?
227. What would you like to celebrate?
228. How do you define "visionary"?
229. Are you more likely to conform or rebel?
230. Would you rather be a worried genius or a joyful simpleton?
231. Whom do you envy?
232. Are you embracing something you need to release?
233. If you could have three personal wishes granted—something for yourself—what would they be? (Caveat: none of your wishes can be to have unlimited wishes.)
234. If you could have three global wishes granted—other than for yourself—what would they be? (Caveat: none of your wishes can be to have unlimited wishes.)
235. In what areas of your life do you feel like you're running?
236. How are you an inspiration?
237. How would you define a great relationship?
238. What life experience would you happily repeat?
239. What would you do if you lost everything?
240. What do you miss most about being a child?
241. Do you think of yourself as a curious person?
242. What is your relationship to compromise?
243. What does growing up mean to you?
244. If you could be an acknowledged expert in one area, what would it be?
245. What are you looking forward to?

246. What difficulties have you caused the most important person in your life?

247. When you were younger, what did you want to be when you grew up?

248. How has your life been different than what you imagined? Does the difference bring you joy or sorrow?

249. Are you authentic, or are you a reflection of what you perceive others want you to be?

250. What keeps you from being in the present moment?

251. How would you describe your self-esteem?

252. Do material possessions boost or enhance your self-esteem?

253. How are you similar to your parents? How are you different from your parents?

254. In five or fewer words, what would you like to see improve in our society?

255. What is the relationship between health and spirituality?

256. What are the characteristics of a true friend? Are you that kind of friend?

257. What is your relationship to prayer or meditation?

258. If you could blink your eyes and become any color—not change your skin color but actually become a humming orb of pure light—what color would you become, and why?

259. What aspects of yourself do you deny or reject?

260. What does personal freedom mean to you?

261. What is your relationship to revenge?

262. What is the difference between wants and needs?

263. What is the best thing about being you? What is the hardest thing about being you?

264. Do you make consistent time for nurturing your creativity?

265. When was the last time you laughed until you cried?

266. What role does community play in your life?

267. What habit do you have that annoys someone else? Why haven't you stopped?

268. How do you present yourself to others?

269. When it comes to financial matters, do you wing it or do you have a budget?

270. Would you rather lose all of your old memories or never be able to make new ones?

271. Have you made the choice to step into your talents and gifts?
272. What are you sensitive about?
273. Who supports your growth?
274. What was the last act of compassion you saw that touched your heart?
275. Whose strength do you admire?
276. Who in your life have you underestimated?
277. What is your personal definition of spirituality?
278. If your life were a book, what would the title be?
279. Has your greatest fear ever come true?
280. To date, what is the most important thing you've learned in life?
281. What is the one thing that makes you who you are; the thing at the core of your being that if you woke up without, you'd be a totally different person?
282. In what way do you hold yourself back?
283. What stops you from listening?
284. Who or what keeps you going when times are tough?
285. What in life is free?
286. How do you initiate friendship? When was the last time you made a new friend?
287. What is troubling you?
288. How did you get where you are now?
289. Do you eat to live or live to eat?
290. How do you respond when you find out you've been lied to?
291. With whom can you spend extended periods of silence and enjoy your time together?
292. If life is all about change, is resisting change resisting life?
293. What question would you like to be asked each day?
294. What have you lost in your life?
295. Is it hard for you to assert yourself?
296. What are your top five favorite smells?
297. What are your top five favorite sounds?
298. What practical skill has served you well?
299. What expectations do you have of those closest to you? What expectations do those closest to you have of you?
300. Do you believe honesty is always the best policy?
301. What does enlightenment mean to you? Are you enlightened?

302. What choice would you like to be given the opportunity to make?
303. If you could have the honest answer, what single question would you want the answer to?
304. What makes something sacred?
305. In your experience, what is the best part about getting older?
306. What would you like to be remembered for?
307. What role does art play in your life?
308. If you could play any instrument flawlessly, what would it be?
309. If you won a million dollars, what—exactly—would you do with it?
310. What is the worst predicament you've ever found yourself in? How did it happen?
311. What is your favorite hour of the day or night?
312. What motivates you?
313. Are you good at accepting compliments?
314. To what do you aspire?
315. Do you believe in love at first sight?
316. What nourishes your soul?
317. What is the purpose of difficulty?
318. Who is the most intriguing person you have ever met?
319. How do you define caring? Are you a caring person?
320. Are you living or existing?
321. What is missing in your life?
322. Are you afraid to make mistakes?
323. If you had the absolute confidence that no one would judge you, what would you do differently?
324. Which do you prefer, planning or spontaneity?
325. What have you been putting off?
326. What distracts you?
327. Are you doing what you love? If not, why?
328. How can you create more peace in your life?
329. Do you have a special name for that inner spark?
330. What problem would you most like a solution for?
331. In what area of your life do you follow your heart, instead of your head?
332. Whom do you watch over? Who watches over you?
333. What would you like to accept?
334. Where do you belong? What, specifically, contributes to that sense of belonging?

335. What does greatness mean to you?

336. What do you like most about your life right now?

337. If you could remove one emotion from your life, which one would it be?

338. What single tool could you not live without?

339. Where do you feel the most misunderstood?

340. What was the last lesson you learned? Did you learn it the hard way?

341. What have you needed to be reminded of recently?

342. Whom do you love? Can they tell by your actions?

343. Would you be willing to exchange ten years of your life expectancy to alter your physical appearance in any way?

344. What words would you take back if you could?

345. What does your inner dialogue sound like? What do you say when you talk to yourself?

346. Who has had the greatest positive impact on your life? Who has had the greatest negative impact on your life?

347. What is the greatest compliment someone could give you?

348. What dream have you carried with you the longest? What would it take to realize this dream?

349. How often do you sing out loud?

350. What part of life confuses you the most?

351. If you could be any age for just a day, what age would you choose?

352. How do you respond when someone is in need?

353. If you could choose one—strength, courage, or wisdom—which one would it be?

354. What was the last thing you hid from? Did it find you?

355. What connects life and death?

356. Do you work for your money, or does your money work for you?

357. How does the loss of pride (when you lose face) affect you?

358. In your heart of hearts, what matters most?

359. Who are you when no one's looking?

360. What would be the most difficult thing for you to give up?

361. What have you been meaning to do yet keep putting off?

362. Who or what is in charge of your life—*really?*

363. Where have you settled for less than your ideal?

364. What is your personal definition of "beautiful"? Are you beautiful?

365. If you had to sum it up in a single word, what kind of person would you say you are?

366. What's next?

THE SEVEN SELVES

SELF-PRESERVATION is responsible for survival and physical wellness; its purpose is to enhance our sense of groundedness. When healthy, this self functions from a place of courage. Corresponding to the base chakra, it resonates with the color red. An inspiring affirmation for this self is: I am safe. Its shadow side is self-destruction.

SELF-GRATIFICATION is responsible for pleasure and occupational wellness; its purpose is to increase our sense of delight. When healthy, this self functions from a place of personal respect. Corresponding to the sacral chakra, it resonates with the color orange. An inspiring affirmation for this self is: I am radiant. The shadow side is self-denial.

SELF-DEFINITION is responsible for personal power and social wellness; its purpose is to cultivate our inner landscape. When healthy, this self functions from a place of humble dignity. Corresponding to the solar plexus chakra, it resonates with the color yellow. An inspiring affirmation for this self is: I am empowered. The shadow side is self-importance.

SELF-ACCEPTANCE is responsible for love and emotional wellness; its purpose is to develop our emotional empowerment. When healthy, this self functions from a place of compassion and forgiveness. Corresponding to the heart chakra, it resonates with the color green. An inspiring affirmation for this self is: I am loved. The shadow side is self-rejection.

SELF-EXPRESSION is responsible for creativity and environmental wellness; its purpose is to unleash our creative flair. When healthy, this self functions from a place of original thought. Corresponding to the throat chakra, it resonates with the color blue. An inspiring affirmation for this self is: I am creative. The shadow side is self-repression.

SELF-REFLECTION is responsible for intuition and intellectual wellness; its purpose is to boost our awareness. When healthy, this self functions from a place of endless possibilities. Corresponding to the brow chakra, it resonates with the color indigo. An inspiring affirmation for this self is: I am insightful. The shadow side is self-absorption.

SELF-KNOWLEDGE is responsible for divine connection and spiritual wellness; its purpose is to strengthen the connection with our higher self. When healthy, this self functions from a place of present-moment awareness. Corresponding to the crown chakra, it resonates with the color violet. An inspiring affirmation for this self is: I am divine. The shadow side is self-unawareness.

Acknowledgments

The stories in this book are true. I thank my clients who shared their souls, providing me with passage into otherwise-secret places. I'm deeply humbled by their trusting hearts and confidence. Although your names have been changed, you'll recognize yourself in these pages.

Thank you to Christine DeSmet at University of Wisconsin-Madison, who held my feet to the fire and said, "Wring emotion from me, Laurie—make me care!"

Thank you to the dynamic team at She Writes Press: Brooke Warner, publisher, and Cait Levin, author liaison and project editor, maestros who seamlessly conducted a symphony of creatives—each an expert in her field: Julie Metz, Tabitha Lahr, Megan Rynott, Krissa Lagos, and Annie Tucker, copyeditor, who dotted my i's, crossed my t's, and attentively tucked in my participles to avoid indiscreet dangling.

Thank you to Crystal Patriarche, Taylor Vargecko, and Robert Soares—marketing and publicity rockstars at BookSparks where they cultivate big ideas and outstanding executions.

Thank you to Rucinski & Reetz Communication, creators of the inspiring book trailer for this body of work.

Thank you to my sister, Julie Hunter, for her incredible eye for detail. We're the only two people on this planet who bear the indelible touch of Delle; who share the mystery and magic of that long ago, faraway place that we still call home.

I'm grateful to my son, Evan without whom I'd know so much less about what really matters. I'm a better person because of his presence in my life.

Finally, I thank my husband, Len, for his generous faith in this book and in me. He's a continuous source of strength. Ever ready to laugh, he never allows me to take myself too seriously (and he almost never ran away when I asked him to review a chapter).

. . . .

"The only people with whom you should try to get even are those who have helped you."

—JOHN E. SOUTHARD, author

. . . .

About the Author

Board certified by the American Association of Drugless Practitioners, Laurie Buchanan is a holistic health practitioner and transformational life coach. Her areas of interest include energy medicine, inner alchemy, spiritual awareness, writing, and laughter. *Definitely* laughter!

Embracing the belief that life is an expression of the choices we make, Buchanan is a teacher and student of purposeful living. With tremendous respect for the earth's natural resources, she strives to leave the slightest footprint on the planet while at the same time making a lasting impression on its inhabitants—one that is positive, uplifting, constructive, and healing.

A minimalist by intent, she lives a beautiful life with fewer things—simple yet full. Please visit Laurie's blog, *Tuesdays with Laurie*, at www.tuesdayswithlaurie.com.

"Generally, by the time you are Real, most of your hair has been loved off, and your eyes drop out and you get loose in your joints and are very shabby. But these things don't matter at all, because once you are Real you can't be ugly, except to people who don't understand."

—*THE VELVETEEN RABBIT,* by Margery Williams

----

author photo credit: Len Buchanan

Bibliography

ARTICLES

Allen, Colin. "The Benefits of Meditation." *Psychology Today,* April 1, 2003.

Easterbrook, Gregg. "RX for Life: Gratitude." *Beliefnet,* accessed November 24, 2000.

Ekman, Paul. "Why Don't We Catch Liars?" *Social Research* 63, no. 3 (1996): 801–17.

Furlow, F. Bryant. "The Smell of Love." *Psychology Today* 29, no. 2 (1996): 38–43.

Kabat-Zinn, Jon. "Alterations in Brain and Immune Function Produced by Mindfulness Meditation." *Psychosomatic Medicine* 65, no. 4 (2003): 564–70.

Meadow, Mary Jo. "The Dark Side of Mysticism: Depression and 'The Dark Night.'" *Pastoral Psychology* 33, no. 2 (1984): 105–25.

Myers, David G. "The Emerging Scientific Understanding of Sexual Orientation." *Psychology,* 9th edition. New York: Worth Publishers, 2010.

Orme, Geetu, and Bar-On, Reuven. "The Contribution of Emotional Intelligence to Individual and Organizational Effectiveness." *Competency & Emotional Intelligence Quarterly: The Journal of Performance Through People* 9, no. 4 (summer 2002): 23–8.

Webb, David. "The Many Languages of Suicide." Suicide Prevention Australia Conference, Sydney, June 2002.

Zak, Dan. "The Truth About Lying." *Washington Post,* November 25, 2007.

BOOKS

Avila, St. Theresa of. *Interior Castle, or, the Mansions.* Charleston, SC: Biblio Bazaar, 2007.

Baron-Reid, Colette. *Remembering the Future: The Path to Recovering Intuition*. Carlsbad, CA: Hay House, 2006.

Bloom, Bob. *Taming the Tiger of Emotion: A Radical Change of Mind*. Phoenix, AZ: Little Handbooks LLC, 2008.

Borysenko, Joan. *Pocketful of Miracles: Prayer, Meditations, and Affirmations to Nurture Your Spirit Every Day of the Year*. New York: Warner Books, 1994.

Braden, Gregg. *Secrets of the Lost Mode of Prayer: The Hidden Power of Beauty, Blessings, Wisdom, and Hurt*. Carlsbad, CA: Hay House, 2006.

Buscaglia, Leo. *The Fall of Freddie the Leaf: A Story of Life for All Ages*. Thorofare, NJ: Slack Inc., 1982.

Cameron, Julia. *The Artist's Way: A Spiritual Path to Higher Creativity*. New York: Jeremy P. Tarcher/Putnam, 1992, 2002.

Casserly, Julie Murphy. *The Emotion Behind Money: Building Wealth from the Inside Out*. Chicago: Beyond Your Wildest Dreams LLC, 2008.

Emoto, Dr. Masuro, and Thayne, David A. *The Hidden Messages in Water*. New York: Atria Publishing, 2005.

Ford, Dr. Charles V. *Lies! Lies! Lies!: The Psychology of Deceit*. Arlington, VA: American Psychiatric Publishing, Inc., 1999.

Fronsdal, Gil. *The Issue at Hand: Essays on Buddhist Mindfulness Practice*. Redwood City, CA: Insight Meditation Center, 2002.

Glazov, Sheila. *What Color Is Your Brain? A Fun and Fascinating Approach to Understanding Yourself and Others*. Thorofare, NJ: Slack Inc., 2007.

Goldsmith, Joel S. *The Art of Spiritual Healing*. San Francisco: HarperOne, 1992.

Hay, Louise L. *Heal Your Body A-Z: The Mental Causes for Physical Illness and the Way to Overcome Them*. San Diego: Hay House, 1998.

Hyde, Catherine Ryan. *Pay It Forward*. New York: Simon & Schuster, 2000.

Jacoby, Peter. *Unlocking Your Creative Power*. San Diego: Ramsey Press, 1993.

McClellan, Dr. Michelle. *The Way Back Home*. Crystal Lake, IL: e-book, 2008.

Petit, Philippe. *To Reach the Clouds*. London: Faber and Faber, 2004.

Ponder, Catherine. *Dynamic Laws of Prayer*. Marina del Rey, CA: DeVorss & Company, 1987.

Rowling, J. K. *Harry Potter and the Chamber of Secrets*. New York: Arthur A. Levine Books, 2003.

Stein, Garth. *The Art of Racing in the Rain*. New York: Harper, 2008.

Walker, Alice. *There Is a Flower at the Tip of My Nose Smelling Me*. New York: Harper-Collins, 2006.

Weiner, Eric. *The Geography of Bliss: One Grump's Search for the Happiest Place in the World*. New York: Twelve, 2008.

Welch, Terrill. *Leading Raspberry Jam Visions Women's Way: An Inside Track for Women Leaders*. Vancouver, BC: Trafford Publishing, 2005.

Willard, Dallas. *The Divine Conspiracy: Rediscovering Our Hidden Life in God*. San Francisco: HarperOne, 1998.

Wisehart, Susan. *Soul Visioning: Clear the Past, Create Your Future*. Woodbury, MN: Llewellyn Publications, 2008.

AUDIO CDS

Hay, Louise. *The Power of Your Spoken Word*. Carlsbad, CA: Hay House, 2005.

Naparstek, Belleruth. *Guided Imagery, Meditation, and Affirmations*. Akron, OH: Health Journeys, 2002.

"I am a part of all I have read."

—JOHN KIERAN, American author, journalist, amateur naturalist, and
radio and television personality

SELECTED TITLES FROM SHE WRITES PRESS

She Writes Press is an independent publishing company founded to serve women writers everywhere. Visit us at www.shewritespress.com.

Falling Together: How to Find Balance, Joy, and Meaningful Change When Your Life Seems to be Falling Apart by Donna Cardillo. $16.95, 978-1-63152-077-8. A funny, big-hearted self-help memoir that tackles divorce, caregiving, burnout, major illness, fears, and low self-esteem—and explores the renewal that comes when we are able to meet these challenges with courage.

Tell Me Your Story: How Therapy Works to Awaken, Heal, and Set You Free by Tuya Pearl. $16.95, 978-1-63152-066-2. With the perspective of both client and healer, this book moves you through the stages of therapy, connecting body, mind, and spirit with inner wisdom to reclaim and enjoy your most authentic life.

The Thriver's Edge: Seven Keys to Transform the Way You Live, Love, and Lead by Donna Stoneham. $16.95, 978-1-63152-980-1. A "coach in a book" from master executive coach and leadership expert Dr. Donna Stoneham, The Thriver's Edge outlines a practical road map to breaking free of the barriers keeping you from being everything you're capable of being.

Think Better. Live Better. 5 Steps to Create the Life You Deserve by Francine Huss. $16.95, 978-1-938314-66-7. With the help of this guide, readers will learn to cultivate more creative thoughts, realign their mindset, and gain a new perspective on life.

Stop Giving it Away: How to Stop Self-Sacrificing and Start Claiming Your Space, Power, and Happiness by Cherilynn Veland. $16.95, 978-1-63152-958-0. An empowering guide designed to help women break free from the trappings of the needs, wants, and whims of other people—and the self-imposed limitations that are keeping them from happiness.

The Complete Enneagram: 27 Paths to Greater Self-Knowledge by Beatrice Chestnut, PhD. $24.95, 978-1-938314-54-4. A comprehensive handbook on using the Enneagram to do the self-work required to reach a higher stage of personal development.